The Shrinking Perimeter

The Shrinking Perimeter

**Unionism and Labor Relations
in the Manufacturing Sector**

Edited by
Hervey A. Juris
Myron Roomkin
Northwestern University

LexingtonBooks
D.C. Heath and Company
Lexington, Massachusetts
Toronto

Library of Congress Cataloging in Publication Data

Main entry under title:
  The shrinking perimeter.

  1. Trade-unions—United States—Congresses. 2. Industrial rela-
tions—United States—Congresses. 3. United States—Manufactures—
Congresses. I. Juris, Hervey A. II. Roomkin, Myron.
HD6508.S524   331.88'7'0973   79-1864
ISBN 0-669-02939-4

Copyright © 1980 by D.C. Heath and Company

Published simultaneously in Canada

Printed in the United States of America

International Standard Book Number: 0-669-02939-4

Library of Congress Catalog Card Number: 79-1864

Contents

List of Tables

Preface and Acknowledgments

The decade of the 1930s was one of immense growth for the trade union movement. Membership expanded from nearly 3.8 million in 1935 to 7.2 million in 1940. The CIO's drive to create industrial unions in the manufacturing industries spurred the AFL to new heights, and together they transformed the industrial landscape. The 1930s saw the nation's labor policy move from hostility toward unions, through the neutrality of the Norris-La Guardia Act, to the Wagner Act's creation of a protected environment for organizing and bargaining. Out of this decade came George Meany, Pat Gorman, John L. Lewis, Phil Murray, and other giants of this nation's industrial history.

In the postwar years, industrial democracy and due process became firmly established as part of American industrial relations. These years also saw collective bargaining evolve into a power relationship. As unions in the major manufacturing industries such as steel, automobiles, rubber, meat packing, and electrical equipment became more powerful, society became concerned with the possible abuses of union power and the question of whether that power would ever be checked.

By the 1960s, however, market forces began to restrict union power in the manufacturing sector. Manufacturing employment in the United States, with the slight exception of the Vietnam years, began to decline relative to the total labor force as employers substituted capital for labor, exported jobs to countries offering lower labor costs, moved to nonunion plants in the South and elsewhere, and became more sophisticated at resisting unions. These trends continued through the 1970s, and by the end of the decade the business press began to question whether the manufacturing labor movement in this country had a future.

The editors of this volume looked at the future of the manufacturing labor movement from a slightly different perspective. We were concerned that scholars had become so engrossed in unionism in emerging sectors that insufficient attention was being paid to manufacturing unions at a time when they were under great stress. No one from the research community had asked: "What is the effect of this shrinking perimeter on unions and collective bargaining in manufacturing?" We wanted to know whether the classical paradigm developed in the 1930s, 1940s, and 1950s still held, or whether thirty years later, in a significantly different environment, a new paradigm would be required.

It is around this question that we convened a conference in June 1978 at Harrison House in Lake Bluff, Illinois. Major contributors to the development of the classical paradigm were invited to exchange views with persons from both labor and management. Each of the participants was asked to reexamine the assumptions underlying received theory and to project whether these assumptions might hold in the 1980s.

In part I, Lee Preston lays out his impression of the future of manufacturing enterprises. Frank Cassell draws some implications of Preston's predictions for industrial unionism and the political economy.

Albert Rees, in part II, looks at union membership and the future of domestic organizing. He extrapolates from current trends to show that, at best, the labor movement will probably maintain the status quo in the future. Milton Derber reminds us, however, that the history of trade union growth is often episodic and not necessarily subject to interpolation. Richard Prosten, also commenting on union membership and the future of domestic organizing, points out that the situation may be even worse than the data would suggest.

Jack Barbash examines the union as an evolving organization. He defines the concept of bargaining effectiveness, which is the objective he says unions attempt to maximize. Arthur Loevy takes exception to this strict application of business unionism.

In part III, George Hildebrand looks at the structure and process of bargaining in the manufacturing sector over the next few years and finds little change. However, he does find that the changing environment will affect the administration of union contracts. Clifford Hathway and John Zancanaro support Hildebrand's analysis.

The quality of worklife and worker participation in management as bargaining issues are explored by George Strauss. He predicts that these issues will not become a major factor in U.S. bargaining over the next few years. Strauss sees bargaining remaining with bread-and-butter issues.

In part IV, Michael Jedel finds that the increasing incidence of foreign-owned manufacturing companies in the United States will not have a significant impact on U.S. labor-relations practices. Joseph Tierney files a mild dissent to this observation.

In part V, Michael Piore suggests that the labor movement, if it is to retain any political influence, must throw in its lot with the new consumer and minority interest groups. Stanley Ruttenberg and Lloyd Ulman take strong exception. The editors observe in a closing summary that while the possibility of a new paradigm exists, most evidence seems to suggest that the classical paradigm is still valid and in force.

We were fortunate that the international management consulting firm A.T. Kearney, Inc. shared our interest in these questions. It is through their generosity in providing funds that this conference was made possible. We are indebted further to James R. Arnold and to Gordon Scott of A.T. Kearney for their help and counsel throughout the project. The J.L. Kellogg Graduate School of Management of Northwestern University and its Department of

Policy and Environment provided additional funds and services that made it possible to bring the volume to publication. We acknowledge our debt and gratitude to Sanna Hans Longden, who helped us prepare each of the chapters for publication. Responsibility for all errors, of course, remains with us.

Finally, we thank the conference participants themselves. The text of this book, which is comprised of papers and discussions prepared and distributed prior to the conference, is no measure of their total contribution. Rather, there exist several hundred pages of transcript that capture the full flavor of their participation. While we tried in the concluding chapter to summarize the salient discussion points, the economics of publishing preclude our sharing the full richness of this experience. It was also in the interest of economy that we edited from each chapter the author's dictum that he was unable to predict the future with certainty. Each said it with his own particular elegance; we say it for all of them: if we could predict the future with complete certainty, we would no doubt be in some other occupation.

Part I
The Future of Manufacturing
Enterprises

1 The Manufacturing Environment in the 1980s

Lee E. Preston

The Unpredictable Future

The Joint Economic Committee (JEC) has recently produced a series of forty-one commissioned studies under the general title, "U.S. Economic Growth from 1976 to 1986: Prospects, Problems and Patterns." These reports discuss the idea that every significant social, economic, and technological trend within our society, and those in other societies with which ours is linked by international power or trade relationships, will contribute to the evolving industrial environment of the future. In summarizing the studies, the committee's staff wrote:

> Several participants in the Committee's deliberation stated categorically that the United States is "entering a new era" in its economic development with circumstances fundamentally different from those of the past. Among the characteristics of this new era are the persistent slowing of labor force growth foreseen for the 1980's, slower gains in the contribution of higher education, rising real costs of acquiring raw materials, a maturing of major postwar industries, and possibly, shifts in popular values to place less emphasis on economic growth. Partially offsetting these influences is the prospect of a return to somewhat higher productivity growth through technical progress as the economy recovers and labor becomes more scarce. (U.S. Congress, 1978, p. 1)

The JEC Staff Study is essentially a plea for new long-term economic and social policies. However, it makes no attempt to forecast such policies, or even to suggest the range of policy choice that may be available. Moreover, neither the Staff Study nor the underlying research reports make what is probably the single most critical point: the future economic environment requires analysis as a public policy environment, rather than simply as the result of interacting demographic, resource, and technological forces. The studies commissioned by the committee dwell at length on demographic factors, an emphasis justified by their fundamental importance as well as by the fact that they can be most easily projected forward for the decade. However, the decade economic growth forecasts suggested by various contributors range from a low of 3 percent per year to 6 percent or more; even

The assistance of numerous faculty colleagues in locating and selecting data sources is gratefully acknowledged, as well as the data development and computational work of William Lorenz and Bernard Ramos.

3

the detailed econometric forecasts reviewed by Gary Fromm vary between 3.2 percent and 5.0 percent, with a median of 4.1 percent (1976, pp. 22-23).

In searching for an explanation for this high degree of uncertainty about the future path of the economy, it seems useful to distinguish between the roles of marketplace forces and policy variables. My own view of the relevant distinctions is suggested by the following tabulation:

Factor	Determinants and Relative Importance		Reliability of Forecast Estimates
	Real Economy	*Public Policy*	
Labor	90	10	High
Capital	75	25	Medium
Resources	50	50	Medium (?)
Productivity	?	?	?
Overall economy	50	50	Medium (?)

The sources of uncertainty about the future state of the economy are not hard to identify, if this presentation is even approximately correct. First, there is basic uncertainty about the relationships among factors in the real economy, particularly with respect to the connection between real economic variables and the rate and direction of productivity change. (Is necessity or research and development expenditure the true mother of invention?) Second, there is considerably more uncertainty as to the impact of public policy variables, whatever they may prove to be, on the real economic factors and their interaction. And finally, there is still greater uncertainty as to the actual policies that will be chosen, their timing, and the effectiveness of their implementation.

In the context of this high degree of uncertainty, even on the part of so distinguished and varied a panel of experts as those selected by the JEC, this chapter will focus rather narrowly on some of the major trends involving the manufacturing sector of our economy over the past couple of decades, highlight some features of the current scene (insofar as available data permit), and raise questions about the likely persistence and implications of these developments for the future. Since we all know that "nature does not make jumps," it seems inevitable that a survey of recent and current conditions would yield considerable insight into future possibilities, at least within the relatively limited timespan of the decade of the 1980s. This type of analysis is a contribution to the evolving field of meso-economics—the study of multiple industries and economic sectors at an intermediate level of aggregation between the micro-analysis of firms and markets, on one hand, and the conventional focus on the macro-economic aggregates on the other.

Some Larger Issues   `

The JEC staff conspicuously omitted discussing one important social force: the strong and continuing trend toward centralization of economic decision-making in both the private and public sectors. Developments with respect to concentration and integration in the private sector will be discussed in more detail below. However, the growth of public regulation as a major factor in the future environment of manufacturing industries merits brief attention here.

Paradoxically, the recent growth of regulation apparently arises from many of the same broad social forces that have stimulated emphasis on individual rights and values, and the legitimacy of varied life-styles, in recent years. One manifestation of this trend has been increased participation of individuals throughout society in decisions affecting their personal and working lives. Some aspects of this development are clearly decentralizing, and constitute a departure from rationalistic and efficiency-oriented values and behavioral norms.

The economizing mode of thought and action, defined by Daniel Bell (1973), gradually spread from its origins in private economic affairs to become a dominant theme in our culture. It is now widely believed that this economizing mode is being replaced throughout our society with more participative, communitarian, and political modes of thought and behavior. Bell characterizes this as a shift toward a "sociologizing mode, or the effort to judge a society's needs in more conscious fashion, and . . . to do so on the basis of some explicit conception of the 'public interest'" (1973, p. 283). His emphasis is on the societal aspects of "sociologizing," but the effects of a shift from individualist-rationalist to communitarian-behaviorist modes of thought and action within organizations are certainly parallel and of equal importance. Such a shift has, for example, clear implications for employee participation in managerial decision-making, and for greater emphasis on social roles and quality-of-life considerations in worklife relationships.

However, one conspicuous and important manifestation of increased participation in the conduct of economic life is the expansion of public regulation, particularly with respect to the manufacturing sector, in recent years. Lilley and Miller (1977) cite the enactment of thirty major pieces of federal legislation, the establishment of seven new regulatory agencies, and an increase of approximately 200 percent in federal regulatory agency budgets during the short period 1970-1975. These calculations take no account of increased activity at the state and local level, or of the private cost and procedural requirements of expanded public regulation. Although one is initially impressed—and many serious analysts are alarmed or dismayed—by the sheer volume and cost of this increased regulatory activity, its greater general significance is the implication that the mixed economy, as we have heretofore conceived it, has undergone a radical transformation. While some of the traditional regulated industries—finance, transportation, and public utilities—have experienced minor changes in the direction of deregulation, the bulk of this unregulated activity in the private economy (and, again, particularly manufacturing) has been drawn within a significantly more comprehensive regulatory framework.

It is true, of course, that all industries have been regulated to some extent since the late nineteenth century, but the substantial recent expansion in the scope and character of regulation has rendered largely invalid the conventional regulated/unregulated distinction among classes of economic activity. Partially as a result, participative, political, and public interest-oriented modes of analysis and decision-making are now required—and required by concern for social legitimacy as well as strict legality—thoughout the great bulk of the private economy, and certainly in all major industries and large firms.

There is, at the same time, a major distinction between the old forms of regulation and the new. The old regulation was client-oriented in some sense, whether the clients in question included only some or many participants to a market-exchange relationship. By contrast, the new regulation is essentially function-oriented and is concerned primarily with the welfare of persons who may not be parties to a market relationship, either because they are excluded from participation (equal employment opportunity) or because no such relationship exists (environmental protection). Even where an exchange relationship lies in the background, the new regulation is not aimed at exchange conditions themselves (character and quality of service, rate of compensation), but rather at ancillary issues such as safety, privacy, and availability of information.

Again, the new regulation can be seen in an evolutionary context. The protection of employees, customers, and even the general public has a long and varied history at every level of government; some features of the new regulation simply codify and extend the coverage of well-established arrangements. The total impact of the new regulation represents, however, a substantial change in the status quo because of the pervasiveness, variety, specificity, and enormous cost of this vast expansion in public regulatory authority. Indeed, during the current period of adjustment to these new conditions, it seems likely that some modification in goals, and some reduction in their specificity and in compliance cost, will take place all across the regulatory agenda.

These short-run adaptations will not, however, alter the basic situation. Traditional economizing will no longer provide, by itself, socially legitimate solutions to economic problems involving any substantial social side-effects, whether internal to the organization or external in the larger society. The range of external impacts in which a formal public interest is manifest has expanded to a point that few, if any, areas of economic life remain excluded.

A final note on this subject: there is considerable argument and some evidence that much of the old regulation either (1) arose in response to a demand on the part of the regulatees, or (2) whatever its origins, was eventually "captured" by the regulatees and made to serve their own interests, rather than those of intended clients or the general public. The new regulation can scarcely be described as involving responses to regulatee demand, and the cross-sectional character of much of the new regulation (that is, focus on a specific function across all industries, rather than on multiple characteristics of a single industry) creates such a large and varied regulatee constituency that the likelihood of capture is substantially reduced.

The Manufacturing Sector in the Postindustrial Economy

Relative Decline in the Manufacturing Sector

Although there may be some question as to whether or not the United States has evolved into a "postindustrial society" in the complete sense in which Bell (1973, p. 14) uses that term, there is no doubt about the post-industrial status of our economy. Victor Fuchs's analysis (1968) clearly demonstrated that service-producing activities—including government, finance, and trade, as well as "services proper"—surpassed goods-producing activities as sources of employment by the late 1950s; the balance with respect to sources of national income has now also shifted in the same direction.

The relative decline of agriculture and relative growth of government have been the most striking trends in the income and employment structure of our economy for many decades. Agriculture accounted for just under half of all labor utilization and more than one-fifth of national income (*Historical Statistics of the U.S.*, 1975) in 1869; it now accounts, according to table 1-1, for well under 5 percent of each. Government at all levels accounted for under 5 percent of both labor utilization and income in 1869, and now accounts for more than 15 percent of each.

This relative growth of government and other service activities necessarily implies a corresponding decline in the shares of income and employment for other sectors over the same period. Recently, however, the relative decline in the share of manufacturing in both labor and income has been substantially greater than that of the private domestic economy as a whole, and now seems to be clearly established as a long-term trend. The sharp shift in employment and income structure that has taken place over the past decade can be clearly observed in table 1-1.

A long-term perspective reveals that manufacturing accounted for an increasing share of persons engaged in production throughout the nineteenth century and with a fair degree of continuity up until the early 1950s,

Table 1-1
Composition of National Income and Employment, 1963 and 1976; Employment Projections, 1985

Sectors	1963 National Income Originating Amount ($ billions)	1963 National Income Originating %	1963 Employment Number (000)	1963 Employment %	1976 National Income Originating Amount ($ billions)	1976 National Income Originating %	1976 Employment Number (000)	1976 Employment %	1985 Employment (Projection) %
Total	481.9	100.0	67,762[a]	100.0	1399.3	100.0	87,485[a]	100.0	100.0
Rest of world	3.4	0.7	—	—	14.4	1.02	—	—	—
Government & government enterprises	64.7	13.4	9,226[a]	13.6	214.9	15.35	15,088[a]	17.24	17.7
Total private domestic	413.9	85.9	58,536	86.4	1170.0	83.61	72,397	82.75	82.3
Agriculture	18.6	3.9	4,687	6.9	40.8	2.91	3,297	3.76	2.1
Construction & mining	30.2	6.2	3,598	5.3	87.1	6.22	4,153	4.74	5.1
Transportation & public utilities	40.1	8.4	3,903	5.8	106.8	7.63	4,507	5.15	4.9
Finance, insurance, & real estate	53.6	11.1	2,877	4.2	160.8	11.49	4,316	4.93	5.4
Manufacturing	143.8	29.8	16,995	25.1	365.0	26.08	18,954	21.66	20.6
Wholesale trade	26.8	5.6	11,778	17.4	91.1	6.51	17,490	19.99	4.7
Retail trade	46.6	9.7			129.6	9.26			16.5
Services	54.1	11.2	8,325	12.3	188.2	13.44	14,602	16.69	22.1
Proprietors, self-employed & others not enumerated by industry			6,373[b]	9.4			5,078[b]	5.80	

Source (1963): national income—*Survey of Current Business*, July 1966, table 1.12, p. 15; employment—*Economic Report of the President*, 1970, tables C-22, C-27.

Source (1976): national income without capital consumption adjustment by industry—*Survey of Current Business*, November 1977, table 17, p. 9; employment—*Economic Report of the President*, 1977, tables B-32, B-27.

Source (1985): Charles T. Bowman, "The Labor Force, Employment, and Economic Growth," *U.S. Economic Growth from 1976 to 1986: Prospects, Problems, & Patterns*, for JEC, 95th Congress, Washington, D.C., 1977, table 6, p. 79.

[a]Excluding armed forces.
[b]By subtraction.

apart from the interruption of the Great Depression. Since that time, however, there seems to be no question as to the declining trend in the relative share of manufacturing in total private employment, a decline that has become even more striking during the 1970s, as shown by the year-by-year data in table 1-2. Indeed, again apart from the Depression, the relative importance of manufacturing employment is lower now than at any time in this century, and all recent studies project a continuing decline into the 1980s (Mooney and Tschetter, 1976). A JEC study by Charles T. Bowman

Table 1-2
Manufacturing Employment as Percent of Total Private Employment, 1947-1976

Year	Total Private Employment Number (000)	Manufacturing Employment Number (000)	Manufacturing Employment as %
1947	38,407	15,545	40.47
1948	39,241	15,582	39.70
1949	37,922	14,441	38.08
1950	39,196	15,241	36.76
1951	41,460	16,393	39.53
1952	42,216	16,632	39.39
1953	43,587	17,549	40.26
1954	42,271	16,314	38.59
1955	43,761	16,882	38.57
1956	45,131	17,243	38.20
1957	45,278	17,174	37.93
1958	43,524	15,945	36.63
1959	45,230	16,675	36.86
1960	45,881	16,796	36.60
1961	45,448	16,326	35.92
1962	46,706	16,853	36.08
1963	47,477	16,995	35.79
1964	48,735	17,274	35.44
1965	50,741	18,062	35.63
1966	53,163	19,214	36.14
1967	54,459	19,447	35.70
1968	56,106	19,781	35.25
1969	58,240	20,167	34.62
1970	58,359	19,349	33.15
1971	58,334	18,572	31.83
1972	60,373	19,090	31.62
1973	63,157	20,068	31.77
1974	64,235	20,046	31.20
1975	62,330	18,347	29.43
1976	64,493	18,956	29.39

Source: *Employment and Training Report of the President*, 1977, table C-1, p. 218.

showed manufacturing accounting for 21.5 percent of total employment by 1980 and 20.6 percent by 1985 (1977, p. 79). It is notable that the projected 1980 level had already been reached by 1976, as shown in table 1-1.

Location of Manufacturing Activity

Patterns of change in the location of manufacturing activity, on both an employment and a value added basis, are shown in table 1-3. In general, the detailed data confirm popular impressions: a continuing decline in the relative importance of traditional manufacturing centers in the Northeast, and a corresponding expansion in the South and West. Prior to about 1970, these changes took place in the context of expanding total manufacturing employment (see table 1-2), so that relative decline did not necessarily involve a corresponding absolute reduction in production and employment. In more recent years, relative and absolute changes have tended to be in the same direction, and this situation seems certain to hold for the foreseeable future.

Another point demonstrated by the data in table 1-3 is the relatively higher value added per employee in the two regions of greatest recent growth—West South Central and Pacific—as compared to both the older industrial areas and the expanding South Atlantic and East South Central regions. This difference is not necessarily a pure productivity differential, since regional differences in the composition of manufacturing activities and price-cost margins are also involved.

The Centrality of Manufacturing

Despite the evident shift toward postindustrialism, the manufacturing sector remains the single largest subdivision of the economy. This may be something of an artifact of the classification system, but both the classifications themselves and the specific data reflect an important underlying reality.

The manufacturing sector is characterized by a special strategic importance suggested by the term "centrality": manufacturing provides the physical and functional linkage between virtually all raw materials production, on one hand, and the distributive trades and final utilization (both investment and consumption) on the other. Not only is this physical and economic linkage both obvious and important, but inspection of the summary input-output matrix (table 1-4) shows that the manufacturing sector is the largest user of its own output and that of agriculture, mining, trade, transportation, and service as well.

This central role of manufacturing in an industrialized economic system simply means that whatever happens in the manufacturing sector leads to repercussions in other sectors and thus throughout the economic system. One specific manifestation of this pervasive impact is the increasing integration

Table 1-3

Manufacturing Employment and Value Added—Percent Distribution by Geographic Divisions: 1950-1975

Geographic Division	1950	1954	1958	1963	1965	1967	1970	1972	1974	1975
Employment										
New England	9.8	9.0	8.7	8.4	8.2	8.1	7.6	7.2	7.2	7.1
Middle Atlantic	26.9	26.6	25.7	24.0	23.4	22.6	21.8	20.7	19.7	19.5
East North Central	30.0	28.6	26.6	26.4	27.2	26.7	26.0	25.9	26.1	25.3
West North Central	5.6	6.0	6.0	6.0	6.0	6.2	6.2	6.3	6.6	6.7
South Atlantic	11.1	11.0	11.8	12.5	12.7	12.9	13.6	14.4	14.3	14.5
East South Central	4.4	4.5	4.9	5.2	5.6	5.7	6.1	6.6	6.7	6.6
West South Central	4.0	4.5	5.0	5.1	5.3	5.6	6.1	6.5	6.7	7.0
Mountain	1.1	1.1	1.4	1.7	1.6	1.6	1.8	2.0	2.2	2.2
Pacific	7.0	8.8	10.0	10.6	10.0	10.6	10.3	10.4	10.7	10.9
Value Added										
New England	8.3	7.8	7.4	7.1	7.1	7.2	6.8	6.4	6.1	5.9
Middle Atlantic	26.2	26.0	24.6	22.7	22.5	21.9	21.4	19.9	18.6	18.6
East North Central	33.2	31.2	28.9	29.3	30.2	28.6	27.5	28.2	28.3	26.8
West North Central	5.7	6.1	6.3	6.1	6.2	6.4	6.9	6.7	6.7	7.1
South Atlantic	9.4	9.1	10.1	11.0	11.1	11.2	11.8	12.5	12.2	12.5
East South Central	3.8	4.0	4.5	4.8	5.1	5.2	5.7	6.0	6.1	6.1
West South Central	4.3	4.9	5.5	5.7	5.8	6.3	6.7	7.0	8.1	8.8
Mountain	1.2	1.2	1.6	1.8	1.6	1.7	1.9	2.1	2.3	2.3
Pacific	7.9	9.7	11.1	11.5	10.7	11.3	11.1	11.3	11.6	12.0

Source: *Statistical Abstract of the United States 1977*, U.S. Department of Commerce, Bureau of the Census, table 1373, p. 799.

Table 1-4
Input-Output Flow Table, 1970
(billions of dollars; for inputs read down; for outputs read across)

	Agriculture	Mining	Construction	Manufacturing	Wholesale & Retail Trade[b]	Transportation	Services	Other	Final Demand	Total Output
Agriculture	22.34	0.0	.29	35.69	.14	.14	3.35	.24	10.81	72.99
Mining	.15	1.75	1.03	21.18	.01	.04	5.06	.22	2.03	31.46
Construction	.59	6.94	.04	3.48	.72	1.71	14.47	2.50	103.50	127.72
Manufacturing	.92	2.89	44.43	272.21	10.29	5.78	34.50	9.72	319.58	708.61
Wholesale & retail trade	.35	.46	10.19	23.28	4.42	2.13	9.15	.25	153.77	207.11
Transportation	.15	.44	3.12	16.01	1.66	6.94	3.63	7.81	24.64	65.68
Services[a]	.65	5.42	8.49	49.61	33.20	6.31	27.14	5.22	275.18	417.07
Other	.15	2.95	1.03	33.97	6.17	5.43	18.56	10.44	83.99	164.05
Employees, owners, and government (value added)	27.79	16.86	59.11	253.20	150.50	37.19	301.21	127.64	973.50[c]	—
Total input	72.99	31.46	127.72	708.61	207.11	65.68	417.07	164.05	—	1794.69

Source: U.S. Department of Commerce, Office of Business Economics. For basic explanation of data see *Survey of Current Business*, November 1969, pp. 16-47.

[a]Finance, insurance, and real estate, as well as communications and public utilities are classified as services in this tabulation; in other respects the data are approximately comparable to those in table 1-1.

[b]The output of wholesale and retail trade is estimated on a "value added" basis; that is, the value of merchandise purchased and resold is not included in total output of the distributive trades.

[c]Total Value Added = Total Final Demand = Gross National Product. (This GNP figure does not correspond precisely to that available from other sources due to omissions and rounding adjustments in the input-output table.)

of manufacturing and nonmanufacturing activities within the same large, diversified business enterprise, a development to which we now turn detailed attention.

Diversification and Integration

When the largest industrial merger in history—the acquisition of Utah International by General Electric—occurred in 1977, it drew considerable attention because of its size, its special approval by the Justice Department, and the apparent informality of the merger negotiations themselves (Kraar, 1977). Much of the discussion about this merger focused on the apparent lack of direct competitive overlap between the two companies, but possibilities for significant compatibility and growth support existed. Less widely noted was the fact that this merger, although impressive in size and in many unique details, constitutes simply an example of the continuing integration of manufacturing and nonmanufacturing activities within the same industrial enterprises, whether via merger or through internal growth and expansion. This continuing process of intersectoral (as well as interindustry) diversification can best be observed in *Enterprise Statistics* prepared periodically by the Census Bureau as part of the Economic Census program.

Multi-Industry Activities

Enterprise Statistics (originally named *Company Statistics*) was initiated in 1954 in an effort to present an integrated picture of the multi-industry activities of entire business enterprises, as opposed to the conventional industry and sectoral tabulations arising from traditional census procedures. The coverage and character of the data collection have changed significantly over time so that few detailed comparisons among data for 1958, 1963, and 1967 can be easily made. However, the 1967 and 1972 reports are the most comprehensive produced thus far, and probably constitute benchmarks for the analysis of future trends.

Although some data in this collection include dollar value items such as sales and payrolls, the principal basis for analysis is the distribution of enterprise employment among establishments according to their various functional activities. It should be noted that *Enterprise Statistics* employs a set of industrial classifications somewhat different from, but entirely compatible with, the usual Standard Industrial Classification (SIC) system. The data do not cover enterprises primarily engaged in agriculture, transportation and public utilities, finance, insurance and real estate, and other service activities outside the scope of the economic censuses. Thus, coverage varies by sectors from 95 percent of all manufacturing employment to 77 percent of all private nonagricultural employment.

Table 1-5
Diversification among Manufacturing and Nonmanufacturing Enterprises, 1972
(number of employees, except as noted)

Type of Employment Activity	Single-Industry Manufacturing Companies	Multi-Industry Manufacturing Companies	Multi-Industry Nonmanufacturing Companies	Single-Industry Nonmanufacturing Companies	Totals
	257,201 companies	7,851 companies	2,242 companies		
Manufacturing activity	5,901,584	11,790,595	345,693		
Manufacturers' sales branch/office and CAO	59,112	1,885,178	30,398[a]		
Total	5,960,696	13,675,773	376,091		Total manufacturing employment (95% of all manufacturing employment) 18,037,872
		Mineral 171,885	23,801 companies	4,737,890 companies	
		Construction 120,870			
Nonmanufacturing activity[b]		Wholesale 241,116	6,570,083	17,807,418	Total nonmanufacturing employment production activities only 25,263,151
		Retail 434,219	(CAO—485,999)	(CAO—78,206)	Including sales branches/offices and CAO 27,772,932
		Services 304,406			
		Other 207,359			
		Total 1,479,855			
Total Employment	5,960,696	15,155,628	6,946,174	17,807,418	Total covered employment (77% of all private nonagricultural employment) 45,710,804

Source: *Enterprise Statistics*, 1972.

[a]Excludes CAOs of Nonmanufacturing companies.
[b]The number of manufacturing companies diversified into nonmanufacturing activities cannot be ascertained from available census sources.

The 1972 data have been synthesized in table 1-5 to show the extent to which manufacturing companies have become integrated into nonmanufacturing activities, and vice versa. It is obvious that a relatively small number (7,851) of diversified manufacturing companies account for about 65 percent of all manufacturing employment covered by this data. This amounts to about 78 percent of the total employment of such companies, a figure that has declined only slightly (from 79.4 percent) since 1963 (Preston, 1971, p. 6). These companies have an additional volume of employment (12 percent) in sales branches and offices and in central administrative offices (CAO) which are primarily related to their manufacturing activities.

An additional group of employees, amounting to just under 10 percent of the total employment of these companies, is engaged in nonmanufacturing activities other than sales and central administration. The actual number of firms engaging in such nonmanufacturing activities cannot be determined from census sources, but since it is certainly less than the total, the importance of diversification for those companies is somewhat greater than indicated by this figure.

The extent of enterprise diversification is, of course, much greater within the manufacturing sector itself. Table 1-6 breaks down the manufacturing employment of the 7,851 diversified manufacturing companies into two categories: employment within each company's home industry and employment in other *manufacturing* activities. These data are tabulated according to the major industry group of each enterprise, but are developed from the basic *Enterprise Statistics* industry classifications themselves (115 industries). Thus, for example, the diversification of a meat packing company into dairy products will be reflected in these data, even though both activities fall within the broad "Food and Kindred Products" industry category.

The striking fact illustrated by table 1-6 is that even when the broader mode of classification is utilized, 41 percent of the employment of diversified manufacturing companies (and 27.5 percent of the employment of all manufacturing companies) is accounted for by manufacturing activities outside the home industry of the enterprise. This table also reveals that the extent of intramanufacturing diversification varies significantly among home manufacturing groups. In two industry groups—paper and allied products, and electric and electronic equipment—manufacturing employment outside the home industry activity exceeds that in the home industry activity itself; in no instance is diversification employment less than one-fifth of the total.

Although these precise results are to some extent artifacts of the particular classification system being utilized, their overwhelming implication—and that of the underlying data itself—is that multi-activity diversification is now the typical pattern of enterprise structure within the manufacturing sector.

Table 1-6
Manufacturing Employment of Multi-Industry Manufacturing Companies, by "Home" Industry of Company and Other Manufacturing Activity[a]

| Major Industry Group of "Home" Industry | Manufacturing Employment | | B as Percent A |
	Total (A)	Outside "Home" Industry (B)	
20. Food & kindred products	965,061	370,706	38.35
21. Tobacco manufacturers	89,925	31,951	35.53
22. Textile mill products	596,251	201,578	36.40
23. Apparel & other textile products	418,992	154,824	36.95
24. Lumber & wood products	193,497	67,514	28.01
25. Furniture and fixtures	151,174	49,865	32.98
26. Paper & allied products	525,648	294,207	55.97
27. Printing & publishing	453,935	102,537	22.59
28. Chemical & allied products	770,278	332,546	43.17
29. Petroleum & coal products	151,503	59,117	39.02
30. Rubber & miscellaneous plastic products	368,809	143,634	38.94
31. Leather & leather products	166,803	60,184	36.08
32. Stone, clay, & glass products	378,696	137,337	36.26
33. Primary metal industries	1,003,036	352,718	35.16
34. Fabricated metal products	626,606	278,553	44.45
35. Machinery, except electrical	951,991	341,638	35.83
36. Electric & electronic equipment	1,455,289	750,025	51.54
37. Transportation equipment	2,043,367	884,967	43.31
38. Instruments & related products	323,965	118,979	36.72
39. Miscellaneous manufacturing industries & ordinance & accessories	156,769	63,252	40.35
Totals	11,790,595	4,858,519	41.21

Source: *Enterprise Statistics 1972*, table 2.
[a]Data computed from 115-industry classification, summarized by major industry group for presentation purposes.

Mergers

To what extent are these diversification patterns due to mergers? That question is virtually impossible to answer because, among other reasons, (1) merger data are generally reported by dollar value, not number of employees, and (2) in any event, allowance must be made for postmerger growth or decline in the size of the merged units. However, it is well known that the merger wave of the 1960s reached a sharp peak, both in number and in dollar volume, during 1967-1969. By 1976, large merger activity ($10 million or more in assets) had dropped to about half of its previous peak—seventy-seven large mergers, involving almost $6 billion in assets in that year. Mergers are not, however, easily summarized in terms of diversification impact since they frequently involve companies that are themselves already diversified, so that a sequence of overlapping diversification relationships results.

By contrast, the larger universe of all mergers recorded by the Federal Trade Commission may be arrayed by major industry group of acquired and acquiring company, and inspection of the most recent data gives some impression of the importance of diversification mergers within total merger activity. As shown in table 1-7, 139 (26 percent) out of the 526 acquisitions made by manufacturing companies in 1976 involved firms within the acquiring company's own major industry group. An additional 32 percent were acquisitions of other manufacturing companies, and the remaining 42 percent of all manufacturing acquisitions (including the "unknowns," since it is likely that a manufacturing company would have been correctly identified) involved intersectoral diversification. In addition, 115 (20 percent) of the acquisitions of nonmanufacturing companies involved manufacturing activities.

Thus, although the data reveal nothing about the magnitude of these acquisitions in either value or employment terms, the superficial evidence is that there was substantially more merger-diversification of manufacturing firms into nonmanufacturing activity than the other way around, although there was a significant amount of activity in both directions. More recent data indicate that the pace of merger activity is accelerating, that diversification mergers are continuing to grow in importance, and that acquisition of U.S. companies by foreign buyers is a new and growing aspect of the current merger wave (*Wall Street Journal*, April 11, 1978, p. 1).

There is some suggestion in these data, supported by inspection of the annual merger series in more detail, that industries in which enterprises are already characterized by high levels of diversification—as revealed by the 1972 employment data in table 1-6, for example—are also those in which diversification mergers are continuing to take place at relatively high rates. For example, firms primarily engaged in manufacturing electric and elec-

Table 1-7

Completed Acquisitions, Classified by Industry of Acquiring Company and Sector of Acquired Company, 1976

Acquiring Company SIC Code	Acquired Company					
	Same Industry	Other Manufacturing	Mining	Wholesale & Retail	Other & Unknown	Total
20. Food & kindred products	26	6	0	14	14	60
21. Tobacco manufacturers	0	1	0	0	2	3
22. Textile mill products	5	3	1	0	2	11
23. Apparel & other textile products	3	1	0	0	4	8
24. Lumber & wood products	2	8	0	1	2	13
25. Furniture & fixtures	1	3	0	0	1	5
26. Paper & allied products	2	5	0	2	3	12
27. Printing & publishing	22	5	0	2	8	37
28. Chemical & allied products	13	19	0	8	15	55
29. Petroleum & coal products	2	0	4	1	4	11
30. Rubber & miscellaneous plastic products	5	2	0	0	5	12
31. Leather & leather products	0	3	0	0	0	3
32. Stone, clay, & glass products	4	5	2	1	5	17
33. Primary metal industries	2	17	0	6	6	31
34. Fabricated metal products	3	31	1	8	11	54
35. Machinery, except electrical	20	17	3	5	19	64
36. Electric & electronic equipment	15	23	1	2	17	58
37. Transportation equipment	3	7	0	2	12	24
38. Instruments & related products	8	8	0	3	15	34
39. Miscellaneous manufacturing industries & ordinance & accessories	3	2	0	0	9	14
Total manufacturing	139	166	12	55	154	526
Mining	—	8	14	2	9	33
Wholesale & retail	—	22	1	52	35	110
Other & unknown	—	85	14	53	260	412

Source: U.S. Federal Trade Commission, *Statistical Report on Mergers and Acquisitions*, November 1977, p. 16.

tronic equipment, shown to be highly diversified in their 1972 employment, engaged in fifty-eight mergers during 1976, and three-quarters of these involved firms outside the electric and electronic equipment industry. Similar high incidence of diversification mergers is noted for firms in machinery manufacturing, chemicals, and fabricated metals, all of which showed relatively high levels of diversification in the 1972 employment data. By contrast, firms in printing and publishing showed the lowest level of employment diversification in 1972; twenty-two of the thirty-seven mergers recorded for firms in this industry group in 1976 were within their own sphere of economic activity.

Major Trends within the Manufacturing Sector

Changing Composition of Manufacturing Activity

The data in table 1-8 show the percentage distribution of employment by major manufacturing industry group for the census years 1958-1972 and for 1976. It is scarcely surprising that the changes revealed even over this two-decade time span are typically of small magnitude. Relative decline in employment in the food industries, and corresponding increases in areas of heavy manufacturing (metals and machinery other than automobiles) are probably the most significant observations.

The broad stability of the relative employment structure masks an important underlying reality: a decline of more than 1.5 million manufacturing jobs between 1967 and 1976. Even if this particular statistic is viewed as a short-term phenomenon, the more striking point may be that the absolute level of employment declined in fifteen out of twenty major manufacturing industry groups over the decade. This decline was led by a drop of almost 400,000 jobs in electric and electronic equipment, more than 200,000 in both transportation equipment and primary metals, and nearly 200,000 in the food industries. The five groups registering employment increases over the decade were instruments, nonelectrical machinery, fabricated metals, printing and publishing, and lumber and wood products.

Recent output projections for the period 1978-1982 for 143 selected manufacturing industries produced by the Department of Commerce (*U.S. Industrial Output, 1978*) identified only three large-employment industries—paper and paperboard, industrial organic chemicals, and computers—for which unusually high rates of employment growth were anticipated. The largest industries covered by the study—automobiles, meat packing, and steel—were projected to lag significantly in output growth over this period. (See Appendix, table A-1, for detailed data.) Inspection of these and other analyses suggests that the pattern of gradual change in the structure of manufacturing employment observed over the past couple of

Table 1-8
Percentage Distribution of Manufacturing Employment, by Major Industry Groups, Selected Years

SIC Code	Industry Groups	1958	1963	1967	1972	1976
20.	Food & kindred products	11.11	10.11	8.93	8.74	8.68
21.	Tobacco manufacturers	.51	.49	.43	.39	.37
22.	Textile mill products	5.70	5.20	4.93	5.17	4.95
23.	Apparel & other textile products	7.41	7.60	7.10	7.32	7.13
24.	Lumber & wood products	3.68	3.35	2.90	3.69	3.56
25.	Furniture & fixtures	2.22	2.24	2.22	2.46	2.41
26.	Paper & allied products	3.57	3.61	3.47	3.50	3.48
27.	Printing & publishing	5.43	5.45	5.44	5.70	6.14
28.	Chemical & allied products	4.89	5.00	5.08	5.22	4.81
29.	Petroleum & coal products	1.54	1.29	1.09	1.10	.92
30.	Rubber & miscellaneous plastic products	2.22	2.51	2.74	3.33	3.55
31.	Leather & leather products	2.23	1.90	1.74	1.50	1.40
32.	Stone, clay, & glass products	3.58	3.55	3.20	3.47	3.39
33.	Primary metal industries	7.04	6.88	6.87	6.23	5.25
34.	Fabricated metal products	6.80	6.54	7.10	8.00	8.32
35.	Machinery, except electrical	8.64	8.96	9.98	10.14	11.08
36.	Electric & electronic equipment	7.60	9.50	10.25	9.46	8.93
37.	Transportation equipment	10.24	9.96	10.01	9.54	9.43
38.	Instruments & related products	1.83	1.86	2.11	2.52	2.93
39.	Miscellaneous manufacturing industries & ordinance & accessories	3.55	3.80	4.30	2.39	2.32
	Total	100%	100%	100%	100%	100%
	Total number of employees	16,025,200	16,958,400	19,322,900	19,026,800	17,682,700

Source: *Census of Manufactures, 1972* and *Annual Survey of Manufacturers, 1976*.

decades, with large absolute changes confined to a few critical sectors, is likely to continue during the 1980s.

Because they share the greatest responsibility for air and water polluting activity, the industries most likely to be directly affected by environmental protection are pulp and paper mills, chemicals, petroleum refining, and primary metals (Tolley and Graves, 1978).

Concentration in Manufacturing

The concentration of economic activity—control by a small number of units (households, firms, or whatever) of a large portion of some economic magnitude (wealth, income, production)—remains a subject of continuing interest. By far the greatest attention has been paid to concentration within the manufacturing sector, although the importance of concentration in manufacturing with respect to the functioning of the entire economy, whatever the actual level may be, is subject to change over time as a result of other long-term trends. For example, the relative growth of government and of economic sectors, such as distribution and services which are not characterized by high concentration levels, may suggest a relative deconcentration of the entire economy. On the other hand, expansion of large manufacturing firms into nonmanufactuirng activity raises the possibility that patterns of manufacturing concentration may spread by contagion to other sectors of the economy. Whatever the net result of these developments, the pattern of concentration within manufacturing itself retains some intrinsic interest, particularly in relation to patterns of unionization among manufacturing employees.

Aggregate Concentration. The term "aggregate concentration" refers to the share of some small number of large companies in the activity of the total sector of the economy in which they participate, or conceivably, of the economy as a whole. The significance of aggregate concentration has nothing directly to do with the presence or absence of monopoly in specific industries and markets. Given the tendency of large manufacturing firms to be highly diversified, aggregate concentration indicates the participation of the largest of such enterprises across a broad spectrum of economic activities, and by implication, the ability to participate in still other spheres if they should find it attractive to do so. (I omit here discussion of the possible political impact of aggregate concentration, although it may not be a less important consideration than those discussed.)

The data tabulated in table 1-5 already shed some light on aggregate concentration, since they reveal that 7,851 large diversified manufacturing companies account for some two-thirds of all manufacturing employment, and for a slightly larger share if the sales and administrative employees are taken into account. These relationships cannot be conveniently traced back to previous years because of the absence of data.

More precise information indicates that the share of a much smaller number of very large firms in total U.S. manufacturing activity has increased gradually, but substantially, for the past several decades, and probably since the beginning of the industrial era. The data in table 1-9 show the share of the fifty and 100 largest companies in total manufacturing value added for census years 1947-1972, as well as the share of the specific fifty and 100 largest companies, 1972, for each of the previous census years. This latter series is significant because it demonstrates the relative rise to prominence of firms that were not within the top ranks in previous years. As a matter of fact, only half of the firms that were among the top fifty in 1972 were also among the top fifty in 1947 (although twenty of the twenty-five replacement firms were among the top 200 in that year).

Measures of concentration in terms of employment and payroll as well as value of output, shown in table 1-10, reveal some curious relationships. Although one would do well to treat small differences in these extremely aggregated data with great caution, it appears that the fifty largest firms accounted for a more substantial share of output value—whether shipments or value added—than of employment or compensation payments, although the latter were clearly greater than the former. Perhaps these largest firms are more able to increase prices (and therefore output values) above costs, or are more efficiently run—or both—than other firms in the manufacturing sector. Furthermore, these comparisons indicate that whatever the source of the high output values, some of them are paid out to employees. The fact remains, however, that a very small number of giant enterprises engage the productive services of a substantial portion of the manufacturing

Table 1-9
Share of Total Value Added by Manufacture Accounted for by the 50 and 100 Largest Identical Manufacturing Companies: 1972 and Earlier Years

Year	Share of Largest Companies of 1972 in Each Year		Share of Largest Companies in Each Year	
	50 Largest	100 Largest	50 Largest	100 Largest
1972	25	33	25	33
1970	23	31	23	32
1967	23	30	22	30
1966	23	30	22	30
1963	22	29	21	29
1962	22	28	22	29
1958	20	26	20	27
1954	19	25	20	27
1947	12	17	17	24

Source: *Census of Manufactures 1972, Concentration Ratios in Manufacturing Industries.* Bureau of the Census, 1975.

Table 1-10
Share of Value Added, Employment, Payroll, Value of Shipments, and Capital Expenditures Accounted for by the 200 Largest Companies: 1972 and 1967
(percent)

Company Rank Group Based on Value Added by Manufacture		Value Added by Manufacture	All employees[a]		Production Workers			Value of Shipments[b]	Capital Expenditures, New
			Number	Payroll	Number	Man-hours	Wages		
50 largest	1972	25	17	22	17	18	24	24	26
	1967	25	20	25	18	18	23	25	27
51st to 100th largest	1972	9	6	6	6	6	7	8	9
	1967	8	6	7	5	6	6	8	13
101st to 150th largest	1972	6	5	5	5	5	6	6	6
	1967	5	4	5	4	4	4	6	6
151st to 200th largest	1972	4	3	3	3	3	4	5	5
	1967	4	4	3	3	3	3	4	4
200 largest	1972	43	31	37	32	32	40	43	46
	1967	42	34	40	30	31	37	43	51

Source: *Census of Manufactures 1972*, Special Report Series, Bureau of the Census.

Note: all percentages are independently rounded and do not necessarily add to totals.

[a]Includes employees in central administrative offices and auxiliaries serving manufacturing establishments.

[b]Includes a substantial, but unmeasurable amount, of duplication because of shipments of materials and products among manufacturing establishments for further processing.

workforce. When the few additional large concentrations of employee-employer relationships from the public sector are added into consideration, it is apparent that a very small number of massive employment connections—although involving an incredibly wide range of labor functions and employment activities—dominate the entire employment structure of our economy.

Industry Concentration. "Industry concentration" refers to the share of a small number of firms in the total activity of more narrowly defined industries or product classifications. It is interesting to note the level of concentration and the changes in that level with time, in both individual industries and in the aggregate. Data from 1963 and 1972 for 367 SIC industries are analyzed in tables 1-11 and 1-12. More than 400 industries are covered in each year, but it is necessary to exclude a number of industries, many of them small, involved in reclassification between the two years, as well as a few important high-concentration industries for which relevant data are withheld to avoid disclosure. However, the remaining data collection is large enough to reveal major patterns of change throughout the manufacturing sector.

The share of the four largest firms in value of total industry shipments increased over the decade in 45.0 percent of the comparable industries, decreased in 37.6 percent, and remained unchanged (within a range of ± 1 percentage point) in 17.4 perent. Thus, for those industries in which changes in concentration occurred, increases were more frequent than decreases. However, the net impact of these changes was not sufficient to change the overall weighted average of four-firm concentration, which was 36.7 percent for the 367 comparable industries in both years.

Data in these tables reveal considerable diversity in both levels and patterns of change in four-firm concentration among industries classified into the twenty major manufacturing industry groups. Aside from tobacco manufacturing, two high-concentration industry groups in 1963, transportation equipment and chemicals, experienced substantial declines over the decade. By contrast, instruments and related products, a smaller but rapidly growing industry, experienced a major increase in concentration, such that it became the third most highly concentrated industry group by 1972. Significant increases in concentration also occurred in the moderately concentrated electrical and nonelectrical machinery industries, although these latter remained among the least concentrated groups within manufacturing.

Overall, average concentration increased in twelve groups over the decade, and declined in eight. The number of industries with value of shipments of $1 billion and over increased from ninety-five to 155 over the period, and the number of such industries with four-firm concentration of 60 percent or more increased from twelve to twenty-four. Thus, even taking

Table 1-11
Distribution of Four Firm Concentration Ratios by Major Industry Group and Size of Industry, 367 Comparable Manufacturing Industries, 1963-1972; Data for 1963

SIC Code	Industry Group	Value of Shipments Concentration Ratio for Four Largest Companies												Weighted Average
		Total		80 to 100		60 to 79		40 to 59		20 to 39		Less than 20		
		No. Industries	Value Shipments	No. Industries	Value Shipments	No. Industries	Value Shipments	No. Industries	Value Shipments	No. Industries	Value Shipments	No. Industries	Value Shipments	
20.	Food & kindred products	42	59022.5	2	869.9	8	5485.9	11	10509.3	17	36939.8	4	5217.6	34.9
21.	Tobacco manufactures	4	4519.9	1	2655.3	1	1366.6	2	498.0	—	—	—	—	74.6
22.	Textile mill products	26	14441.0	—	—	3	689.8	4	2333.7	16	8853.9	3	2563.6	33.2
23.	Apparel & related products	33	17087.1	—	—	—	—	2	705.5	9	3712.7	22	12668.9	16.5
24.	Lumber & wood products	7	6314.6	—	—	—	—	—	—	4	1907.6	3	4407.0	15.4
25.	Furniture & fixtures	11	3986.1	—	—	—	—	—	—	7	1967.4	4	2018.7	19.6
26.	Paper & allied products	15	15728.0	—	—	2	1093.1	4	2056.9	8	12352.2	1	225.8	31.0
27.	Printing & publishing	15	16165.9	—	—	—	—	2	983.7	6	4675.3	7	10506.9	18.6
28.	Chemicals & allied products	21	23285.7	2	2135.0	8	4641.2	4	7084.9	7	9424.6	—	—	48.2
29.	Petroleum & coal products	5	17994.7	—	—	1	71.5	—	—	3	17495.7	1	427.5	33.8
30.	Rubber & plastic products n.e.c.	4	6518.2	1	48.9	2	3303.9	—	—	—	—	1	3165.4	39.6
31.	Leather & leather products	9	4157.8	—	—	—	—	—	—	6	3052.0	3	1105.8	22.7
32.	Stone, clay, & glass products	26	12009.9	2	974.5	3	1073.8	10	3798.8	7	2114.3	4	4048.5	37.6
33.	Primary metal industries	19	23079.0	—	—	4	3076.2	5	12433.4	7	6694.5	3	874.9	43.5
34.	Fabricated metal products	26	20689.0	1	165.1	2	2358.4	5	950.4	6	5880.6	12	11334.5	26.6
35.	Machinery, except electrical	34	25286.3	1	616.4	1	318.6	12	10291.9	15	9328.0	5	4731.4	33.3
36.	Electrical machinery	30	27237.5	6	1762.3	6	4014.2	11	9300.4	5	8668.9	2	3491.7	43.5
37.	Transportation equipment	11	26737.2	1	437.9	1	11433.9	5	9956.0	4	4909.4	—	—	61.5
38.	Instruments & related products	11	6831.7	—	—	1	1851.2	6	2386.1	4	2594.4	—	—	44.8
39.	Miscellaneous manufacturing	18	5419.8	1	204.1	—	—	3	550.3	10	2881.1	4	1784.3	29.3
	Industry Size Class													
	$1,000,000,000 & over	95	232329.1	2	4058.5	10	27747.6	22	48937.9	36	105052.5	25	46532.6	
	$500,000,000 to $999,999,999	81	56719.8	5	3097.2	9	6566.0	21	14182.9	28	19827.6	18	13046.1	
	$200,000,000 to $499,999,999	114	37620.3	7	2129.0	16	5445.0	24	7961.3	44	14710.1	23	7374.9	
	$100,000,000 to $199,999,999	54	8199.9	3	535.8	6	897.2	17	2599.7	20	2967.4	8	1199.8	
	$50,000,000 to $99,999,999	19	1494.7	—	—	2	122.5	2	157.5	10	795.6	5	419.1	
	Less than $50,000,000	4	148.1	1	48.9	—	—	—	—	3	99.2	—	—	
	Total, all industries	367	336511.9	18	9869.4	43	40778.3	86	73839.3	141	143452.4	79	68572.5	36.7

Source: *Census of Manufactures 1972, Concentration Ratios in Manufacturing Industries.* Bureau of the Census, 1975.

Table 1-12

Distribution of Four Firm Concentration Ratios by Major Industry Group and Size of Industry, 367 Comparable Manufacturing Industries, 1963-1972; Data for 1972

SIC Code	Industry Group	Total No. Industries	Total Value Shipments	80 to 100 No. Industries	80 to 100 Value Shipments	60 to 79 No. Industries	60 to 79 Value Shipments	40 to 59 No. Industries	40 to 59 Value Shipments	20 to 39 No. Industries	20 to 39 Value Shipments	Less than 20 No. Industries	Less than 20 Value Shipments	Weighted Average
						Value of Shipments Concentration Ratio for Four Largest Companies								
20.	Food & kindred products	42	78818.7	2	1508.1	8	9090.9	14	21776.9	15	30493.4	3	15949.4	37.3
21.	Tobacco manufactures	4	5920.3	1	3744.6	2	1837.0	1	338.7	—	—	—	—	77.2
22.	Textile mill products	26	23546.6	1	685.1	3	604.1	6	2484.6	14	17468.4	2	2304.4	33.6
23.	Apparel & related products	33	27809.5	—	—	1	1133.0	2	438.1	18	12817.0	12	13421.4	22.9
24.	Lumber & wood products	7	12096.5	—	—	—	—	—	—	5	3146.2	2	8950.3	22.2
25.	Furniture & fixtures	11	8108.4	—	—	—	—	2	1226.0	3	1815.0	6	5067.4	30.0
26.	Paper & allied products	15	27181.0	—	—	2	2234.6	5	3830.1	6	16486.2	2	4630.1	31.6
27.	Printing & publishing	15	29159.1	—	—	1	755.4	2	1466.5	5	6311.2	7	20626.0	19.3
28.	Chemicals & allied products	21	43113.3	1	589.5	8	10587.2	3	10529.4	8	19204.9	1	2202.3	42.6
29.	Petroleum & coal products	5	28694.6	—	—	1	137.6	1	1010.3	2	26624.2	1	922.5	31.3
30.	Rubber & plastic products n.e.c.	4	17072.7	—	—	2	5776.8	1	600.0	—	—	1	10695.9	31.8
31.	Leather & leather products	9	3134.4	—	—	—	—	—	—	5	1342.1	4	1792.3	24.4
32.	Stone, clay, & glass products	26	20872.2	2	1577.4	4	2178.9	9	6507.9	6	2922.5	5	7685.5	36.2
33.	Primary metal industries	19	35214.2	—	—	3	1381.3	6	18501.1	9	14104.1	1	1227.7	38.4
34.	Fabricated metal products	26	37474.8	—	—	2	4733.3	5	1605.5	9	13140.3	10	17995.7	25.8
35.	Machinery, except electrical	34	42475.2	1	2189.0	1	1296.1	14	19839.1	10	8576.8	8	10574.2	36.8
36.	Electrical machinery	30	45066.6	7	5844.3	3	3442.5	13	20070.2	6	6569.4	1	9140.2	47.0
37.	Transportation equipment	11	47145.0	—	—	4	31412.5	3	6845.1	3	7839.2	1	1048.2	55.2
38.	Instruments & related products	11	14063.2	—	—	1	5623.9	6	4532.8	4	3906.5	—	—	54.4
39.	Miscellaneous manufacturing	18	10452.4	1	342.3	—	—	4	1461.4	10	6655.7	3	1993.0	30.6
	Industry Size Class													
	$1,000,000,000 & over	155	458846.4	6	11231.0	18	69894.8	34	93549.5	59	162925.1	38	121246.0	
	$500,000,000 to $999,999,999	87	63257.0	5	3548.5	11	8315.3	26	18412.9	32	23172.6	13	9807.7	
	$200,000,000 to $499,999,999	86	29933.3	5	1700.8	9	3089.8	28	9786.5	32	11254.5	12	4101.7	
	$100,000,000 to $199,999,999	29	4695.9	—	—	4	646.1	7	1204.9	12	1831.9	6	1013.0	
	$50,000,000 to $99,999,999	7	572.5	—	—	3	249.4	1	73.1	2	191.9	1	58.1	
	Less than $50,000,000	3	113.6	—	—	1	29.7	1	36.8	1	47.1	—	—	
	Total, all industries	367	557418.7	16	16480.3	46	82225.1	97	123063.7	138	199423.1	70	136226.5	36.7

Source: *Census of Manufactures 1972, Concentration Ratios in Manufacturing Industries.* Bureau of the Census, 1975.

into account changes in the distribution of firms by size due to inflation, the incidence of high concentration among the largest industries in the manufacturing sector appears to have increased substantially. However, the net effect of increases and decreases, and changes in industry size, was such as to leave the overall weighted average level of concentration in manufacturing industries unchanged.

International Aspects

The increasing importance of world trade relationships is a significant element of the future manufacturing environment. A discussion of this subject is derived primarily from the *International Economic Report of the President*, 1977.

In spite of year-to-year fluctuations, world trade has increased at a substantially greater rate than world GNP over the entire period since 1960. Further, over the same period the U.S. world trade balance on current account, in the aggregate, has been positive more frequently than negative, never between 1950 and 1970, and the few recent years of negative balance are accounted for very substantially by the price increase of petroleum imports. The balance with respect to manufactured goods is even more strongly favorable: they accounted for 71 percent of exports and only 56 percent of imports; the relevant dollar values are $76.6 billion and $60.6 billion.

The relatively favorable trade situation is no doubt due to many factors, but one of them does not seem to be extensive export promotion activity. U.S. export promotion expenditures in 1975 amounted to $23.7 million in total, or $338 per million dollars worth of exports, a figure substantially smaller than that for any major industrial trading country except West Germany. The special strength of U.S. manufactured exports appears to be in technology-intensive products, chemicals, machinery, and instrumentation, for example. Furthermore, in spite of a great deal of comment and controversy, unit labor costs in U.S. manufacturing appear to have increased much less rapidly than those in other major industrial and trading countries. On a base of 1967 = 100, the U.S. figure 156.6 for 1976 compares very favorably with 181.9 for Canada, 256.3 for West Germany, and 259.8 for Japan.

Therefore, in a world where trade is growing faster than output, U.S. manufacturing appears to be doing rather well and subject to trends which may be more favorable than those confronting other industrial trading countries. Furthermore, given the domestic political problems confronting several important trading countries, and the potential impact of rising oil prices on industrial activity in both Europe and Japan, the relatively stable and potentially energy-sufficient environment of the United States should prove an advantageous location for the expansion of world manufacturing activity.

The Role of Inflation

Only one matter remains to be mentioned: inflation and the policy responses it engenders are probably the most important aspects of the manufacturing environment in the coming decade. They are certainly the most difficult to anticipate. Multiple levels of analysis are involved. Among them are (1) the inflation process itself, including its underlying public policy elements; (2) the impact of inflation on the economy, both in the aggregate and in specific areas and industries; (3) the sequence of eventual policy responses over time, and the impact (if any) of these responses on inflation; and (4) the perpetual feedback or feed-forward relationships among these processes.

I know of no way to deal with this highly conjectural area, much less with its multiple, complex dimensions. I simply note its overwhelming presence.

Conclusions

The major structural trends involving the manufacturing sector over the past couple of decades may be briefly summarized.

1. There has been a gradual decline in the relative importance of manufacturing as a source of employment and income.

2. Rates of productivity change in manufacturing are not markedly different from those of the private economy as a whole.

3. There have been only minor and extremely gradual shifts in the overall composition of manufacturing activity, although specific changes in key industries are of critical importance.

4. Intersectoral and interindustry diversification of manufacturing enterprises is increasing, arising both from mergers and from gradual evolution and adaptation.

5. There have been very gradual tendencies toward increasing concentration, both with respect to manufacturing activity in the aggregate and with respect to individual industries and industry groups.

6. Continued strength exists in international markets for U.S. manufactured goods, coupled with increasing penetration of the U.S. markets by imported products and even establishment or acquisition of U.S. manufacturing facilities by foreign firms.

7. Perhaps the most dominant influence on the future environment of

manufacturing is the inflation process and how government chooses to deal with it.

These developments have taken place within a social environment characterized by increasing participation, both on the part of individuals and groups within large managerial organizations and between organizations and other entities in the external environment such as business firms, trade associations, unions, government, and organized interest groups. A particularly conspicuous form of such external participation is formal regulation of many aspects of economic activity, often by several levels of government. These expanding regulatory operations have been modeled on the pattern of the Federal Trade Commission and the National Labor Relations Board, involving regulation of a specific activity in multiple industries, rather than on the traditional regulated-industries model. Both the cost and the effectiveness of this so-called New Regulation are currently matters of considerable dispute; however, the adjustment of the economy to this new set of regulatory circumstances should be a major phenomenon of the 1980s.

References

Bell, Daniel. *The Coming of Post-Industrial Society.* New York: Basic Books, Inc., 1973.

Bowman, Charles T. "The Labor Force, Employment, and Economic Growth." In *U.S. Economic Growth from 1976 to 1986: Prospects, Problems & Patterns.* U.S. Congress (95th), Joint Economic Committee, Washington, D.C., 1977.

Fromm, Gary. "Forecasts of Long-Run Economic Growth." In *U.S. Economic Growth from 1976 to 1986: Prospects, Problems & Patterns.* U.S. Congress (94th), Joint Economic Committee, Washington, D.C., 1976.

Fuchs, Victor R. *The Service Economy.* New York: National Bureau of Economic Research, General Series No. 87, 1968.

Kraar, Louis. "General Electric's Very Personal Merger." *Fortune,* August 1977, pp. 187-194.

Lilley, William, III, and Miller, James C., III. "The New 'Social Regulation.' " *Public Interest,* no. 47 (Spring 1977):49-61.

Mooney, Thomas J., and Tschetter, John. "Revised Industry Projections to 1985." *Monthly Labor Review* 99 (November 1976):3-9.

Preston, Lee E. *The Industry and Enterprise Structure of the U.S. Economy.* New York: General Learning Press, 1971.

Tolley, George S., and Graves, Philip. "The Locational Impacts of Environmental Policies." A paper presented May 5-6, 1978, at a conference in Buffalo, New York, entitled "The Urban and Regional Impact of Government Policy."

U.S. Congress (95th), Joint Economic Committee. *U.S. Long-Term Economic Growth Prospects: Entering a New Era*. Washington, D.C., 1978.

U.S. Department of Commerce. *Historical Statistics of the United States: Colonial Times to 1970*. U.S. Bureau of the Census, Bicentennial Edition, 93rd Congress, 1st Session, House Doc. No. 93-78, Pt. I.

Appendix A

Table A-1
Rankings of Projected Growth and Employment for Selected Manufacturing Industries

Rank by Size[a]	Industry SIC Code(s)	Value of Industry Shipments (in millions of current $) 1977	1978	Rank by Annual Real Rate of Growth[b] 1977-1982	Rank by 1977 Employment
1.	Automobiles (37111)[d]	47,000	46,500	100	7
2.	Meat packing plants (2011)	38,228	42,815	128	15
3.	Steel (3312, 3315, 3316, & 3317)[d]	38,051	42,238	103	1
4.	Paper & paperboard	22,000	24,600	5	9
5.	Industrial organic chemicals, n.e.c. (2869)	21,800	24,000	10	30
6.	Truck and bus chassis (37112 & 37113)[d]	19,800	19,000	88	49
7.	Softwood plywood (24361 & 24362)	18,400	18,450	100	n.a.
8.	Aircraft (3721)	15,154	19,809	24	11
9.	Commercial printing (2751, 2752 & 2754)	14,600	16,000	40	3
10.	Electronic systems & equipment (3662)	13,500	14,400	18	4
11.	Newspapers (2711)	13,400	15,000	40	2
12.	Drugs & pharmaceuticals (283)[d]	13,350	14,550	27	21
13.	Aluminum (3334, 3353, 3354, 3355, 3361; & parts of 3341, 3399, & 3463)[d]	13,339	14,882	30	9
14.	Electronics components (367)	13,000	14,050	32	5
15.	Converted paper and paper board (264)[d]	12,140	13,600	53	18
16.	Steel castings (3325)[d]	11,645	13,450	67	8
17.	Computers and related equipment (3573)	11,500	13,230	4	13
18.	Construction machinery and equipment (3531)	10,790	11,650	122	20
19.	Tires & inner tubes (3011)	10,200	11,000	34	29
20.	Household appliances (363)[d]	10,090	11,150	60	16
21.	Bread and other bakery products, except cookies and crackers (2051)	9,842	10,088	105	12
22.	Sawmills and planing mills (2421)	9,800	10,000	130	14
23.	Household furniture (251)[d]	9,565	10,325	65	6
24.	Farm machinery & equipment (3523)	9,200	9,200	127	24
25.	Plastics materials & resins (2821)	9,000	10,300	21	61
26.	Photographic equipment and supplies (3861)	8,898	9,520	16	32
27.	Guided missiles and space vehicles (3761) and space vehicle equipment (3769)	8,820	9,455	100	26
28.	Sausages and other prepared meat products (2013)	8,142	9,119	105	55
29.	Refrigeration & heating equipment (3585)	8,115	8,602	130	23
30.	Metal cans (3411)	8,000	8,700	117	58
31.	Industrial inorganic chemicals, n.e.c. (2819)	7,646	7,953	77	47
32.	Aircraft engines and engine parts (3724) and space propulsion units & parts (3764)	7,503	9,387	6	27
33.	Fiber boxes (2653)	7,125	7,770	60	32
34.	Ready-mixed concrete (3273)	6,900	7,750	86	41
35.	Malt beverages (2082)	6,865	7,552	67	65

Rank by Size[a]	Industry SIC Code(s)	Value of Industry Shipments (in millions of current $) 1977	1978	Rank by Annual Real Rate of Growth[b] 1977-1982	Rank by 1977 Employment
36.	Telephone & telegraph equipment (3661)	6,845	7,255	23	25
37.	Canned fruits, vegetables, preserves, jams and jellies (2033)[e]	6,782	7,294	133	43
38.	Drawing & insulating of nonferrous wire (3357)	6,650	7,250	67	47
39.	Poultry dressing plants (2016)	6,121	6,733	122	42
40.	Paints & allied products (2851)[d]	6,075	6,655	67	52
41.	Toiletries (2844)	5,940	6,420	60	22
42.	Soaps & detergents (2841)	5,920	6,570	28	84
43.	Fabricated structural metal products (for buildings and bridges) (3441)	5,660	5,850	89	32
44.	Periodical publishing (2721)	5,592	6,319	40	44
45.	Consumer electronics (3651)	5,475	5,700	59	45
46.	Valves & pipefittings (3494)	5,450	5,890	40	31
47.	Pumps and compressors (3561 & 3563)	5,310	5,790	117	37
48.	Plastics packaging bags, except textile bags (26432, 27512 & 30794)	5,145	5,625	49	40
49.	Aircraft equipment (3728)	4,969	5,364	52	32
50.	Elevators, conveyors, hoists, & industrial trucks (3534, 3535, 3536 & 3537)	4,780	5,130	128	39
51.	Cyclic intermediates (2865)	4,690	5,150	10	86
52.	Book publishing (2731)	4,175	4,535	89	63
53.	Rolling, drawing, & extruding of copper (3351)	3,950	4,250	122	83
54.	Motors & generators (3621)	3,937	4,240	83	36
55.	Glass containers (3321)	3,800	4,100	115	46
56.	Oilfield machinery (3533)	3,700	4,035	119	62
57.	Nonrubber shoes & slippers (314)	3,620	3,950	136	17
58.	Special dies, tools, jigs, & fixtures (3544)[d]	3,567	3,949	63	28
59.	Frozen specialities (2038)[e]	3,263	3,570	86	n.a.
60.	Lighting fixtures and equipment (3645, 3646, 3647 & 3648)	3,250	3,600	67	52
61.	Fertilizer, phosphatic (2874)	3,150	3,275	67	118
62.	Hydraulic cement (3241)	3,125	3,575	84	86
63.	Mobile homes (2451)	3,100	3,650	1	71
64.	Frozen fruits, juices, and vegetables (2037)[e]	3,089	3,383	119	77
65.	Industrial fasteners (3452)	3,050	3,265	53	58
66.	Cookies and crackers (2052)	2,936	3,009	105	80
67.	Steam, gas, and hydraulic turbines (3511)	2,911	3,406	119	70
68.	Pesticides (2879)	2,900	3,200	47	113
69.	Switchgear (3613)	2,880	3,080	89	51
70.	Pulp mills (2611)	2,723	2,821	18	114
71.	Surgical appliances and supplies (3842)	2,710	2,980	40	55
72.	Manifold business forms (2761)	2,672	2,992	21	73
73.	Concrete products, n.e.c. (3272)	2,600	2,950	34	60
74.	Ball and other roller bearings (3562)	2,530	2,710	53	67
75.	Industrial controls (3622)	2,500	2,700	65	52
76.	Electrical measuring instruments (3825)	2,480	2,710	14	50
77.	Distilled liquors except brandy (2085)	2,411	2,664	89	n.a.
78.	Truck & bus bodies (3713)	2,255	2,510	8	76

Rank by Size[a]	Industry SIC Code(s)	Value of Industry Shipments (in millions of current $) 1977	1978	Rank by Annual Real Rate of Growth[b] 1977-1982	Rank by 1977 Employment
79.	Sporting goods (3949)[d]	2,186	2,547	14	37
80.	Surgical & medical instruments (3841)	2,180	2,465	10	65
81.	Fertilizer, nitrogenous (2873)	2,175	2,250	67	124
82.	Games & toys (3944)[d]	2,107	2,298	105	64
83.	Synthetic rubber (2822)	2,100	2,250	98	118
84.	Folding paper boxes (2651)	2,095	2,265	122	73
85.	Mining machinery (3532)	2,005	2,185	115	86
86.	Engineering & scientific equipment (3811)	1,935	2,170	40	68
87.	Alkalies & chlorine (2812)	1,900	2,100	99	114
88.	Current-carrying wiring devices (3643)	1,860	2,045	89	n.a.
89.	Food products machinery (3551)	1,840	2,006	77	82
90.	Precious jewelry (3911)[d]	1,835	2,020	77	78
91.	Transformers (3612)	1,790	1,910	105	78
92.	Wines and brandy (2084)	1,790	2,014	26	n.a.
93.	Screw machine products (3451)	1,770	1,910	67	68
94.	Prefabricated wood buildings and components (2452)	1,700	1,975	18	104
95.	Machine, tools, metal cutting (3541)[d]	1,620	1,705	77	57
96.	Truck trailers (3715)	1,600[d]	1,771[d]	53[e]	93
97.	Perishable cutting tools (35451)[d]	1,500	1,640	32	n.a.
98.	Concrete block and brick (3271)	1,500	1,650	105	95
99.	Hose & belting (3041)	1,500	1,650	53	86
100.	Process control instruments (3823)	1,480	1,600	47	73
101.	Book printing (2732)	1,465	1,580	67	71
102.	Leather tanning & finishing (3111)	1,390	1,475	142	97
103.	Noncurrent-carrying wiring devices (3644)	1,365	1,515	89	n.a.
104.	Plumbing fittings, brass goods (3432)	1,325	1,475	84	107
105.	Power boilers (34433)	1,310	1,180	30	86
106.	Welding apparatus (35493 & 3623)[d]	1,300	1,450	39	80
107.	Phonograph records (3652)	1,300	1,400	3	124
108.	X-Ray apparatus & tubes (3693)	1,290	1,550	2	100
109.	Flat glass (3211)	1,200	1,290	63	104
109.	Primary smelting & refining of lead (3332)	1,200	1,230	89	132
109.	Inorganic pigments (2816)	1,200	1,310	67	19
112.	Printing trades machinery (3555)	1,194	1,290	53	95
113.	Automatic environmental controls (3822)	1,140	1,255	34	84
114.	Selected industrial pollution control equipment (35645 & 35646)[d]	1,068	1,180	24	107
115.	Textile machinery (3552)	1,056	1,110	34	91
116.	Optical instruments and lenses (3832)	1,040	1,125	6	92
117.	Poultry and egg processing (2017)	994	1,093	136	111
118.	Other measuring and controlling devices (3829)	960	1,045	49	97
119.	Costume jewelry (3961)	945[d]	1,040[d]	77[e]	100
120.	Motorcycles, bicycles, & parts (3751)[d]	935	1,018	8	132
121.	Dental equipment and supplies (3843)	905	1,023	10	111
122.	Calculating & accounting machines (3574)	762	702	136	110
123.	Plastic tableware (30797)[d]	690	750	49	n.a.
124.	Glass tableware (32291)[d]	660	727	28	n.a.
125.	Metal sanitary ware (3431)	650	725	105	121

Rank by Size[a]	Industry SIC Code(s)	Value of Industry Shipments (in millions of current $)		Rank by Annual Real Rate of Growth[b] 1977-1982	Rank by 1977 Employment
		1977	1978		
126.	Industrial heating equipment (3567)[d]	644	721	17	99
127.	Machine tools, metal forming (3542)[d]	620	670	77	93
128.	Luggage (3161)	525	560	132	107
129.	Fluid meters and counting devices (3824)	520	570	40	116
130.	Small arms (3482)[d]	501	510	136	106
131.	Small arms ammunition (3484)[d]	500	550	122	118
131.	Vitreous china plumbing fixtures (3261)[d]	500	560	89	100
131.	Primary smelting & refining of zinc (3333)	500	495	89	130
134.	Carbon black (2895)	460	530	105	132
135.	Women's handbags & purses	435	460	140	116
136.	Dolls (3942)[d]	420	462	105	127
137.	Silverware (3914)[d]	405	425	143	124
138.	Personal leather goods (3172)	380	405	135	121
139.	Leather & sheep lined clothing (2386)	315	330	134	121
140.	Foundry machinery & equipment (35592)[d]	272	313	34	100
141.	Leather gloves & mittens (3151)	165	180	141	128
142.	Chinaware (3262)[d]	102	105	103	130
143.	Earthenware (3263)[d]	85	89	105	129

Source: *U.S. Industrial Outlook 1978.*

n.a.: Not Available.

n.e.c.: Not elsewhere classified.

[a]1977 industry shipments except where noted.

[b]Based on 1977 constant dollars.

[c]Estimated by Bureau of Domestic Commerce.

[d]Product shipments.

[e]Value of production.

Comment

Frank H. Cassell

A major contribution of Preston's chapter is the manner in which it highlights the political economy of the manufacturing environment for the 1980s. The economics of this sector favor increased concentration. However, many elements of the polity are concerned that these new concentrations are not responsive to the needs of society. Moreover, they complain that these continuously growing concentrations are not reluctant to use political power to shape the environment to their advantage. As the concentration grows, the number and magnitude of potential political challenges increase. When the public believes that this power is too great, it resorts to government to regulate in the public interest. A more extreme—some would say realistic—statement of this view is that many concentrations have become so large and powerful that they take on the form of a private government which is responsive not to the citizenry but to its owners and must therefore be made accountable to the elected government. This charge has been leveled at supranational corporations by individual European countries.

The need for centralized resource allocation in the concentration and the acquisition of political power by the concentration alters the dynamics of its relationship to its work force and unions as well as its relationship to government. The aggregation of political power by concentrations helps prevent passage of legislation favorable to unions and encourages the election of political candidates who do not favor unions. Moreover, growth in the range of interest of the concentration, the centralization of internal economic control, and the ability to mobilize and reallocate its resources at will—regardless of impact on the work force—may result in demands from the concentration's various work forces (unionized or not) that their interests, job rights, continuity of employment, and values be preserved even as the concentration preserves its own interests.

Finally, the ability of the concentration to move its resources from place to place, combined with its operations in the political arena, can frustrate worker, environmental, and consumer groups in the workplace and in the community. That is to say, the activities of the concentration in pursuing its market function, and its effective use of the political mode to preserve its position, set in motion other decentralized forces—workers, unions, and community organizations—who also utilize the political mode to establish a countervailing power.

Each of these competing methods for ordering priorities in the society has its own set of values. The economic mode emphasizes the standards of efficiency and continuity of the organization in a competitive market. The political mode emphasizes citizen, worker, and community standards of performance such as the quality of products and services, safety, health, equal opportunity employment, and environmental preservation, among other issues. Thus the political mode represents an effort to have the visible hand of the citizen replace, or at least serve as a check on, the invisible hand of competition as the regulator—allocator of resources—in areas that affect workers and citizens. The profit system can decide among efficiencies, but the political system may ultimately decide whether the service or product should be provided at all.

If the foregoing has any validity, it is not hard to see why concentrations both attract political attention and attempt to dominate the political mode. The unanswered question is, however, are the complex dynamics of the political mode a limiting factor on growth and concentration? Is there a point at which growth and concentration become too costly? What is this point?

Inquiry should be made into the possible growth of slack (as discussed by Hirschman, 1970) in its operations as the concentration attempts to control or frustrate externally imposed social performance criteria. This, it would seem, is one means for gaining greater insight into the uncertainty which business feels about social policies and the impact of their implementation.

A further word contributed by Preston's paper about the political mode which illustrates the development of slack is the contrast between the "old regulation" and the "new regulation." In the former, the client of the federal agency turned out to be the regulated, not the public, as intended. In contrast, the "new regulation" specifically represents people who are excluded from a market relationship, such as minorities by the Equal Employment Opportunity Commission (EEOC), or citizens whose lives and health may be affected by corporate decisions but who have no market relationship by the Environmental Protection Agency (EPA). In the case of the "old regulation," the slack argument could lead to the conclusion that it permitted or even encouraged inefficiencies (slack) to be rewarded. In the case of the "new regulation," the result might be more efficient utilization of the work force and other resources, thus less slack in the system, and presumably greater productivity. However, these tendencies might be offset by managerial inefficiencies in responding to externally imposed performance criteria, or by costs incurred by management in opposing regulation. From this Preston concludes that

> traditional economizing will, by itself, no longer provide socially legitimate solutions to economic problems involving any substantial social side effects, whether internal to the organization or external in the larger society. (page 9)

One consequence is the application of two sets of performance criteria to corporate decisions and results: the "bottom line" and an extension which must include an accountability for the consequences or social costs imposed on the society of decisions which led to the "bottom line" in the first place. Preston suggests that this accountability is the basis for the social legitimacy of corporate economic decisions.

If the possibility of political limits on growth and concentration exists, there is also the probability of productivity limits on concentration. The number of these limits seems almost countless, but for purposes of this commentary, only three are selected, with a brief comment on each. The first is the power of concentrations to mobilize political forces to reduce competition and thus increase the opportunity for slack. The second is the growth of segmented internal labor markets which impede labor's mobility and limit its utilization. The third is growth of administrative rigidities arising out of the concentration's coordination needs and the possibility that size and diversity may outrun present managerial capabilities.

The political power of firms or concentrations, hard pressed by foreign competition, to secure legislative and executive support for limiting such competition can and does preserve in specific domestic industries essentially monopolistic prices and dependent wage levels. This, Hirschman would argue, leads to acceptance of inefficiencies at the "cell" level of the organization—on the shop floor. Existence of conditions which preserve both employment and wage levels from competition encourages union support of these policies, thus maximizing the efficiency of the firm's political action. At the same time, these policies increase both labor and management's tolerance for slack in the production system inasmuch as costs can be shifted to other people and sectors in the economy. Thus, the limits of concentration may lie in (1) its inability to export its products or price itself out of the domestic market, or (2) such an increase of slack that the possession of political power to establish compensating price levels becomes worthless.

With reference to the second of the limits discussed here, segmented internal labor markets seem to arise in concentrations from a number of causes, two of which are relevant at this point. The first is the growth of the number and diversity of units, products, and services under a concentration which increases the variety of occupations and accompanying training programs, avenues of progression, and of course the amount of segmentation. The second cause of segmented internal labor markets is the impact of management techniques to assure coordination and control resource allocation, and incentive mechanisms to increase performance. Oversimplified systems to assure accountability and promote internal competition frequently find expression in protective mechanisms for preventing loss of talent to competing units (managerial competition); this tends to limit full utilization of manpower in a unit of the concentration or firm, and often prevents the development and growth of the personnel. This is an example of slack at the cell level.

Often in assembling a conglomerate or concentration, the basis for

union protection is generated by fear of loss of jobs, often to unions in
other areas of firms or geographical locations—which together with internal
work rules and customs governing entrance into a unit or occupation effectively limits utilization of even the most highly skilled and scarcest workers.
This likely increases search, training, and turnover costs, and quite possibly
adds to slack. Not infrequently, "head-hunters" employed by competing
divisions of a conglomerate can be found recruiting talent from one division
for another simply because rules and managerial competitors' self-interest
prevent internal search and recruiting.

At a more complex level, slack may develop as the concentration grows,
especially as its units become more diversified and the processes of reconciling the organization's internal interests become more complicated and time-
consuming. In addition, the complexity of the mediation process among interests such as stockholders, workers, unions, consumers, suppliers, and the
various publics seems to increase geometrically as units of the concentration
increase arithmetically. In brief, it might be speculated that it is this type of
change—complexity outrunning man's capability to cope with it efficiently—that helps define the limits of concentration.

This brings us to the third limit, the growth of administrative rigidities.
To help manage these complexities and maintain control over its units, and
to take advantage of new technology, management has expanded its staff of
highly skilled persons equipped with modern methods of quantitative and
qualitative analysis and computers. Although staff has grown rapidly, more
rapidly than the balance of the work force, and become a haven for college-
trained persons, questions could be raised as to their contribution to preven-
tion of slack. Whether their expertise and information really improve the
quality and speed of decision-making is also a question. It is clear, however,
that each of the increasingly numerous varieties of staff has interests which
are added to other existing interests, that there are competing interests
among various staff units and with the operating organization, and that this
increases complexity, time, and cost of mediating among interests as well as
decision-making. If the fact of slack does not exist, and this is hard to
believe, the opportunity for it to develop certainly does. This ultimately has
to be examined and measured along with an equally careful measurement of
staff contribution; any assessment of limits of concentration would be incomplete without some appreciation of staff contribution to productivity or
cost of slack.

For purposes of these comments, the question is whether there is any
longer such a thing as a pure business problem: when few decisions of the
private sector can be made without an expression by the public of its
legitimate concern for the consequences of those decisions (Cassell, 1972, p.

13). So pervasive has this trend become that support for it comes from such unlikely sources as the chairman of Allegheny Ludlum Industries, who has asserted that "nations, government, and people look upon industries as national assets" and that though

> America's foreign policy for generations has been influenced by military and political considerations . . . economic considerations must assume first priority. . . . We [are] now trying to compete . . . with entire economies in which a central decision-making body . . . governs and directs the entire national economic entity. (Ahlbrandt, 1972)

This public concern is reflected in Preston's data in the form of concentration growth, its magnitude, diversity, and pervasiveness. Direct public concern, though implied by his data, does not show the government-concentration connection as regards national defense, including railroads and defense material, or the government as a market and a massive supplier of employment, both directly and indirectly. The geographic data suggest, but do not make clear, the possible economic and employment impact of geographic shifts in government expenditures (often to locations where concentration resources exist), which also affect regional economies and employment patterns. These resource shifts and allocations are not without political overtones, and thus are subject to public interest in government-corporate decisions as they affect people's lives.

For example, the steel industry is perceived by many people, including Ahlbrandt, as central to the economy and its defense and therefore to be protected; however, this makes it a potential target for regulation, if not nationalization. Other examples include AMTRAK, CONRAIL, and the Post Office, which are partly dependent on government financing, and under stress would be candidates for further government intervention. And finally, there are firms which are heavily dependent on government for markets, such as General Dynamics, Mathematica, McDonnell-Douglas, Rand, and perhaps Brookings. All are especially susceptible to public criteria of performance.

The limits to concentration in such settings may lie not in efficiency but in national need, and in the willingness of the polity to socialize the costs of slack in those organizations as the price of national security readiness, including research capability, and maintaining a high level of community convenience.

Preston's chapter suggests the future direction of the economy. These supplementary comments suggest some implications if concentration trends continue, and they are supportive of his observations of increasing concentration and centralization, and consequent increasing public concern over their power, relations with government, and their ability to shape the economics of areas, regions, and even nations.

References

Ahlbrandt, Roger S. "For Whom the Steel Bell Tolls." Speech given at Steel Industry Economics Seminar, Wayne State University, Detroit, April 12, 1972.

Cassell, Frank H. "Public-Private Management." *MSU Business Topics*, (Summer 1972).

Hirschman, Albert O. *Exit, Voice and Loyalty*. Cambridge, Mass.: Harvard University Press, 1970.

**Part II
Unions in Manufacturing**

2

The Size of Union Membership in Manufacturing in the 1980s

Albert Rees

In order to predict the future, even unreliably, we must examine the present and the past, and search for trends that might continue. A discussion of manufacturing union membership in the 1980s should begin with an examination of this subject in the previous decades.

Table 2-1 shows reported union membership in manufacturing for the even-numbered years 1956 to 1976, compared with total manufacturing employment and production worker employment in manufacturing. The initial year, 1956, is the first in which unions were asked to report an industrial breakdown of their membership to the Bureau of Labor Statistics (BLS), and 1976 is the latest year for which this breakdown is available.

The period covered by table 2-1 is long enough so that trends should emerge from the shorter-term fluctuations. However, 1956 was a year of full employment, with an average unemployment rate of only 4.1 percent, while 1976 had an average unemployment rate of 7.7 percent. For this reason, the decline in union membership over the whole period may be overstated.

Unions are asked to report their membership as an average figure for the year. Recession years can produce drops in the figure reported; note the decline in 1958 and the low figure for 1962, which seems to reflect the continuing effect of the recession of 1961.

Because of the recession that began in late 1974, manufacturing employment declined from 20 million in 1974 to just under 19 million in 1976. Union membership dropped by almost 700,000, and the percentage of manufacturing workers who were union members continued to decline slightly. To avoid confusion of trends with the effects of the recession, the analysis in the rest of the chapter will be for the period 1956-1974.

Comparisons between reported union membership and employment are necessarily rough because some unions include unemployed, retired, and Canadian members in their membership figures. However, there is no particular reason to think that this lack of correspondence has changed over the period. It should also be kept in mind that, except in union shops, the

I am indebted to my colleague Richard A. Lester for helpful suggestions.

Table 2-1
Reported Union Membership and Employment in Manufacturing, 1956-1976

Year	(1) Union Members (thousands)	(2) Total Employment (thousands)	(3) Production Workers (thousands)	(4) (1) as % of (2)	(5) (1) as % of (3)
1956	8,839	17,243	13,436	51.3	65.8
1958	8,359	15,945	11,997	52.4	69.7
1960	8,591	16,696	12,586	51.5	68.3
1962	8,050	16,853	12,488	47.8	64.5
1964	8,342	17,274	12,781	48.3	65.3
1966	8,769	19,214	14,297	45.6	61.3
1968	9,218	19,781	14,514	46.6	63.5
1970	9,173	19,349	14,020	47.4	65.4
1972	8,920	19,090	13,957	46.7	63.9
1974	9,144	20,016	14,607	45.7	62.6
1976	8,463	18,956	13,625	44.6	62.1

Sources: BLS *Bulletin* 1865, tables 39 and 41, and *Handbook of Labor Statistics, 1975.*

number of workers covered by collective bargaining agreements will be larger than the number of employed union members.

Table 2-1 shows that reported union membership in manufacturing changed very little from 1956 to 1974; it fluctuated from a low of 8.1 million members in 1962 to a high of 9.2 million in 1968. The growth from 1956 to 1974 was 3.5 percent. Since this is lower than the growth of total employment in manufacturing (16.1 percent) or of production worker employment (8.7 percent), reported union membership as a percentage of both employment series declined (see the last two columns of table 2-1).

It is worth noting that both employment series rose over the period despite increases in labor productivity and sharply increased competition from imported manufactured goods. Since nonproduction worker employment rose faster than production worker employment, the percentage of all manufacturing employees who are production workers declined from 77.9 percent in 1956 to 73.0 percent in 1974. This shift is adverse to the unions, whose membership is heavily concentrated among production workers.

The same rather flat membership trend reported for all unions in manufacturing is evident for most of the individual unions whose membership is concentrated in manufacturing. Table 2-2 shows the reported membership in 1956 and 1974 of eleven unions with 1974 membership of 150,000 or over concentrated in manufacturing. Of these, only the United Automobile Workers shows substantial growth. Six of the eleven unions reported membership declines. There are several other unions with substantial membership in manufacturing that are not included in table 2-2 because

Table 2-2
Reported Membership of Selected National Unions
with Membership Concentrated in Manufacturing
(thousands)

	1956	1974
United Auto Workers	1,321	1,545
United Steel Workers	1,350[a]	1,300
International Assn. of Machinists	950	943
Ladies Garment Workers	451	405
Amalgamated Clothing Workers	385	350
Pulp and Paper Workers	295[b]	301
International Union of Electrical Workers	397	298
United Rubber Workers	178	191
Oil, Chemical, and Atomic Workers	183	177
Textile Workers Union[c]	303[b]	167
United Electrical Workers	100	163

Source: BLS *Bulletin* 1937, Appendix D.
[a]Includes Mine, Mill, and Smelter Workers, separate in 1956.
[b]Total of two national unions in 1956.
[c]Merged with Amalgamated Clothing Workers in 1976.

much of their membership is in other industrial sectors. These include the International Brotherhood of Teamsters, the International Brotherhood of Electrical Workers, and the Amalgamated Meat Cutters. In fiscal 1977, the Teamsters won representation rights in 511 manufacturing bargaining units, including every two-digit industry except tobacco (NLRB 42nd Annual Report, 1978). Many of these may have been units of truck drivers employed by manufacturing firms.

No time series data are available that would permit the computation of changes in union membership as a percentage of employment for individual manufacturing industries. However, industry data have been published for the year 1970, based on the May 1971 Current Population Survey, which asked a representative national sample of households about the union membership of workers sixteen years of age and over. The industry classification is that of the longest job held in 1970. Table 2-3 shows these data for all workers, separately for males and females. Combining membership in durable and nondurable goods, using employment weights from establishment data, we find that 33.7 percent of manufacturing employees were union members in 1970. This is substantially lower than the corresponding figure in table 2-1 (47.4 percent). Some of the difference is due to the inclusion of unemployed, retired, and Canadian members in the union membership reports, and some may be due to the failure of household respondents to report union membership.

Table 2-3 shows a higher percentage of union members in durable than

Table 2-3
Percent of Manufacturing Wage and
Salary Workers in Labor Unions, 1970

Industry of Longest Job Held in 1970	Total	Male	Female
Durable goods	37.4	41.2	24.4
Lumber	24.3	24.5	—[a]
Furniture	25.0	25.9	22.1
Stone, clay, glass	39.6	42.3	27.1
Primary metals	59.8	62.0	38.1
Fabricated metals	38.2	42.7	21.2
Machinery	33.0	36.7	15.1
Electrical equipment	31.0	33.9	27.1
Automobiles	66.2	68.6	50.3
Other transportation equipment	32.0	33.7	22.3
Instruments	15.7	15.4	16.4
Miscellaneous	26.5	31.4	18.3
Nondurable goods	28.7	33.3	22.5
Food	36.2	39.5	27.5
Tobacco	24.2	—[a]	—[a]
Textiles	10.5	14.7	6.9
Apparel	30.7	25.9	31.8
Paper	48.7	51.8	37.7
Printing	22.4	30.8	9.9
Chemicals	23.6	26.9	11.7
Petroleum	30.0	35.5	—[a]
Rubber and plastics	30.3	34.0	23.9
Leather	29.4	33.0	26.6

Source: *BLS Report 417, Selected Earnings and Demographic Characteristics of Union Members, 1970*, table 2.

[a]Not available. Base less than 75,000.

in nondurable goods. Automobiles and primary metals stand out as the industries with the highest percentage of union members, with paper in third place. Textiles, not unexpectedly, has by far the smallest percentage of union members, with instruments next.

Establishment data for 1970 show that 72 percent of all manufacturing employees were production workers in that year. Even if all the union members reported in the household survey were production workers, less than half the manufacturing production workers would have been reported to be union members.

The percentage of membership reported for women was lower than for men in all industries except apparel and instruments. In part, this is because in most manufacturing industries a substantially larger proportion of women than men are nonproduction workers. For both men and women, a higher proportion of nonwhites than of whites were union members. For men, 37.8 percent of white manufacturing workers were union members and 43.4 percent of nonwhites; for women the corresponding percentages were 22.4 and 30.8. One major source of the difference may be the higher fraction of nonwhites who are production workers.

According to establishment statistics, the employment of women in manufacturing grew 31 percent from 1956 to 1974, or substantially more than total employment. Taken together with the lower proportion of women who are union members, this again helps to explain the relatively slow growth of union membership. However, the employment of women grew slightly *less* rapidly than the employment of all nonproduction workers in manufacturing, which rose 42 percent over the period. Thus there is no reason to assume that the fraction of women employees rose among either production workers or nonproduction workers.

The increase in production worker employment from 1956 to 1974 was slightly smaller in the most heavily unionized industries than in all manufacturing. Six of the industries shown in table 2-3 (automobiles; primary metals; paper; stone, clay, and glass; fabricated metals; and food) had a higher percentage of union members than all manufacturing. Four of these also had a larger increase in production-worker employment than all manufacturing. However, the remaining two (primary metals and food) are the largest and they had declines in production worker employment. For the six industries together, production worker employment rose 4.8 percent; in all manufacturing it rose 8.7 percent.

A major reason for the slow growth of manufacturing unionism from 1956 to 1974 was the geographical shift of manufacturing employment toward states with a low extent of union organization. Table 2-4 shows the change in manufacturing employment in the ten states with the smallest proportion of union members in all nonagricultural industries in 1974. These states each had reported union membership less than 15 percent of total nonagricultural employment; the national average was 26.2 percent. From 1956 to 1974, their manufacturing employment grew 67 percent; for the United States as a whole, manufacturing employment grew only 16 percent. All of the states shown in table 2-4 (except New Mexico) had a right-to-work law in 1974. It is not clear what the direction of causality is between union membership and the presence of right-to-work laws. Right-to-work laws no doubt discourage union membership; however, low union membership helps to permit the passage of right-to-work laws by state legislatures.

At the other extreme are the ten states with the greatest extent of union organization; these data are shown in table 2-5. All of these states had reported union membership of more than 32 percent of total nonagricultural employment. Their manufacturing employment declined almost 3 percent from 1956 to 1974, although only three of the ten states had actual declines. Washington and Indiana were the only states among

Table 2-4
Change in Manufacturing Employment,
Ten States with Lowest Percentage
of Union Membership

State	Union Membership as Percent of Nonagricultural Employment	Manufacturing Employment 1974	
		Thousands	Index 1956 = 100
North Carolina	6.9	795.2	169.0
South Carolina	8.0	376.1	160.7
South Dakota	11.0	20.7	166.9
Mississippi	12.0	219.3	205.1
Florida	12.5	369.0	231.1
Texas	13.0	830.5	170.6
Virginia	13.8	399.4	151.7
Kansas	14.1	166.5	131.1
New Mexico	14.1	29.3	207.8
Georgia	14.5	483.3	142.6
Total		3,689.3	166.7

Sources: BLS *Bulletin* 1865 and *Bulletin* 1370-12.

the ten in which manufacturing employment rose more than the national average. None of the states included in table 2-5 had a right-to-work law in 1974.

Of course, tables 2-4 and 2-5 do not show that a high extent of unionization causes a slow growth of manufacturing employment or that a low extent of unionization causes rapid growth of employment. Many other factors contributed to the employment shifts. Some manufacturing industries such as baking or cement manufacturing serve local product markets, and their location is therefore influenced by the general change in population. Many of the states in table 2-4 have warmer climates and lower energy costs than those in table 2-5, and have benefited recently from the high cost of energy in other areas.

Most of the states in table 2-5 have been centers of manufacturing activity for many years and have a high proportion of old industrial plants; this contributes to a high rate of relocation. But whatever causes the manufacturing industry to shift away from the centers of union strength, this shift makes it harder for unions to gain members.

The size of establishments is usually considered to be an important factor in union organization. Workers in large establishments are more likely to feel the need for grievance procedures, seniority, and other forms of protection that unions offer. The costs per member to the union of organizing very small establishments may be disproportionately high. Table 2-6 shows the percentage distribution of manufacturing employment by employee size

Table 2-5
Change in Manufacturing Employment,
Ten States with Highest Percentage
of Union Membership

State	Union Membership as Percent of Nonagricultural Employment	Manufacturing Employment 1974	
		Thousands	Index 1956 = 100
Michigan	38.4	1,105.9	102.3
West Virginia	38.2	130.0	97.8
New York	38.0	1,573.9	77.1
Pennsylvania	37.5	1,461.8	95.2
Washington	36.7	253.6	118.9
Hawaii	36.2	22.8	100.9[a]
Illinois	34.9	1,347.2	102.4
Indiana	33.2	737.2	118.3
Ohio	33.2	1,413.8	101.6
Missouri	32.3	450.0	113.8
Total		8,496.2	97.1

Sources: BLS *Bulletin* 1865 and *Bulletin* 1370-12.
[a]Index base is 1958.

class for the years since 1954 for which a Census of Manufactures was taken. The distribution is remarkably stable. There was a decline in the share of the very largest size class in 1972, but this was at the expense of the intermediate size classes. The smallest size class has been declining in share over the period. Changes in the size distribution of employment in manufacturing thus do not seem to be a factor of any importance in influencing the size of union membership.

The period 1956-1974 was also one in which developments in international trade were adverse to American manufacturing industries. Over this period the dollar value of machinery exports increased by a factor of almost four, but that of machinery imports increased more than six-fold. The value

Table 2-6
Percentage Distribution of Manufacturing
Employees by Size of Establishment, 1954-1972

Year	Under 20	20-99	100-249	250-299	1,000 and Over
1954	7.7	18.1	15.5	26.0	32.6
1958	7.8	19.2	16.2	26.3	30.5
1963	7.3	18.9	16.8	26.5	30.5
1967	5.6	17.7	16.6	27.3	32.8
1972	6.2	18.6	17.9	28.6	28.7

Source: *Statistical Abstract of the United States, 1976*, p. 763.

of transportation equipment exports increased by a factor of four, but that of imports increased by a factor of ten (U.S. Department of Commerce, 1975).

Import competition also increased for a variety of other manufactured products including steel, television sets, shoes, and apparel. The direct effects of these foreign trade developments on employment are already included in the employment figures reviewed earlier, and one might question whether they have any additional effects on the percentage of manufacturing employees in unions. However, where there are subtantial union-nonunion wage differentials, nonunion firms may be better able than union firms to meet import competition. This would lead employment declines to be concentrated in or confined to the unionized portion of the industry. This may have happened in the apparel industry, where both major unions report membership declines from 1956 to 1974 (see table 2-2), while production worker employment in the industry rose slightly, from 1,088,000 in 1956 to 1,163,000 in 1974.

The statistical record reviewed so far presents a moderately cloudy outlook for manufacturing unionism. However, there are also some encouraging factors. First, there have been a number of mergers of national unions which should produce larger, more efficient organizations that are better able to serve their present members and to recruit new members. These include the mergers of the Textile Workers Union with the Amalgamated Clothing Workers, the United Packinghouse Workers with the Amalgamated Meatcutters, the Papermakers with the Pulp and Sulphite Workers, and the Printing Pressmen with the Stereotypers.

There are still possibilities for additional mergers which could strengthen small manufacturing unions. Several national unions in manufacturing had fewer than 50,000 members in 1974. These include the Aluminum Workers, the Cement Workers, the Distillery Workers, the Glass Workers, the Grain Millers, the Hatters, the United Shoe Workers, the Tobacco Workers, and the Toy Workers. There are still two different national unions of leather workers affiliated with the AFL-CIO, one with reported 1974 membership of 47,000 and the other with 3,000. Of course, it does not follow that just because a national union is small it is necessarily weak or ineffective. Some of these national unions may be doing very well, thus having no incentive to merge.

A second favorable factor is that several major manufacturing unions have installed new presidents within the last two or three years. Some of these new leaders seem to be exceptionally able and energetic, and determined to revitalize their organizations.

A third factor favorable to unions is that there has been a recent increase in the number of manufacturing plants with union-management committees to improve productivity (Batt and Weinberg, 1978). To the extent that such committees succeed in checking the rise in unit labor costs in unionized plants, they may help to encourage the growth of union membership.

A final favorable factor, perhaps related to the first two, is that unions in manufacturing have stepped up their organizing efforts. In fiscal year 1956, unions participated in 3,457 collective-bargaining representation elections in manufacturing; in fiscal year 1977 they participated in 4,337 such elections. However, the percentages of elections in which unions won representation rights dropped over the period, so that the number of manufacturing units in which unions won representation declined from 2,302 units in 1956 to 1,941 units in 1977. The number of units in which no representative was chosen rose from 1,115 to 2,396. In the 1977 elections the number of valid votes cast for unions (140,962) was smaller than the number of valid votes for no union (153,879) (NLRB, 1957 and 1978).

The decline in the number of NLRB elections won and the percentage of votes cast for unions in manufacturing parallels a similar decline across a wider range of industries. The reasons for this decline are not fully understood. Unions blame it on tougher resistance to unionization by management. Some of it may result from the shift of economic activity to areas of the country, like the South, that are traditionally more hostile to unions.

Recent research offers another possible explanation. It has been shown that unions have a pronounced leveling effect on the wage structure—that is, they narrow the dispersion of wage rates within the unionized segment of an industry (Bloch and Kuskin, 1978). This narrowing of wage differentials could more than offset for high-wage workers the effect of the union in raising the average level of wages. A recent analysis of votes cast in a sample of NLRB elections shows that having a high relative wage sharply lowers the probability that a worker will vote in favor of a union (Farber and Saks, 1978). It may be that this behavior on the part of high-wage workers has become more important recently and tips the balance in a larger fraction of elections.

Congress has considered and rejected legislation that would amend the National Labor Relations Act (NLRA) in the area of procedures for union recognition and for holding representation elections. Clearly, both labor and management believe that the passage of such a bill would increase the extent of unionization, and should it be reintroduced we can assume that both sides will make the same strenuous efforts to influence the decision.

No doubt the proposed changes in the NLRA would help unions in manufacturing as well as elsewhere, although the magnitude of this effect may be considerably less than some have estimated. In fiscal year 1977, 120,000 employees in manufacturing chose unions. Even if the changes in the law increased this number by 50 percent, these 60,000 employees would represent only .7 percent of union membership in manufacturing.

Of course, under more favorable laws, unions might engage in more elections and win a larger fraction of them. Even so, the effect of winning more elections in one year leaves fewer good targets for organization in the next; thus an estimate of effects for a single year cannot safely be cumulated over several years to get a total number for a longer period. For manufacturing unions to add a million members by 1985 through new organizing efforts would represent a large increase over present organizing success, and much of this might be offset by declines in employment in units now represented.

Having sacrificed several volumes of statistics and examined their entrails, I can no longer postpone the question, "What will union membership in manufacturing be in the 1980s?"

I believe that total employment in U.S. manufacturing will continue to grow, though not rapidly. The present imbalances in merchandise trade will diminish as a combined result of the lower value of the dollar relative to the yen and the deutsche mark, and of policy measures to lower the trade deficit taken by both the United States and its trading partners. Nevertheless, the principal growth of American manufactures will be in high technology products where the United States has a comparative advantage—in aircraft, computers, and instruments rather than in shoes, apparel, or textiles. Employment of production workers will grow more slowly than total employment, as the proportion of manufacturing employees who are managerial, professional, sales, and clerical workers continues to rise. Manufacturing industry will continue to shift from the snowbelt to the sunbelt, although the shift may be slowed by equalization of the interstate and intrastate price of natural gas and by redistribution of federal government expenditures. In short, if the 1980s are to be very different from the 1970s, I am not clever enough to see how or why.

All of this suggests that the membership of manufacturing unions will continue to grow more slowly than total manufacturing employment, and probably more slowly than production worker employment. Sometime in the 1980s the reported number of union members in manufacturing will exceed the 1968 peak of 9.2 million, and may even cross the 10 million mark. For this to happen, however, total employment in manufacturing would probably have to rise above 22 million, some 10 percent above its present level, for it seems very unlikely that the fraction of all manufacturing employees who are union members will rise appreciably.

References

Batt, William L., Jr., and Weinberg, Edgar. "Labor-Management Cooperation Today." *Harvard Business Review* (January-February 1978).
Bloch, Farrell E., and Kuskin, Mark S. "Wage Determination in the Union

and Nonunion Sectors." *Industrial and Labor Relations Review* 31 (January 1978).

BLS, *Handbook of Labor Statistics*, 1975.

BLS, Report 417. *Selected Earnings and Demographic Characteristics of Union Members,* 1970.

BLS, *Bulletin* 1370-1412.

BLS, *Bulletin* 1865.

Farber, Henry S., and Saks, Daniel H. "Why Workers Want Unions: The Role of Relative Wages and Job Characteristics." Unpublished manuscript, March 1978.

NLRB, 21st Annual Report, 1957.

NLRB, 42nd Annual Report, 1978.

Statistical Abstract of the U.S., 1976.

U.S. Department of Commerce. *Business Statistics*, 1975.

Comment

Milton Derber

Professor Rees has concluded through statistical analysis that the structural components of manufacturing employment and union membership are not likely to be very different in the 1980s than they have been in the 1970s. If anything, the prospects for union growth in membership are negative because of the declining percentage of production workers, the rise in female employment, the relatively larger decline of production workers in the most heavily unionized industries, the adverse trend in foreign trade, and, perhaps most of all, the geographical shift of manufacturing employment to states with a low extent of union organization, mainly in the South.

He finds some feeble rays of hope for the union movement only in a number of national union mergers, the emergence of several energetic and able national union leaders, an increase in union-management committees to improve productivity (an arguable point), and the stepped-up (although thus far not very successful) union organizing campaigns. One might add to this list by inference from his statistics the increased employment and unionization of nonwhites, although their higher union ratio may be attributed to their relatively greater proportion of production workers. Even the possibility of revision of the basic labor law favorable to union organizing gets short shrift.

As Professor Rees has noted, the government's statistics on union membership contain many defects, and comparisons with employment data over a twenty-year period may not reflect the stable correspondence that he assumes. Moreover, he makes no allowance for the possibility of new industry growth beyond the twenty-year trend line. However, I am not inclined to dispute his statistical findings, particularly since I have no better substitutes to offer.

Instead I want to suggest a somewhat different line of analysis, not to replace his but to supplement it. The history of unionization has not been that of a simple straight line, although a long-term growth curve can be shown in absolute membership terms, largely reflecting the growth of the nation. Rather, union growth has occurred in sharp spurts over comparatively short periods of time: 1897-1904, 1915-1920, 1933-1947 (really two phases), 1950-1953, and 1965-1970. Usually, in these boom periods, some exceptional and often unexpected combination of factors occurred to promote large-scale union organization. At the risk of oversimplification, I offer the following examples. In the 1897-1904 period, the nation experienced the start of a long-term upsurge in prices following a prolonged period of falling prices and recovery from a major depression and a minor war. The 1915-1920 union growth was tied in closely with World War I. The 1933-1937 period involved first the New Deal and then World War II. The 1950-1953 expansion occurred during the Korean War. The last period, 1965-1970, coincided with the Vietnam War and an inflationary trend, and entailed a dramatic drive for collective bargaining rights by public sector employees as well as the conversion of professional and quasi-professional associations into unionlike organizations.

This history suggests that if there is to be a rapid upward deviation from the pattern of comparative stability in manufacturing unionism envisaged by Professor Rees, we must look for some rather exceptional (difficult to anticipate) developments or circumstances. Changing events must intensify the motivation of workers to organize, the forces in favor of organization must be strengthened by economic, political, and institutional conditions, and the barriers of employers' resistance and their allies must be rendered relatively less effective.

Without trying to predict whether and when we can expect such changing circumstances, I suggest that the possibilities lie in the following directions:

1. The outbreak of another sustained war involving the United States. This is the most distasteful prospect; however, if it occurs, the consequences are perhaps most readily predictable. War increases the demand for factory workers. It also greatly enhances the bargaining power of unions. Moreover, workers turn to unions to cope with the inevitable inflationary pressures and to gain protection against wartime dislocations. In addition, government depends upon unions to fulfill a variety of essential functions in furthering the war effort. Finally, employer resistance declines or becomes less effective.

2. Organization of the South. As Professor Rees has demonstrated, the past two decades have witnessed a shift of industry from the East and Midwest to the South, which is the least unionized geographic section of the nation. If the South were organized to the same degree as the East or Midwest, there would be about 1.5 million more union members. With increasing industrialization, urbanization, and affluence, as well as the continuing influx of companies and personnel from more union-minded regions, the traditional (mainly rural) southern values opposing unionism and collective bargaining will probably become diluted.

In some of the larger industrialized southern cities, factory unionism has been well established for several decades. The future elimination of right-to-work laws on a state-by-state basis or through repeal of Section 14(b) of the Taft-Hartley law could occur. Or if labor law revisions were enacted and a few key organizational successes ensued, a take-off stage might speedily develop. One of the significant qualities of organizing campaigns is their epidemic like nature. Once a new organizational climate materializes, the process accelerates rapidly until a period of consolidation and absorption is required.

3. Unionization of white-collar factory workers. As Professor Rees has shown, the proportion of nonproduction, mainly white-collar, workers in manufacturing rose from about 22 percent in 1956 to 27 percent in 1976. This ratio will probably continue to grow. Since white-collar employees in factories are far less organized than production workers, this trend seems to augur poorly for unionization. However, the spectacular (and largely unexpected) rise of unionism and unionlike associations in the public sector has demonstrated that white-collar employees are not insensitive to the appeal of organization, particularly if the legal environment is encouraging and the employee organizations develop appropriate organizing techniques and programs.

It is true that private employers can be expected to offer greater and more effective resistance than public employers have done. On the other hand, in many democratic countries white-collar employees in manufacturing have shown that they can become active and even militant union members. If white-collar factory unionization rose from its present level of 2-5 percent to 20 percent (on an industry basis it varies from 0 to perhaps 10 percent in steel and electrical products), this would represent an increase of between 800,000 and a million union members.

4. Unionization of the weakly unionized industries. A recent study by Gus Tyler for the ILGWU calls for drastic changes in American society to redress the economic imbalances existing between the capital-intensive and labor-intensive segments of enterprise. According to Tyler a majority of all wage and salaried persons in the private sector belong in the category of "America's Working Poor."

If Tyler's analysis is correct, and it manifestly applies to such important manufacturing industries as garments, textiles, and furniture, a union-led movement for a "New Deal" for the working poor could conceivably attract a sizable number of new members. What sparks a social movement—a widely held sense of grievance; dynamic, charismatic leadership; organizational skills; political clout? What in particular might arouse the hundreds of thousands of minorities—blacks, Mexican-Americans, Puerto Ricans, Appalachians—who now fill the bulk of positions in low-paying industries? Many of these persons already belong to unions, but a substantial proportion do not. Reliable statistics for estimating the potential increase in union members in these industries are unfortunately not available.

I have suggested four alternatives to the stability pattern projected by Professor Rees; all show a substantial increase in factory union membership. It is possible, of course, to conceive of a swing in the opposite direction, although at this stage our society is probably too organization-minded to permit it for long. Such a downward swing would emanate from a number of factors listed by Professor Rees: the continuing shift of industry to the less-unionized South; the declining proportion of production workers; and the intense adverse opposition that many employers bear toward unions. The last point is reflected in the increasingly sophisticated techniques that employers are using to combat union organizing campaigns, and the spread of consulting firms whose main mission is to counteract unionization. The history of American unionism in the twentieth century, however, suggests that a strong advance is more likely to occur than a precipitous decline.

I conclude by echoing the editors' general disclaimer about the ability of the forecaster. We are constantly being surprised by sudden shifts in social behavior patterns. An external crisis, a new charismatic leader, a turnabout in public attitudes—these have repeatedly altered an apparently stable trend of organization. It is tempting to project into the future the line of development connecting the present with the recent past, as Professor Rees has done. However, sooner or later a sharp turn in the road occurs. The question is when, where, and under what circumstances.

Comment

Richard Prosten

When speculating about union membership in manufacturing in the 1980s, it may well be more important to examine declines in manufacturing employment rather than the trends in membership which parallel that decline. People who are not working are unlikely candidates for union membership, at least in the traditional job-centered context of industrial union membership in this country. Thus, we must be certain that we are examining the correct end of the animal.

A cursory look at a few statistical references reveals that manufacturing employment in general, and production work in particular, is a component of our total store of jobs that is edging toward extinction. However, there is no Endangered Species Act for workers who, like the Tennessee snail darters, need all the friends they can get.

Between 1950 and 1976, nonagricultural employment in the United States increased by 76 percent (from 45 million to 79 million). During the same period the civilian labor force increased from 62.2 million to 94.8 million people, a jump of over 52 percent. The concurrent increase in production workers was less than 9 percent. If we look at all manufacturing employment (production and nonproduction) as a percentage of total nonagricultural employment, it has declined from almost 34 percent to 24 percent during the same span of years. In 1950, 28 percent of those in nonagricultural employment were production workers; in 1976 only 17 percent could be so described. Obviously there were minor fluctuations from year to year, but the trends are clear and unmistakable.

The decline in job opportunities in the manufacturing sector goes a long way toward explaining the lack of union growth in manufacturing. A variety of factors has created the conditions, which are reflected in table 2-1.

Professor Rees listed a number of external factors which might have affected union membership in recent years, although he places different weights on them than I do. I agree that recent developments in international trade were adverse to American manufacturing industries; however, they were even worse for their employees. He suggests that imports have affected unionized firms more severely—or at least more quickly—than nonunionized firms. He also notes the shift in production worker employment from the frostbelt to the sunbelt, leaving open the question of whether these relocations have any relationship to antiunion attitudes of the involved state governments.

In addition, Rees says that the decline in unionization, at least as marked by the results of NLRB elections, shows a parallel drop-off between manufacturing and nonmanufacturing sectors. According to my figures, from 1962 to 1976 the percentage of workers participating in NLRB elections that ended up choosing bargaining units was lower in communication, construction, mining, finance, and trade than in manufacturing. The rates have been higher only in services and utilities, and unionization in the services sector has increased as a definite result of including hospitals under NLRB jurisdiction in recent years.

One area where I do disagree with Dr. Rees's observations is in the effect of unit size on election outcome. Of all manufacturing elections closed by the NLRB in 1977, 53 percent resulted in no union (1,039 of 1,953). Unions won 54 percent of the contested units with populations of nine or less, 49 percent of those with ten to thirty-nine members, 41 percent of those with forty to ninety-nine members, thirty-seven of those with 100 to 199, and only 33 percent of the units with 200 or more voters. Whatever the reasons for such a situation, there was nothing new about it: The last year in which a majority of manufacturing units of 500 or more people chose unions was 1967.

Rees's table 2-6 may have more significance than he attributes to it. I suspect that the size of the parent company (and not just the establishment) has a great impact on the eventual outcome of an election. Concentration in manufacturing has increased in recent years—a situation that I find to be of significance in this discussion.

While labor law reform seems to have received more attention as symbolic rather than as substantial legislation, it is important to look at some of the reasons such legislation was originally proposed, and how abuses of the National Labor Relations Act have contributed to the declines in union membership noted in Professor Rees's chapter. He suggests that unions blame tougher resistance on the part of management. This is not mere speculation; it can be documented by an almost endless supply of evidence.

More important, however, are the things that management does to thwart efforts by employees to organize themselves. For instance, management delays the actual election process. In 1962, according to an Industrial Union Department (IUD) survey, 11.3 percent of all NLRB elections were conducted in the same month as the original filing, and 59.2 percent of the elections had been concluded by the end of the month after the month of filing. The corresponding figures for 1977 were only 2.2 percent and 40 percent, respectively. While many rationalizations can be given for such figures, I think the facts clearly point to concerted employer resistance.

Another example: in 1962, 46.1 percent of all NLRB elections were "consent" elections—the process which requires the least red tape and most quickly resolves the issues of representation. Last year, only 8.6 percent of elections were consent elections, with employers forcing employees into costly administrative proceedings by refusing to consent to elections once the union had proved appropriate employee interest.

Even where unions win elections, employer resistance to their aspirations is adamant. A few years ago, the IUD conducted a survey to determine the eventual disposition of NLRB election victories. The study looked at all elections administratively closed during 1970 which were won by any union. Over 22 percent of the units (13.64 percent of the people) choosing a union in NLRB elections during 1970 were never brought under contract; 13.2 percent of the units (10.5 percent of the people) were brought under contract for a while, but were no longer under contract five years after the union victory.

In short, 35 percent of the units (containing 24 percent of the people) for whom bargaining rights were won in 1970 were not under contract five years after the election. The reasons for this were varied, and certainly included some plants which closed because of natural disasters. However, for the most part, the results reflect the fact that employers outspend employees in postelection legal proceedings.

Dr. Rees has also correctly suggested trade as a problem for our unions. Industry after industry has succumbed to a system which encourages the exportation of advanced American technology, and thus American job opportunities, in order to pad the pockets of certain multinational operators. In other cases, we allow certain foreign powers to export their joblessness by dumping products in the United States. Since such processes most readily affect manufactured items, it might be concluded that the U.S. government is an active partner in the erosion of our manufacturing workforce and industrial capacity.

Obviously there is no future for manufacturing unionism in the absence of manufacturing activity. Assuming we do not commit suicide by selling off all of our developing technology and systematically stripping away our productive capacities, I would in general concur with Professor Rees's scenario of a gradual growth in manufacturing unionism in the next few years.

None of this should be construed as a labor "excuse" for what we all agree is a fall-off in union membership. Certainly a portion of the blame rests on labor's shoulders, but the bulk of causality is external to the labor movement.

3

The Union as an Evolving Organization

Jack Barbash

The objective of the modern industrial union is the enhancement of what I have labeled bargaining effectiveness. Bargaining effectiveness goes beyond the union's pursuit of "more," in Gomper's terms, and includes a desire for power vis-à-vis both the employer and constituent groups within the organization. Bargaining effectiveness is the central theme underlying the basic union functions of organizing, negotiating, striking, politics, legislation, and governance. The relationship of bargaining effectiveness to each of these functions is considered separately in the sections below, after briefly reviewing the characteristics of the industrial union.

A question posed for this conference is, "What form will the union take?" I believe that the union has already evolved into an appropriate form in response to changes in its environment. Given the belief of those at the conference, which I share, that the environment will remain relatively stable, it is reasonable to infer that the union as an institution will undergo no fundamental changes.

The Industrial Union as a Bargaining Organization

Industrial unionism's characteristic environment is the factory worksite, capital-intensive employment, high or middling technology, complex management organization, and an expanded product market. Industrial unionism mainly regulates the work through work rules, leaving the employer in control of entry. Its base of operations in collective bargaining is principally the internal labor market of the enterprise. The output of this process is a complex agreement and an active and stratified shop floor society.

John R. Commons's construct of industrial government is appropriate for the kind of collective bargaining relationship which has emerged.

> Out of the wage bargain a constitution for industrial government is being constructed by removing cases from the prerogative of management and the arbitrary power of unions and subjecting the foreman, the superintendents and the business agents to the same due process of law as that which governs the laborers. (Commons, 1924)

The operative words are "due process of law."

Industrial unions are also social organizations, and most of these unions have had to assimilate successive ethnic waves. Because its industries are close to the "center" economy, industrial unionism is also closely associated with wide-ranging political and legislative programs.

All of the above notwithstanding, the union is at its core a bargaining organization; therefore, what it seeks most of all is bargaining effectiveness. It is bargaining effectiveness which represents the highest priority for union leadership. Commentators have for more than a century variously identified the union's primary goal as socialism (or conversely, pro capitalism), job consciousness, business unionism, maximizing (or "satisficing"), monopoly, and organizational survival. At various times, the union does pursue many of these other goals, but when they clash with bargaining effectiveness these goals give way.

Some have tried to view the union as revolutionary. However, I believe the revolutionary goal is excluded by bargaining. First, bargaining means coming to terms with the fundamental structure of the other side. Second, the high priorities attached to immediate gains by the union rank and file forces the union to settle for what it can get now; it has proved impossible to postpone these incremental gains in bargaining to favor a more wholesale strategy. It was the recognition of this narrow time horizon of the rank and file that prompted Lenin and other revolutionary theoreticians to conclude correctly that revolutionary consciousness could only be brought to the trade unionist from without, that trade unionism would compromise away its long-run revolutionary mission and relegate it to slogans.

Bargaining effectiveness is the ability to demand support from the rank and file, including striking where necessary, and the ability to "command respect" from employers (Commons, 1919). Bargaining effectiveness is to be understood in the context of collective bargaining of the North American variety, where the union as the exclusive representative of workers in specified units and appropriate employers negotiate terms of employment. In the final analysis, it is the union's ability to strike, that is, to withhold labor, and the employer's ability to withhold demand for jobs which bring the parties to the bargaining table. The terms of bargaining are, broadly, the price of labor and the power relationships in the work situation, or, more briefly, price and power.

Price

A meaningful price bargain requires implicit or explicit specification of five elements: (1) composition, or the various modes of compensation which comprise the price—pensions and insurance, vacations, holidays, and overtime; (2) effort—hours, work measurement, classification, supervision, and scheduling of work; (3) job tenure, or job security—layoff, recall, promotion, transfer, discipline, discharge, and work and earnings guarantee; (4) equity—the wage structure which fixes jobs and earnings in some equitable (among others) relationship to each other; and (5) adjustment of the terms to expected and unexpected change during the life of the contract, including changes in the cost of living, technology, and ownership and mangement. These specifications cannot all be set out in the written agreement; they need to be detailed later in formal and informal transactions.

Power

To oversee its part of the bargain, the union needs to be able to determine whether these specifications are being enforced. Employer accountability is therefore inherent in the bargain. Without employer accountability, the formal price bargain could be nullified by the employer's unilateral manipulation of essential specifications. With this goes nullification of the essence of the bargain, which is not for a lump of nondescript labor but for labor with very specific characteristics. The transaction, then, only begins with the formal determination of the initial price in an agreement; the transaction is consummated when the union is able to review the employer's price determination, or protest it, if necessary.

Power, in short, must be part of price. Without power to require accountability there can be no meaningful price. Because accountability is commonly enforced through the grievance procedure, bargaining effectiveness entails the effective application of the agreement, too. The grievance-arbitration system is the formal mechanism through which shop floor disputes over individual or group prices of labor and power relations are formally resolved. Even the grievance-arbitration system falls materially short of completing the labor bargain for every employee. This is eventually completed only in the continuous relationship between the employee and the employee's immediate superior. This is the ultimate test of bargaining effectiveness for the worker.

Power provides the leverage necessary for getting the employer to bargain to agreement by inflicting costs on him (or threatening to do so), by withholding labor supply (strike), by withholding product demand (boycott), or sometimes by direct physical interference in the operation of the plant (direct action). In a fundamental sense, the employment terms which result from collective bargaining differ from unilateral determinations because collective bargaining represents employee entitlements or rights and also a sense of power that comes from being able to protest employer determinations without fear or reprisal. To be effective in negotiation and enforcement, the union must undertake collateral functions along with negotiations. These are organizing, striking, politics, and governance.

Bargaining Effectiveness and Organizing

Organizing is essential to bargaining effectiveness. The union's ability to gain its demands from an employer is influenced by whether or not it has been able to organize his competitors and hold them to comparable employment standards. Conversely, the employer's ability to meet the cost of union demands depends on the extent to which the union has standardized employment costs in competitive product/labor markets. Both depend in large part on the extent of union organization in these markets.

Mass organizing as it took place in the New Deal 1930s has evolved into piecemeal organizing. Mass organizing of blue-collar workers in manufacturing was completed, for all practical purposes, by World War II. Since then the only mass organizing efforts in manufacturing have been in textiles, but with little success to date. Another try particularly directed at the sunbelt might occur if a labor reform bill, such as that proposed in 1978, gets enacted.

White-collar and professional employees in manufacturing (as in the private sector generally) continue to evade unionization. However, it is not their white-collar status that prevents them from joining unions; witness unionization across the broad spectrum of white-collar employment in the public sector. It is more likely that large-scale management has bought out the union impulse of white-collar workers by automatically extending the benefits gained by the blue-collar unions. Therefore, unionism in manufacturing continues to be identified with production workers. Among production workers, unionism has adapted itself readily to the changing composition of the manual labor force, as the substantial union-proneness of women and black males indicates.

Bargaining Effectiveness and Negotiation

Unions have imposed two self-denying limitations in negotiations in the interest of bargaining effectiveness. First, they deliberately limit the bargain to the terms of employment. Second, the unions limit themselves to a "grieving," protective, adversary posture as being more compatible with bargaining effectiveness than comanagement, partnership (now codetermination), or any other variation which puts the union in an initiating role.

This self-denial has little to do with a procapitalist ideology. It has more to do with the union's rejecting a position in which it would have to defend management against the claims of its grieving constituents. The union prefers to affect employment policy by grieving incrementally rather than by formulating it wholesale through codecision-making.

American union leaders reject ownership and control of the means of production as unnecessary to bargaining effectiveness so long as they can bargain with those who do own and control. In fact, the union may view bargaining effectiveness as impeded by codetermination because management, faced with an attack on its ownership, may stiffen its resistance to all union demands.

In the American union view, bargaining effectiveness is better enforced through countervailing power rather than through the kind of integration in the management system which codetermination requires. On the one hand, the unions fear that cooptation into the management system will blunt the force of the adversary grieving role which underlies bargaining effectiveness. On the other, the union is short on resources to cope with the vast amount of technical information on which management feeds.

But even more basic is the fact that ideologically American unions lack the Socialist commitment which is one of the mainsprings of codetermination, even though they have been exposed to the argument by American and European intellectuals for more than a century. However, again, it is not so much that the American unions are procapitalist as that codetermination and its variants, including socialism, do not enhance union bargaining effectiveness. American unionists counter the common query, "Why aren't you Socialist?" with, "Why should we be?" Accordingly, the future holds little hope for American union acceptance of the comanagement principle.

But if comanagement does not explain the future, neither does "more." "More" says nothing analytically about union goals in bargaining. It does not begin to comprehend the intraorganizational elements of composition, power, and equity which are structured into price. "More" overlooks the fact that it is not only the absolute sum of labor's price which divides unions and management, or divides unions internally, but also the mix of price and power.

Furthermore, "more" disregards the importance of equity—the maintenance of an acceptable balance among the contending claims of the sectional groups within the union and in relation to the "significant others" on the outside with whom the sectional groups compare themselves. It is "compar[isons that] are important to the worker. They establish the dividing line between a square deal and a raw deal" (Ross, 1948, p. 51).

Ross's "orbits of coercive comparison" (1948, p. 53) are important to the maintenance of the union as an effective bargaining institution. Equity maintains that internal parity which is so decisive for the union's viability as an organization. The union leadership ignores these internal balances at the peril of severance, secession, and lowered morale.

Scientific management is the historical case which demonstrates the union's preference for bargaining effectiveness over "more." Taylor, as he conceded, wanted to remove wages from bargaining and replace them with unilateral determinations by engineers in the service of management. ("A union is absolutely unnecessary. . . . The principles of scientific management will confer far greater blessings upon the working people than could be brought about by any form of collective bargaining" [Kakar, 1970, p. 485]). After a long debate the industrial unions, for all practical purposes, came to terms with industrial engineering when its rules and results became bargainable.

In summary, the goals of the American industrial unions are limited. They are not interested in ownership, comanagement, or revolution. Rather, the agreement is restricted to general rules for enforcing the terms of price and power.

Bargaining Effectiveness and the Strike

The strike or, more importantly, the strike threat is basic to bargaining effectiveness. The costs inflicted by a strike or the threat of one force the parties to listen to each other and discipline their demands and responses accordingly.

An important qualitative change in the strike is that it is not the highly charged struggle—possibly class struggle—of the 1930s. The strike has been normalized: it is no longer an overriding end, but a calculated and measured means to an end—the end being a fixed-term agreement. The strike now represents basically the same kind of withholding which all buyers and sellers must have available in order to make their bargaining credible. Consequently, the parties seek to avoid or minimize strikes if other means are available to resolve differences.

Escalator clauses, periodic productivity allowances, and other automatic adjustments represent resolution of differences by rational formula instead of strikes. Grievance arbitration, long-term contracts, and, to a lesser extent, "precrisis" study committees and interest arbitration represent means to avoid strikes or weaken the strike impulse. Government has established methods and principles to dispose of issues that would previously have led to a strike: National Labor Relations Board (NLRB) elections are available to resolve questions of union representation and recognition; the bargainability of certain contract terms is now settled by adjudication rather than by strike power; mediation services are available to bridge communications gaps between the parties.

Even the conduct of the strike has become routine. Violence is unusual, due largely to management's acquiescence in not hiring strike breakers, although it does erupt from time to time. Where the violence is not mindless, it is designed to shut down an operation after other sanctions have failed, or once in a while as a sanction in interunion or union-nonunion rivalry.

Most often the union and management come to an understanding of how the strike procedures can conform with the union's interest in not working, management's interest in the maintenance of plant safety and security, and their joint interest in minimizing friction which could infect the relationship when the strike is over. In short, the strike has become an agreement on how to disagree.

Nevertheless, strikes have not become inconseqential. Many of the great issues in collective bargaining have had to be resolved through strikes, including, in modern times, pensions, guaranteed employment, union security, work rules, industrywide bargaining, and coordinated bargaining.

The strike has been normalized but it has not withered away; in fact, we may have even experienced a strike resurgence in the last decade. By most measures the United States is more strike-prone than other comparable systems. However, despite this greater strike-proneness, strikes in the United States are more systematically financed and organized, more directly focused on collective bargaining ends (in contrast to political strikes, which are rare here), and more likely to be controlled by the official union leadership. There are, to be sure, many wildcat strikes, but even these are closely related to practical ends. On balance, the strike in the United States is mainly a calculated means employed by the official leadership to get a better contract—the power arm of bargaining effectiveness.

Bargaining Effectiveness and Politics

For American unions politics serves to reinforce the price-power goals of collective bargaining. Political bargaining supplements, or by now complements, collective bargaining. The political bargain is the trade-off of manpower, morale, and money for favorable legislative results.

The quid pro quo for the unions need not be restricted to narrow partisan ends alone, although it often is. For the long term the union position also favors legislation whose benefits are not limited to union members, such as broad redistributive income transfer programs via social security, taxation, and housing; improvement in the quality of labor supply through vocational education; and the elimination of age, sex, and race discrimination—all of which unions share with middle-class liberal elements, on whom it counts for support.

One test for the bargaining effectiveness factor in the politics of trade unions has been the rejection of labor or Socialist party politics in favor of political bargaining. In political bargaining the unions, in effect, negotiate with the major political parties to see which is more likely to favor trade union positions. In the modern period the Democrats have mostly, but not exclusively, won out. In labor or Socialist party politics, by comparison the trade unions are committed to a brand of socialism through a party organically related to the trade union movement.

The labor party question is a dead issue in the United States, mostly because labor party politics clash with bargaining effectiveness. Political bargaining works only if politicians of all stripes have some reasonable expectation of garnering union support in return for their prounion votes. If the unions were already politically committed to a labor party they would not be free to put their support where the votes are. Unions feel that it is difficult enough to deal with opposition to unionism by employers and the general population without also taking on the burdens of anticapitalist politics.

An exception, at the margin, to the pure pursuit of bargaining effectiveness is the union's interest in social justice or social unionism. All labor movements, incuding the American, have their origins in an historic association with social reform and socialism. Something of that social justice impulse is, in varying degrees, embodied in the idea of a labor movement—a spirit of common purpose, elsewhere called solidarity.

However, here is where American and European models diverge. American social justice unionism in practice is not opposed to "business unionism" but is an extension of it. For example, when the price of labor takes the form of a guaranteed annual wage, a comprehensive health and pension program, and a paid four-week-or-so vacation, and when political and legislative goals give the highest priority to full employment and social policy, business unionism may be perceived to have fused into social justice; that is, the union is negotiating not only for the price of a given unit of labor but for improvement in the long-run human condition.

Social justice is also served when collective bargaining means power on the job for the heretofore powerless, especially among the low-paid ethnic minorities. At any rate, it is important to understand that in its own self-image the union is more than a labor "marketing" organization, although it is that, also. In its demands, the union incorporates an extra margin which is largely explainable by its social "uplift" aspirations.

Governance and Leadership

Union governance has been shaped by bargaining effectiveness but also by politics and personalities. Bargaining effectiveness is undoubtedly represented in the changes which have emanated from market requirements, technology, the necessities of political bargaining, pressures for self-determination by sectional groups, and the need for businesslike administration and more economical management of the union as an organization. However, what are interesting are the changes in governance

which have *not* taken place, even though demanded by the logic of bargaining effectiveness, for example, mergers.

Union Governance

The national union's rise to the commanding position in the network of
union government, necessitated by the nationalization of product markets,
brings economies of scale but also introduces the problems of coordinating
sectional interests. Given market conditions in many industries, only the national union has the necessary resources to support the total range of union
functions on the appropriate scale.

On the face of it, the de facto pattern of national union jurisdiction is
not exactly a testament to bargaining effectiveness. Conflicting jurisdictions
were always a vexing problem in the AFL. The rise of the CIO accounted
for some rival unionism but not as much as might have been expected. The
mainstays of CIO strength—steel, auto, rubber, electrical equipment—were
mostly in territories where the AFL jurisdiction was largely theoretical. The
constitution of the AFL-CIO put its stamp of approval on the merger principle. There has been some increase in mergers since then, but by 1965 President Meany could still complain that "many unions [which] by all logic and
common sense could merge" were being perpetuated "for the sake of sentiment and tradition." Since then mergers have "accelerated" (Dewey, 1971,
p. 63), but obvious duplications in manufacturing have continued to exist in
shoes, furniture, and textiles. Bargaining effectiveness does not hold up well
in this aspect of union governance, and further implementation may have to
wait on the passing of incumbent leaders from the active scene.

However, some form of consolidation in the interest of bargaining effectiveness is developing at levels below the national. For example, joint
councils or district councils coordinate, and not infrequently almost
displace, the collective bargaining function of local unions in the large city,
metropolitan, area, or region. Invariably this form of the intermediate body
arose to centralize the responsibility of otherwise competing units of the
same national. Other typical forms of the intermediate body include the
corporation or industry council, which brings together locals of the same
national dealing with a common industry or common employer. The occupational council or department, as in the white-collar council or skilled
workers council, is yet another intermediate vehicle bringing together locals
with a common type of craft constituency. In addition, "industrialization"
within the jurisdictions of former craft unions has spurred the creation of
manufacturing departments in these historic unions.

The most significant development in internal union government has
been the new assertiveness of the industrial rank and file, which can be

dated from the early 1960s. This assertiveness has been expressed through an increasing number of wildcat and authorized strikes during the life of an agreement; local issues bargaining under a national agreement; insurgency, as in steel and electrical equipment, against long-established incumbents; and civil rights confrontations on the shop floor and in the local union.

Bargaining effectiveness has required union governance to fashion orderly channels through which discontent could travel without disrupting the organization. These channels include mechanisms for craft and white-collar representation in industrial unions and the craft "veto," broader-based bargaining committees, local issues bargaining, and "black caucuses."

Furthermore, tribunals in the Federation and several trade and industrial departments chaired by impartial outsiders serve to resolve inter- and intraunion disputes over jurisdiction and representation. Tribunals in several national unions function as courts of final appeal in disciplinary cases, and in one union an independent "ethical practices" committee decides whether officers have been guilty of improper acts. These tribunals mark, first, the use of outsiders to rule on internal affairs, and, second, the acceptance of higher authority to resolve jurisdictional disputes between traditionally autonomous unions.

In addition, legal interventions made possible by Landrum-Griffin and civil rights law have created additional instrumentalities for protest from below. The net effort has been to institute decentralizing forces in union governance and to establish the rank and file as a permanently active check and balance to leadership decision-making. If this commentary had been written a generation or so ago, the emphasis would have been on union democracy, meaning overcentralized authority in the national union. But "the problem [now] may well have become too much rather than too little 'responsiveness.' " Clark Kerr, the author of these words, commented that "one can only be impressed with how quickly trends can be reversed or brought to a stop" (Kerr, 1964, p. xvii).

Another development in union governance necessitated by bargaining effectiveness is the employment of professionals in law, economics, public relations, health, and other fields. Modest as it is, this situation is one element in the trend toward a businesslike organization of union affairs.

Political Influences

The political interests of the labor movement are implemented by a complex organizational network. At the Federation level, this network consists of a Committee for Political Education (COPE), a legislative department, and a technical staff secretariat specializing in economic policy, civil rights, social security, and international affairs. The Federation network is augmented by political departments in several large international unions and political activity units (local versions of COPE) in every state and in every city of any size.

This political organization utilizes specialized techniques in propaganda, education and training, lobbying, registration campaigns, and polling surveys and expends manpower and money in behalf of candidates. "What we're doing now that wasn't done before," George Meany has said, "is that we are going into the localities, right down to the precinct level with our organization, and we're doing it on an educational basis" (*U.S. News and World Report*, 1953, p. 61).

The increasing importance of full-time staff for organizing, servicing, and bargaining represents bureaucracy in another sense: professionalization of the lay volunteers into full-time staff. But this bureaucracy, unlike the classical bureaucracy, is from the ranks, and pressure from the ranks has made its tenure increasingly precarious.

Leadership and Personalities

Walter Reuther is the archetypal figure of modern American industrial unionism. He brought to American trade unionism a synthesis of traditional business and Socialist unionism of the West European style to create social unionism. Reuther fused the incrementalism and practical sense of the former with the articulate social and economic vision of the latter, avoiding at the same time their extremes of excessive protectivism and doctrinaire ideology. The automobile industry as the dynamic growth industry of its time provided the most favorable arena for this sort of leadership.

Reuther was the collective bargaining pacesetter of the postwar period. It is no diminution of John L. Lewis to say that his major impact came in the industrial union breakthrough at the start of this period but waned substantially thereafter. Reuther, by contrast, put his imprint on virtually every landmark in collective bargaining and trade unionism of his time. The United Auto Workers' health care and pension policies transformed the structure of employee compensation. To be sure, Lewis had gotten it first, but in Reuther's hands it became a program and a policy—characteristic words in his vocabulary—not a gamble. More than anybody else, Reuther dramatized the relevance of technological change—"automation"—to collective bargaining. No other union, either, faced up to more squarely or triumphed more decisively and honorably on the issue of Communist penetration.

In the internal affairs of trade unionism the UAW under Reuther gave new content and meaning to political action, workers' education, union democracy, skilled-worker representation, and women's and ethnic civil rights at the workplace. Reuther was the first union leader to raise the question of compatibility between collective bargaining and the general interest. "We are not going to operate as a narrow economic pressure group which says, 'We are going to get ours and the public be damned' " (*New York Times*, 1946).

An important test of Reuther as a leader has been the extent to which a man of his overarching stature was nevertheless able to bring up with him men of comparable mettle. If this point needs substantiation, look at the union in the era after Lewis. His successors have been different from Reuther and came to the office in different times, but neither he nor his successors need be diminished by the comparison.

The United Steelworkers have not had a Reuther figure to dramatize the quality of their union leadership. Nonetheless, steel has been industrial unionism's other major laboratory. USW's early struggles as the Steel Workers' Organizing Committee paved the way for the sweep of industrial unionism in the 1930s. Steel industrial relations pioneered in grievance procedures, rational wage-job structures, and in Supplemental Unemployment Benefits, health insurance, and pensions.

Philip Murray saw the union through its era of turbulence. I.W. Abel especially, but David J. McDonald, too, took political risks to experiment with constructive approaches to bargaining: the Human Relations Committee, crisis bargaining, the Experimental Negotiating Agreement, and Expedited Arbitration. But it is also the steel experience which suggests that the union leadership can move out too far ahead of what its constituency is willing to support by way of "union-management cooperation."

In respect to labor leadership generally we are witnessing the passing of founding fathers, the men who planted the roots of the new industrial union labor movement in the 1930s and who persevered until the roots were sunk deeply into the soil of industrial America. Essentially this is the CIO labor movement personified in Reuther.

Even though the CIO founding fathers eschewed socialism, they embraced a new social or social justice unionism. Social unionism is distinguishable from Socialist unionism in rejecting an explicit Socialist, anticapitalist commitment. At the same time, however, it maintains a running criticism of capitalism's injustice without taking on the system as a whole.

With its roots in the industrial unions closer to the mainstream of economy and society than craft unionism, the concept of social unionism is also applicable to collective bargaining. The industrial union organizations were more broadly based among the ethnic strata of the society.

However, there was also an underlying core of business unionism in the CIO. Its social unionism is an incremental overlay on business unionism. By now the CIO's social unionism has been largely assimilated into the broader trade union movement.

The founding fathers formed their ideas and styles in the struggles of pre-World War II. This era has passed into the legend of labor's golden age; the leaders who are gradually replacing the founding fathers reflect this development, just as the newer leadership is forced to reckon with the changed power relationships in mass production manufacturing and the weakened position of manufacturing industry in the economy generally. All of this means, as a practical matter, that the profits are not there anymore to pay for the kinds of breakthroughs of the earlier decades.

It is hard to see a modern Reuther developing in manufacturing in the new, more restrictive environment. The dynamic center of trade unionism has already begun to shift to the public sector, which, after its brief "golden age," has been experiencing its own hard times.

The circumstances in which factory unionism is likely to find itself in the decades ahead (see chapter 1) do not constitute fertile soil for a factory union renaissance, no matter what the age of the leadership is. It is important to remember that the evangelical zeal of the founding fathers was compressed into a period of two years (1937-1939), or at best a four-year period (1935-1939). From 1939 on, World War II and its aftermath were followed by consolidation, containment, and, in the 1960s, the eruption of public sector zeal perceptibly moving factory unionism away from stage center.

Union leadership of the Reuther style has always been in the minority. The reason is that the union is inherently a reacting, not an initiating, institution. This condition is particularly true of the factory environment, where, if it is a partner at all with management, the industrial union is very much the junior partner. Compare the construction craft unions or the Teamsters, which are more likely to be senior partners in collective bargaining. The unions in women's and men's clothing are the large exceptions to the reacting character of manufacturing union leadership. The apparel unions, unlike the construction unions and the Teamsters, to cite those which are in a comparable power relationship, have at least taken on the critical issues of their industries in an initiating and problem-solving style, even if they have not solved them.

The upshot of this discussion is that the image of the union leader in manufacturing as boss is misleading. Union leaders are constrained mainly by the employer and the economics of the industry, and more generally by the state of the economy and society; the initiative which the organization of work necessarily imparts to management; "the orbits of coercive comparison"; the location of the union leader in the scheme of union government; and the union's resources. The margin for pure union leadership is, in fact, astonishingly thin. And to repeat, the environment is such that no matter what the age of the leadership, a renaissance of factory unionism is unlikely.

The Union as an Evolving Organization

Unionism is likely to remain in an adversary relationship with management. The persistence of the adversary relationship suggests that this is collective bargaining's "natural" state, despite some noteworthy but limited experiments in cooperation.

Unions in apparel, steel, meatpacking, and automobiles have intermittently experimented with collaboration, but it has not really caught hold as a permanent feature of a relationship. Perhaps apparel unions have come closest. The Auto Workers' projects in the quality of worklife may have something new to say on this point. At times the collaboration depends on leading personalities on the union and management sides to give it life and ends when they leave the scene.

It is probably the rank and file which is most likely to become disenchanted with collaborative schemes. The American union member has no formal class-struggle ideology but apparently he wants his leaders to be bargainers and advocates, not partners, acknowledging only the common interest in preserving the fund out of which both wages and profits are financed. Experience, not ideology, is the foundation of the adversary system.

If collective bargaining is still an adversary game, nevertheless the game has been civilized, as in the American College Dictionary's definition, "to bring out of a savage state." Considering the turbulence, class warfare, and violence which ushered in the collective bargaining era of the 1930s, civilized is not an inappropriate term. The adversary relationship is still unmistakably working, but the trial by ordeal and power which it is used to represent has been moderated by John R. Commons's sort of industrial government. Just what industrial relations can be like without industrial government is indicated by the 1978 United Mine Workers' strike.

The rules of the adversary game have been further changed by circumstances to create more than two adversaries. "Third parties" are intervening in the collective bargaining process to expand the traditional bilateral two-party bargaining into multilateral or three-party bargaining. Each of the third parties—the state in behalf of wage-price stability and the civil rights movement (including the state) in behalf of black workers—demands stronger recognition of its particular interests.

The adversary quality in unionism has brought with it related attributes which I label as economism, power, protectivism, decentralization, incrementalism, and capitalism. These attributes, intrinsic to the American brand of unionism, put definite limits to what unions can do that comes "naturally." Economism, expressing the union's preoccupation with the price of labor, implies that nonprice quality of work as conventionally projected cannot make much headway in collective bargaining, even if managements were so inclined. Power is not easily shaped to Theory Y management precepts of trust, flexibility, and informality. Protectivism's negativeness runs counter to the initiative, involvement, and commitment valued in philosophies of participative management. Decentralization makes American unionism inappropriate for the coordination of bargaining and national economic policy. Incrementalism, reflecting the characteristically short-term horizon of workers, combined with unionism's attachment to liberal capitalism, put revolution and wholesale reform off limits.

It is not difficult for unionists to justify these limitations as essential conditions of bargaining effectiveness. Given its limited resources, protectivism is about all the union can successfully accomplish. To go beyond protectivism exposes it to the risk of spreading itself too thin and becoming coopted into the management system.

As to economism's impairment of the quality of work, the unionists might argue that work restructuring is not the only road to the quality of work, that the union-based system of workplace rights—the right to a voice in the conditions of work—can also be read as strengthening the quality of work. Decentralization's disadvantages for the making of a national economic policy need to be measured against the benefits of self-determination, particularly when the efficacy of the economic policy is not all that obvious. Liberal capitalism has so far been the only habitat in which union bargaining effectiveness has been able to flourish for a sustained period.

The relationships between unionism and the state have changed in fundamental ways. In a political sense, the state has become an integral part of the industrial relations structure, departing radically from the voluntaristic model which, until the Great Depression, the AFL ideology had offered as the ideal type.

The state has also become one of the bargaining adversaries in what is now, in many respects, a multilateral relationship. The state as bargainer, not always clearly distinguishable from the state as regulator, has intervened in the two-party bargaining relationship to maintain an active presence on behalf of wage stability—with only indifferent success, it must be said. It has been the unions, of course, which have borne the brunt of this interventionist strategy, one form of which has come to be known as "jawboning."

Civil rights has been the other object of multilateral bargaining by the state, but in this case in concert with the civil rights movement. Major changes in negotiated seniority and hiring policy have been effected as a result of these interventions.

The character of state regulation of unionism has changed materially. The life of the Wagner Act marked the period of the state as union ally, reversing a long period of state intervention in behalf of employers. In Taft-Hartley the state restricted somewhat its role as ally, and in Landrum-Griffin went even further. In any case, the state under all of these three regimens was conventionally interpreted as regulating the process of bargaining, not the substance. Most recently, the enactment of the Employee Retirement Income Security Act (ERISA), the Occupational Safety and Health Act (OSHA), and the Civil Rights Act of 1964, including kindred administrative orders, has forced fundamental changes in substance, that is, in the terms of agreement as negotiated by the bilateral parties.

When the regulatory scheme is seen in its totality, the effect of the state on collective bargaining substance becomes more apparent. Regulation of labor standards such as OSHA, Davis-Bacon, Walsh-Healey, and the Fair Labor Standards Act (FLSA) does not fix a precise bargaining outcome, but the effect of regulation is, nevertheless, to narrow the zone within which the bargaining settlement is likely to fall.

Even the labor relations regulation which the conventional wisdom also holds to be mainly procedural—Wagner, Taft-Hartley, Landrum-Griffin—had substantive results. For the manufacturng unions, the legitimization of the inclusive representation unit created an essential condition of industrial unionism. The employer's legal obligation to bargain paved, if it did not force, the way to agreement on major contract provisions including the vast edifice of health, welfare, and pensions. To be sure, it was legally possible for employers to say no to union demands in these categories, but almost impossible practically.

The debate over the Labor Reform Bill in 1978 did illuminate how closely the parties have associated enactment with major union breakthroughs in the heretofore unorganizable areas of the South. It has become apparent that statutory protection of unionism is indispensable to the acceptance of collective bargaining by the employer.

We are witnessing, in short, the socialization of union relationships to members and employers. While true of unions and collective bargaining in general, socialization operates with particular force on the industrial unions in manufacturing. There are no signs of abatement of this trend; the signs are, in fact, in a contrary direction as the scope of state participation in the economy broadens and deepens.

The North American and West European varieties of trade unionism are unique products of liberal capitalism. They exist nowhere else. However, liberal capitalism is moving rapidly toward an interventionist strategy which will undoubtedly alter trade unionism as delineated here.

References

AFL-CIO. *Convention Proceedings*, 1965.

Commons, John R. *Industrial Goodwill*. New York: McGraw Hill, Inc., 1919.

_____ . *Legal Foundations of Capitalism*. New York: Macmillan, Inc., 1924.

Dewey, Lucretia M. "Union Merger Pace Thickens." *Monthly Labor Review*, June 1971.

Kakar, Sudhir. *Frederick Taylor: A Study in Personality and Innovation*. Cambridge, Mass.: MIT Press, 1970.

Kerr, Clark. *Labor and Management in Industrial Society*. New York: Doubleday & Co., Inc., 1964.

New York Times, December 29, 1946.

Ross, Arthur M. *Trade Union Wage Policy*. Berkeley: University of California Press, 1948.

U.S. News and World Report, November 6, 1953.

Comment

Arthur Loevy

Professor Barbash makes a good number of thought-provoking, stimulating comments. I agree with many of his major points, but I disagree in some areas.

I agree that the basic collective bargaining process hinges on the issues of power and price, but I am not sure that "power" is an adequate term to describe what unions give to or seek for their members. However, power is very much of a factor, especially as related to the organizing process, because workers have no power at all without a union; achieving power through unionization is the first necessary step to gain broader goals.

When unions are organizing in an industry today, it is easier to organize the higher paid rather than the lower paid. For example, people who are working at the minimum wage level in a given industry are very difficult to organize. While the union appeals to workers on the basis of social and economic improvement, self-respect, fair treatment, and so forth—the "power" that Professor Barbash is referring to—people can relate only if they are not already too beaten down. People on the bottom are dispirited and afraid, without options. These are the most difficult people to organize. Workers with better jobs have a better self-image; they have more confidence in themselves that they are going to be able to accomplish something, not exclusively in an economic role but in a power role, and are therefore easier to organize.

Once the bargaining and negotiating process is completed, the main function of the union is to enforce the contract. On a day-to-day basis I think this is what the union staff and union leadership, more than anything else, are really concerned with.

Professor Barbash talks a lot about union preoccupation with bargaining effectiveness rather than fundamental social change. I don't think that these goals are mutually exclusive. There is a need within the labor movement for both, and I don't think that there is any question that the union movement has been a meaningful force for social change. Labor has always recognized that social change is necessary.

A couple of examples point out what I mean. First, while raising the minimum wage is clearly in the self-interest of unions from both organizing and bargaining perspectives, I think it is fair to say that nonunion workers at the lower end of the labor force derive the most benefit from higher minimum wages. The unions have been the major force behind higher minimum wages.

Second, labor's push for full employment—that every American has a right to a job—reflects a deep commitment to social goals. Unions would certainly benefit from a full employment economy, but this is not the major motivating factor behind the drive for the Humphrey-Hawkins Bill. We are discussing fundamental social, economic, and political change here, government planning for a full employment economy.

In the area of national health care, the unions, for the most part, are able to provide decent insurance protection for their members. Nevertheless, the thrust for national health insurance in this country is coming from the trade union movement because those who are excluded from that movement do not have adequate health care or insurance coverage. National Health Insurance will help union members, but mostly it will help workers who are not in unions.

The civil rights activities represent another example of the U.S. trade union movement's interest in social change. The trade union movement was in the forefront of the struggle for racial equality, side by side with the major civil rights organizations. The trade unions took on this battle even though they lost support among their own rank and file in many cases, and even though organizing efforts were thwarted when employers in all regions of the United States took advantage of labor's position by using racially divisive tactics. Still, the unions courageously stood up for civil rights, particularly in industrial unions, even though it might not have been in their short-run self-interest. When there was a strong feeling against busing in Louisville by a large number of AFL-CIO rank and file, George Meany said that if the federations took a position against busing there they would be expelled from the AFL-CIO. There is no short-run benefit from that kind of decision.

Another aspect of union behavior which Professor Barbash discusses is what he calls economism. He says that the union is more interested in money than in the quality of life. However, I must point out that the quality of life, in terms of representing workers in the collective bargaining process, comes down to whether the worker is going to have time and money. That is why vacations and holidays are key elements of every union contract.

Quality of work is also a key factor in wage bargaining. In industries, for example, where an incentive system is involved, it would be very easy for the union to say, "We are going to make the incentive system one in which the worker can earn even more money than he or she is earning now." However, in order to do that the employee will have to work longer hours, thus sacrificing some quality of life. As more and more manufacturing industries add incentive systems, the union has been consistently representing its workers in order to ensure that these systems are structured so the average employee can handle them without undue stress. However, this will often mean a lower average wage than that which might be obtainable.

Professor Barbash defines protectivism as a characteristic which means a rejection of the adversary process in labor relations. I think it is hard to draw firm conclusions in this area. Six years ago the first international president and secretary-treasurer were elected in the apparel and textile industry who were not involved in the formation of the union in 1914. In that election year, the union had its first national clothing strike in over fifty years. I think this was a reestablishment of an adversary process, which is inherent to the representation of workers as opposed to some interests of management. Within the trade union movement, we discussed the reestablishment of the adversary process a good deal; it is not anything to be ashamed of or to back away from.

The interest of workers is not always the same as the interests of management. There are times when the adversary process best represents the workers. Professor Barbash's questions of relevancy become appropriate at the point when the representatives of the workers and the representatives of management believe that their interests are the same. This is not likely to happen under our current economic institutions; in fact, the adversary relationship is now intensifying.

In the garment industry, historically, there has been a concern by the union for management which Professor Barbash accurately identifies. However, it did not come from an altruistic reason; it arose from an effort to stop the employers from destroying one another so that the workers could survive. The basic adversary process has always remained on a day-to-day basis, even through decades of negligible strike activity, and the system has worked fairly well.

It is true that in recent years very few union leaders have advocated fundamental changes in our basic economic system. We must remind ourselves that the trade union movement, as it governs itself, is not an economic institution, but a political one. Fundamentally, in terms of how it governs itself, the movement is a democratic political institution, although certainly not perfect in all of its aspects. Leadership generally has reflected rank-and-file attitudes. This may have prevented the U.S. labor movement from engaging in the radical social change which some might desire. If the mood of workers changes, union leaders will adapt, and younger people with different ideas will move into leadership positions.

Professor Barbash refers to the trade union movement as being a function rather than a mission; I strongly disagree. Some management may successfully eliminate the incentive for unionization by keeping pace with union wages, working conditions, and job security. However, for most employees the mission is still there as much as the function, and the mission relates to the needs that most workers continue to have: the need for self-respect, the need for an organization in which they can bargain for themselves and not wait for handouts. To this degree, the elements of our mission have been maintained within the trade union movement. If anything, this sense of mission is experiencing a resurgence.

It is precisely this sense of mission that meets with the greatest objection from certain representatives in management, because that is the element which seems to challenge the more fundamental power relations in society. This explains management's hysterical response to labor's rather mild labor law reform legislation. The link here is that as the unions turn again to organizing with renewed vigor, we enhance our overall political power. As union leadership watched business destroy the labor reform bill and other union-backed legislation, basic questions were raised concerning the willingness of business to tolerate unions. Now we have the "Council for a Union Free Environment" and other explicitly union-busting firms, organizations, and specialists. In this atmosphere, union leadership will have no choice but to emphasize the adversary relationship with business. If they do not, basic union power, bargaining effectiveness, and the social mission of trade unions will all be weakened.

**Part III
Labor Relations
in Manufacturing**

4

The Prospects for Collective Bargaining in the Manufacturing Sector, 1978-1985

George H. Hildebrand

I propose to begin this chapter with an examination of some of the leading characteristics of present collective bargaining arrangements in manufacturing. Following this general survey, I shall then consider in succession the prospects for contract negotiations in the years now approaching, and the prospects for administration of collective agreements in the sector.

The Present Bargaining Arrangements in the Manufacturing Sector

According to the Bureau of Labor Statistics of the U.S. Department of Labor, on July 1, 1975, the latest survey date, there were 3,750,950 union employees attached to the manufacturing sector involved in 815 collective bargaining agreements covering 1,000 workers or more (p. 3). As of that date, total employment in the sector (seasonably unadjusted) stood at 18.01 million persons, of which 10.43 million were in the durable goods group, and 7.58 million in nondurable goods. Production workers, who are the ones most likely to be union members, numbered 12.74 million within the 18.01 million total, with 7.30 million in durables and 5.44 million in nondurables (*Monthly Labor Review*, December 1975). Thus 20.8 percent of the whole employee group in manufacturing were covered by the 815 agreements, or if one considers production workers alone, then 25.2 percent were involved in these agreements. (According to *Bulletin 1957*, p. 13, 3.21 million of those covered by the 815 agreements were production workers.)

Two observations are in order at this point. The actual number of union members employed in manufacturing in 1975 substantially exceeded these 3.75 million, in units of one thousand persons or more. In 1976, for example, the BLS estimated total union membership in manufacturing at 8.46 million, or 44.5 percent of total sector employment (*Daily Labor Report*, p. B-17). Therefore, about two-thirds of union membership or coverage in

I wish to thank Robert Stewart Smith, Thomas Kochan, John Windmuller, James A. Gross, Robert B. McKersie, Sara Gamm, George W. Brooks, and John Burton for very helpful criticisms and suggestions. None of them, of course, bears any responsibility for what I have to say in what follows.

87

manufacturing were scattered over relatively small bargaining units. At the same time, penetration of the sector by labor organizations was—and still is—far greater than for the entire nonagricultural employee group, where for 1976 the degree of organization stood at only 24.5 percent *Daily Labor Report*, 1977). In 1945, the corresponding figure was 35.5 percent. Between 1970 and 1976, the unions lost a little over 700,000 members in manufacturing.

Varieties of Bargaining Structures

To gain further understanding of the quantitative aspects of collective bargaining in manufacturing, it is worthwhile to examine the 815 agreements according to coverage.

Single-plant Bargaining. Single-employer bargaining involved 661 of the agreements and 3 million members of the bargaining units so covered. (Strictly speaking, the 3 million employees are not all necessarily union members. Some may work in agency shops without belonging to the union, or they may hold the same status in right-to-work states, in that they are covered by the agreement but elect not to join.) Within the single-employer units, 930,850 employees, or one-third, worked under single-plant contracts, while 2.07 million were covered by multiplant agreements. Thus among the large-scale agreements of the sector (1,000 employees or more), the multiplant type predominates. However, it seems certain that if the 5 million manufacturing employees embraced by smaller-scale agreements could be allocated on the same principle, it would reveal that the single-plant unit is clearly predominant for the sector as a whole.

Multiple-plant Bargaining. For manufacturing in 1975, there were only 154 multiemployer or association bargaining agreements, involving 748,200 employees, or just under 20 percent of all those under large-scale contracts. By contrast, within the nonmanufacturing sector, 2.49 million workers were covered by multiemployer contracts, or three-quarters of the entire work force in that sector (U.S. Department of Labor, 1977, p. 12).

Within manufacturing, association bargaining dominates in only two of the twenty-one industries in the sector: apparel, with 408,800 employees under thirty large-scale contracts; and food and kindred products, with 160,750 workers and forty-four contracts. By comparison, the construction industry has 1.07 million employees under 286 agreements; transportation (except rail and air), 534,900 involved in fifty-one agreements; services, 318,650 under fifty-seven agreements; hotels and restaurants, 181,900 under thirty-eight agreements; and retail trade, 178,650 under fifty-one agreements (U.S. Department of Labor, 1977, p. 12).

Clearly, multiemployer bargaining is predominately a phenomenon of the nonmanufacturing sector, where, typically, the units of enterprise are small and numerous.

Industrial Distribution of Bargaining Units. Consider now the industrial composition of contracts and bargaining units in manufacturing. (In this discussion, "contract," "agreement," and "bargaining unit" are used interchangeably.) Of the 815 large-scale units, embracing 3.75 million employees, 80 percent of such employees are under single-employer contracts. Further, 69 percent of these 3 million workers are attached to multiplant single-employer bargaining units, and 31 percent to single-plant single-employer units. Of the twenty-one industries in the manufacturing sector, four of them account for just under three-quarters of all bargaining unit employees in the single-employer category. This information appears in table 4-1.

Unfortunately, the BLS data do not include industry coverage by union. Nor do they include the distribution by industry of some 4,750,000 union members in manufacturing attached to bargaining units with fewer than 1,000 employees.

Within electrical machinery, the principal unions are the Brotherhood of Electrical Workers (IBEW), the International Union of Electrical Workers (IUE), the International Association of Machinists (IAM), and the United Electrical Workers (UE). In machinery, the main organizations are the United Steelworkers (USW) and the IAM. In primary metals, the USW enjoys overwhelming dominance, while in transportation equipment the United Automobile Workers (UAW) control almost the entire field. In the only two manufacturing industries in which multiemployer bargaining is prominent, the Amalgamated Meat Cutters (AMC) and the Bakery and Confectionery Workers (BCW) are the principal organizations in food and

Table 4-1
Distribution of Bargaining-Unit Employees for Four Largest Industries under Single-Employer Contracts
(contracts covering 1,000 workers or more)

Industry	Single-plant Units	Multiplant Units	Total
Electrical machinery	257,550	176,110	433,660
Machinery	111,000	167,750	278,750
Primary metals	86,300	404,650	490,950
Transportation equipment	123,800	911,000	1,034,800
Total	578,650	1,659,510	2,238,160

Source: *Bulletin* 1957, p. 12.

kindred products, while the apparel industry is dominated by the Amalgamated Clothing and Textile Workers Union (ACTWU) and the International Ladies Garment Workers (ILGWU).

In summary, unionism in manufacturing is remarkably decentralized in the organization of its bargaining units. There is relatively little formal association bargaining; indeed, none at all exists in the rubber, instruments, and chemical industries. Nearly 5 million workers covered by union contracts belong to units with less than 1,000 employees. Of the 3 million others who are attached to large-scale units, 80 percent belong to single-employer units, although 70 percent of this group are in multiplant units.

Forms of Bargaining Systems

Of the five principal modes of collective bargaining (single-plant/single-union, coalition bargaining, pattern following, informal multiplant, formal association), the most common form is the single-plant unit of a single employer—a system that, although technically separate from any other, is nonetheless influenced strongly by the "going annual increase" that extends over the entire sector (Eckstein and Wilson, 1962). In short, the case is one of separate negotiations that are influenced in fundamental ways by leading national settlements, but always with the possibility of deviations to reflect local circumstances. Thus this system could well be described as "uniformity with variations," and it embraces basic wage rate, fringe benefits, and other contract provisions capable of interplant comparisons.

The first step away from strictly individual plant and community negotiations is a mode called "coalition bargaining." It may involve several companies, several plants of the same company, several unions and the same company, or several unions and several employers. In all variants, the common feature is that the individual bargaining units and contracts remain technically and legally separate. At the same time, however, the unions agree to act in concert as regards demands, settlements, and a joint decision to return to work. By this procedure the unions can consolidate their power and thereby overcome the disadvantages of fragmentation, disadvantages that diminish strike effectiveness and therefore bargaining power. In its numerous variants, this method has been used successfully in copper, electrical equipment, and petroleum refining.

The third principal mode of collective bargaining, ordinarily described as "pattern following," owes its inception to the UAW, which has employed this approach with remarkable success in the automobile industry. In essence the method calls for singling out one employer for the initial target, threatening him with a strike and a substantial loss of market share if he does not reach agreement mainly on the union's terms. Once settlement is reached, the union proceeds to the next company, exerting even more leverage because the first producer, who is now assured of freedom from a strike, can enlarge his market share if a strike occurs. It will be obvious that markets involving small numbers of sellers (oligopoly) are most appropriate for pattern-following because of the extreme sensitivity of each seller's market share and the policies of his rivals. Although the UAW was the pioneer with this device, it should be noted that in 1977 the USW imposed pattern-following upon copper mining, refining, and fabrication, employing a coalition of some twenty unions to make the technique effective.

However, the preferred mode of bargaining of the USW remains that of the informal multiplant negotiation, the fourth form to be found in manufacturing. Here the leading employers in basic steel production act jointly through a committee that negotiates with the union for what in fact is virtually a uniform set of conditions for settlement, although the actual contracts remain technically separate. The large companies find this approach convenient because it yields uniformity in increases in labor costs, an advantage to an industry that also has the characteristics of oligopoly. To the union there also are certain advantages: it gains uniformity by settling with the core of the industry first, after which it can readily impose similar terms on the smaller companies. However, the principal disadvantage to both parties is the risk of a major strike, which in this industry could be particularly costly. Perhaps it is for this reason that the industry and the union adopted the Experimental Negotiating Agreement in 1974, which provides for the resolution of key issues not settled in negotiations through a process of voluntary arbitration of contract terms. So far, ENA has not actually been used. It is also unlikely to spread because the underlying conditions of bargaining in basic steel are very uncommon in manufacturing.

The final mode of collective bargaining is formal association or multiemployer agreements, a rare variant in manufacturing with prominence only in the foods and apparel industries. Here there is a single agreement covering all of the employer members and the union or unions involved. In this way standardization of terms is made complete, providing certain advantages to both sides, in particular when the average employer is relatively small and his competitors are numerous. In fact, probably the reason why association bargaining is quite rare in manufacturing, while very common in trucking and retail trade, is that much of manufacturing industry tends to run either toward large plants, multiplant companies, and oligopoly, or to widely separated plants or firms. Both situations enable an employer to take a strike more readily than those in which competitors are numerous and highly concentrated geographically, as in retailing or local construction.

Length of Contract Terms

Of the 3.75 million employees covered by large agreements in 1975, only 275,050 were under contracts whose duration was twenty-four months or less, with 204,850 of these employees on a twenty-four-month basis. By contrast, 3.48 million, or 92.8 percent of the whole group, came under contracts of twenty-five months' duration or more (U.S. Department of Labor, 1977, pp. 7-8); 55.2 percent of the whole group on large contracts fell in the three-year category, while 72.1 percent were involved in contracts running for three years or longer. This 72.1 percent included the following large manufacturing industries and some of their principal unions: foods and kindred products (AMC, BCW); apparel (ACTWU, ILGWU); primary metals (USW); machinery (IAM); electrical machinery (IBEW, IAM, IUE, and UE); and transportation equipment (UAW and IAM).

The predominance of these long-term agreements among the large manufacturing unions acquires particular importance in periods of persistent inflation, such as the years after 1965. In the first place, long-term agreements lead the unions to seek protective mechanisms, such as automatic annual increases and cost-of-living adjustments (COLA). Second, because of their automatic contractual nature, these mechanisms make the problem of stabilizing the price level extremely difficult because they perpetuate in rigid mechanical fashion a series of committed increases over lengthy periods, regardless of efforts to reduce the rate of inflation and regardless of changes in the profitability of the industry or of conditions of demand and supply in the labor market.

Moreover, these are the groups that create the recurring "rounds" of wage settlements that now run mostly on a three-year cycle of renewals. To illustrate, the BLS survey of large contracts for mid-1975 revealed that 192 agreements expiring in 1976 would involve 1,000 or more employees in each of the following industries: food (158,200), apparel (271,080), electrical machinery (277,250), transportation equipment (800,450), and machinery (160,100). For 1977, 194 contracts involving 100,000 or more employees would expire: food (102,200), apparel (135,200), electrical machinery (137,800), transportation equipment (189,350), and primary metals (468,800). Then for 1978 no large industry groups were scheduled for expiration. Indeed, the 1975 expectation was that only 313,300 employees would be involved in all manufacturing contract openings, as against 1.5 million in 1977 and 1.3 million in 1976.

The predominance of the three-year agreement in manufacturing sets up a rather regular cycle of negotiations and renewals, although the prevalence of both twenty-four- to thirty-five-month contracts and those exceeding thirty-six months as well introduces an element of irregularity into the three-year cycle. Nonetheless, the pattern is clear enough to make certain years times of crisis in which wage rounds are created that become "orbits of coercive comparison," to use the language of the late Arthur M. Ross, which spread well beyond their points of origin. However, perhaps a better explanation is that when excess demand for labor prevails broadly over the economy, market forces themselves will cause these "orbits" to appear.

In truth, of course, these cycles are not based solely upon settlements in manufacturing, nor are the standards for settlements exclusively derived from this sector. After all, the construction trades, the Teamsters, the mining unions, and the railroad operating crafts all have cycles of their own and exert an independent influence upon the outcome as a whole. The phenomenon is, however, real and an important part of manufacturing collective bargaining.

Prospects for Contract Negotiations in the 1980s

There are several factors to consider when predicting how contract negotiations will fare in the 1980s.

Inflation in the Negotiating Environment

There can hardly be any doubt that inflation has placed a persistent and growing burden on both companies and unions over the last dozen years. During 1966-1967 wholesale prices rose on an average of 6.1 percent annually, while for 1970-1977 the rate of yearly increase was accelerated to 7.9 percent. At the same time, consumers' prices have increased an average of 5.6 percent annually during 1966-1977, and 6.5 percent annually for 1970-1977. Worse yet, the rate of inflation is again showing signs of acceleration.

On the union side, the inflation burden since 1966 has been dominated by the traditional desire to protect both the level and the annual rate of increase in real wages, an objective that has been successful only in part. Despite catch-up adjustments, COLA provisions, and general annual increases, the rate of increase in real hourly wages for production workers in the whole private nonfarm economy has averaged only 1.2 percent a year since 1966, as against 2.5 percent yearly between 1947 and 1962 (Douty, 1977, p. 7: after adjusting the manufacturing figures deflated for overtime and interindustry employment shifts). But the effect of inflation on domestic prices has fostered a growing influx of imports that—given the failure of real wages and/or productivity to adjust—has wiped out several hundred thousand jobs in manufacturing over the past three years.

On the employer side, the central problem has been to find ways to absorb the money costs of increases in nominal hourly wages of 6 to 8 percent

each year. For manufacturing industries which are highly import competitive, such as automobiles and primary metals, the task has been made
immeasurably more difficult by competitive price constraints domestically,
augmented in some cases by possible subsidies to foreign producers by their
own countries' governments.

However, apart from the import factor, the core of the problem for all
manufacturing enterprises is productivity. Productivity gains per worker
hour over the private sector as a whole have declined: For 1947-1966 the
average annual rate of increase was 3.2 percent; for 1967-1973 it fell to 1.7
percent; while for 1967-1976, the rate of gain contracted still further, to 1.6
percent (Kutscher, Mark, and Norsworth, 1977, pp. 3-4). For manufacturing alone, with shift-effects removed, the average annual rate of gain was
somewhat better—3.31 percent during 1959-1966, and 3.23 percent for
1966-1973. However, more complete BLS data show an average annual rate
of increase of output per hour of all employees of 2.9 percent for 1966-1973
and 2.5 percent for 1970-1976 (Norsworthy and Fulco, 1977, p. 4).

These figures are aggregates. To gain greater insight into labor productivity trends within manufacturing, one would examine the three- and four-
digit industries within the twenty two-digit major groups that make up the
sector. However, data at these finer levels of discrimination are seriously incomplete. Entire two-digit groups are unreported, for example, printing,
publishing and allied industries (Code 27), and machinery, except electrical
(Code 35) as well as the leading category, textile mill products (Code 22)
(Executive Offices of the President, n.d.).

Nonetheless, we can get some impression of detailed trends in gross
labor productivity by examining those three- or four-digit manufacturing
industries with at least 100,000 employees as of 1975 for which data were
reported. Table 4-2 indicates the results.

Of course, these various rates of improvement in gross labor productivity tell us nothing about increased or revamped physical capital, improvements in production organization, or changes in the quality of human
capital. But, conceding all that we do not know, we can still interpret these
figures as at least rough measures of the amounts of "wage space" management has created or acquired to pay for higher hourly labor costs without
major encorachment upon its profit margins. Looked at a little differently,
when productivity gains begin to shrink (as they have after 1966) at the same
time that wage pressures are accelerating, we get the kind of profits squeeze
that has afflicted most of American industry for more than a decade.

To bring the matter out even more sharply, consider the behavior of
unit labor costs in manufacturing, a measure that takes both pay and productivity changes into account. When unit labor costs are stable, that is,
productivity gains match closely with wage-costs per hour, profit margins
are not invaded. The manufacturing sector enjoyed such stability between

Table 4-2

Average Annual Rates of Change in Output per Employee-Hour for 1970-1975, in Manufacturing Industries with at Least 100,000 Employees in 1975

Industry	Rate of Annual Change (%)[a]	Total Employees 1975
Footwear	negligible	163,000
Tires and inner tubes	1.6	118,000
Gray iron foundries	2.1	138,000
Bakery products	2.2	236,000
Paper, paperboard, and pulp mills	2.5	258,000
Steel	2.8	545,000
Grain mill products	3.3	138,000
Petroleum refining	3.3	154,000
Canning and preserving	3.7	293,000
Motor vehicles and equipment	3.7	774,000
Bottled and canned soft drinks	3.8	126,000
Pharmaceutical preparations	4.7	130,000
Synthetic fibers	8.3	105,000

Source: U.S. Department of Labor, Bureau of Labor Statistics, *Bulletin* 1938, "Productivity Indexes for Selected Industries, 1976 ed." (Washington, D.C.: GPO, 1977), p. 7.

[a]Based on linear least squares trends of logarithmic values of each index.

1957 and 1967. However, between 1967 and 1977, average nominal hourly wages rose 120 percent while average hourly output advanced only 20 percent. Put another way, between 1967 and 1977 hourly pay rose more than twice as fast as in 1957-1967, while the annual rate of gain in productivity was one-third less than before (*Wall Street Journal*, 1978); thus the squeeze on profits.

The preceding discussion might be interpreted to constitute an endorsement of a wage-push theory of inflation, although that is not my intention. To be sure, from a narrow perspective there *is* a wage-push process, as every employer who has ever had to go along with the prevailing pattern already knows. However, blaming the profit squeeze on union wage policy does not explain the persistence of the push, its acceleration at certain times (as over the past decade), and its spread throughout both the unionized and nonunionized economy. There is a factor, however, which does answer these questions: money.

When fiscal policy is committed unequivocally to the pursuit of full employment and other social programs by resort to an endless string of increasing federal deficits, the likelihood is great that the creation of purchasing power will outrun the production of goods. With annual deficits of $60 billion and more financed mainly through the banking system, the 1970s have become a period of chronic inflation.

By contrast, before 1965 wage settlements regularly were being made at a comparatively trivial 4 or 5 percent, for which increased productivity then provided substantial although not complete coverage. Today's settlements at 9 to 12 percent per year do not occur because of any miraculous increase in union power in the intervening years. On the contrary, they are the result of the chronically inflationary environment created by increasing reliance upon deficit financing, while union power over the labor market has been shrinking. The ensuing inflation squeezes profits as a source of investment funds, while the upward pressure on nominal interest rates excludes many firms from floating stock or loans to raise capital to improve their efficiency. At the same time, the increasing federal deficits also divert savings away from capital formation. If efforts are undertaken to contain the upward pressure on borrowing rates, still more recourse to money formation becomes necessary, and this in turn accelerates the inflation.

Thus soaring unit labor costs, falling rates of increase in real hourly wages, falling rates of gain in labor productivity, and a persistently declining volume of profits in real terms are all interrelated in the same process, a process whose essence is government spending that increasingly has been outrunning revenues for over a decade. Neither more effective bargaining by management nor voluntary concessions wrung from the unions by hortatory appeals from government can turn matters around.

I conclude, then, that if inflation is not brought under control, we may well see in the 1980s an actual decline in real wages and in incomes per head, because of the accumulated erosion in both quantity and quality of the physical capital stock of the nation, and because of a declining will to work, to save, and to invest in an economy in which rational economic calculations have become increasingly difficult. The traditional incentives to form capital have been weakened seriously in the pursuit of a popular version of distributive justice. A faltering economy and a depreciating dollar have been the result.

To be sure, inflation is not inevitable; it can be brought under control, but only with much difficulty and during a protracted period of adjustment. If inflation were brought under control, it would still take much time and some very difficult bargaining to bring the "going annual increase" down, say, eventually to 4 or 5 percent. In the meantime, the agenda for negotiations will be shaped by issues of job security, plant closures, relaxation of work rules, and other matters related to what, frankly, will be a declining economic environment.

Prospective Changes in Manufacturing Labor

In 1955, employment in the manufacturing sector reached its all-time peak at just under 40 percent of the total labor force (Norsworthy and Fulco,

1977). Today the sector accounts for only 25 percent, having been over-taken in 1955 by the information workers (finance, education, communications, scientific and technical research, marketing, and information processing). Today the latter group stands at about 48 percent of the total labor force and may be facing a glut rather than further growth (U.S. Congress, Joint Economic Committee, 1978).

Revised BLS output and employment projections for 1972-1980 and 1980-1985 (Kutscher, 1976, pp. 3-8) suggest that GNP originating in the private economy will increase in the manufacturing sector at 4.1 percent yearly for 1972-1980, and 3.5 percent yearly for 1980-1985. Within manufacturing, durable goods output is expected to grow at 4.5 percent in 1972-1980, falling to 3.5 percent yearly in 1980-1985, while nondurable goods will increase 3.6 percent annually in the earlier period, and 3.5 percent in the latter.

The revised estimates also indicate that there will be 21.87 million employees in manufacturing in 1980, an increase of 2.38 million between 1972 and 1980, or a simple annual average growth rate of 1.6 percent. For 1980-1985, the expected increase is only 660,000 persons, or an annual rate of increase of just 0.6 percent. In short, the sector is expected to offer only 132,000 new jobs yearly for the first half of the decade. Most of this small advance in employment will be concentrated in durable goods. Meanwhile, the private nonfarm sector as a whole is expected to increase by 5.56 million jobs, or 1.35 percent annually.

If manufacturing's net additional labor requirements actually turn out to be around 150,000 per year for the first half of the 1980s, surely there would be no labor shortages necessary. On the outside, the average annual increase in total labor intake by the sector seems unlikely to reach even 1 percent of the force of 21.87 million projected for 1980. However, factors such as the age structure of the present force, changes in labor-to-capital requirements, cyclical swings, and breaks in past trends, including new laws extending retirement to age seventy, constitute unknowns that could upset these projections.

On the supply side, BLS data published at the close of 1976 suggest that the total civilian labor force will reach 101.7 million by 1980 (in 1977 it was 97.4 million). By this date the postwar baby boom will finally be absorbed. For the coming decade as a whole, it is expected that the annual rate of increase will drop to only 1.1 percent. This is despite the continuing upsurge of the participation rate for women, which jumped from 33.9 to 47.3 percent between 1950 and 1976 (Bednarzik and Klein, 1977, p. 3), because there also will be a drop in the absolute number of women reaching the normal age of entry into the labor force (Fullerton and Flaim, 1976, p. 3). Thus it is suggested that the net annual accretions to the whole labor force will run about 1.1 and 1.2 million during the entire decade. Perhaps manufacturing will absorb 15 percent of this annual increment, but this is by no means a certainty. During the 1980s we shall have a labor force dominated by those in the prime age group (twenty-five to fifty-four years), who will represent 65.0 percent of the entire force in 1985, according to the BLS projections (Fullerton and Flaim, 1976, pp. 4, 6-8). The greatest shortage will be among the eighteen to twenty-five age group, and especially among skilled workers.

Given the expected sharp decline in the annual rate of labor force growth, the increased scarcity of job-seekers may prove to be the least of the problems facing management and the unions during the 1980s. For example, there is reason for skepticism about the level of educational preparation for youngsters who will be among the new entrants; there is also the question of whether their fidelity to the traditional work ethic, and their readiness to accept the authority of management and the discipline of factory work, will meet the standards of the 1950s and earlier. Some observers perceive an irreversible shift in values, but others are not so sure. Perhaps one factor that will contribute to the socialization of the comparatively restless and at times rebellious group will be the weighty presence of the new prime-age majority, who, because of lengthier experience and the acquisition of family responsibilities and other obligations of adulthood, may contribute an atmosphere of greater stability to the plant work force.

It should be emphasized that the whole discussion of labor supply and demand for manufacturing rests upon projections which must overlook the possibility of some major unpredictable events—events that could knock all of these estimates badly askew. One would be a popularly based decision to break the present chronic inflation—a course of action that cannot be carried through without severe deflation and therefore unemployment and idle plants. Another would be a continued surge of imports which would cut even more deeply into the vital parts of the manufacturing sector. Either of these developments would impose unprecedented pressure (in modern time) upon management to regain efficiency as the price of survival. Labor negotiations would become tough and bitter, for the pressures would be directed against almost the entire content of existing agreements: rates, fringes, COLAs, annual increases, assignments, crews and manning, and so on.

Attempts to project employment by sector and industry rest upon such fragile assumptions that they do not justify extended discussion. To obtain a figure for employment in some industry, for example, for 1985, one must first estimate expected output, and then expected change in output per worker hour. The projected change of numbers employed is then derived. All of the traditional weaknesses of trend extrapolation are present here.

Changes in Bargaining Structure

We have already noted that single-firm bargaining is by far the most common arrangement in the manufacturing sector. There is very little association bargaining, and informal types of centralization such as the employer-committee system in basic steel and the pattern-following technique typical of automobiles tend to be concentrated in a relatively few industries. The question thus emerges, will a movement develop toward greater centralization of bargaining structures elsewhere in manufacturing over the next several years?

A case for this inference would run roughly as follows. Should the National Labor Relations Act ever be amended in the fashion sought by the AFL-CIO in 1978, the unions would find it easier to organize new plants and firms. If organizing drives were actually mounted and met with some success, would not the employers involved turn to some form of joint action to strengthen themselves? Another scenario would run like this: if either roaring inflation or protracted deflation lies ahead, employers in certain situations might engage in joint action simply to protect themselves in dealing with the difficulties of collective bargaining associated with either set of economic circumstances. A third alternative might be a revival of the union coalition technique, devised originally by the building trades in the late nineteenth century and utilized by Walter Reuther in 1962 when he was head of the Industrial Union Department. Coalition bargaining at that time made considerable progress in forcing centralization without technical change in the structure of bargaining units in a few industries, notably nonferrous metals. Because bargaining units in many parts of manufacturing were established on a plant or partial plant basis simply because this was the easiest way to organize then, today we have fragmentation that sometimes works to the disadvantage of the union, particularly relative to multiplant employers. Although the coalition movement seems to have lost all momentum in recent years, if it were revived it, too, could bring about greater centralization on the employers' side.

To assess the possibilities, perhaps the best place to start is with a crude surmise regarding the industries in which organizing drives or coalitions might be attempted. The indications are that the industries of weakest union penetration in manufacturing are those such as instruments, leather, miscellaneous manufacturing, printing, furniture, lumber, apparel, and textiles (Freeman and Medoff, 1979). In general, these industries contain numerous employers, often with relatively low capitalizations, many of whom are located in the South. Given the precedents in apparel and textiles, it could be suggested that these are the kinds of industries for which the formal multiemployer association would be a likely response, if, of course, organizing is actually attempted and proves successful.

However, I think it very doubtful that we shall witness any startling innovations of this type. Neither would I expect a renaissance of the coalition bargaining movement. Coalitions are very difficult to put together and to hold together, and unless the expiration dates of the various individual contracts can be brought close together—which can take several years of bargaining if it is to be accomplished at all—then the essential basic tools of the joint strike, the joint settlement, and the joint return to work cannot be brought into play. The 1977 imposition of coalition bargaining upon the major nonferrous producers must be considered a special case. At that time, independent and powerful financial motives involving two of the majors made the incentive for a quick settlement, virtually on the coalition's terms, irresistible. For them, the strike lasted less than two days.

Thus I foresee no startling developments in coalition bargaining, either. Then what remains? Essentially, for employers who are impelled toward greater centralization, the choice lies between formal bargaining by commit-tee, with separate agreements after bargaining is completed, and the UAW pattern-following system. Either one seems most likely where oligopoly, or at least high concentration, prevails in product markets which are national or at least regional, characteristics that do not seem to be broadly typical of the manufacturing sector.

Therefore, I do not expect major changes in the structure of present bargaining units or in the various systems through which negotiations are now conducted.

Changes in the Agenda for Collective Bargaining

Earlier we considered some demographic changes in the labor force of the 1980s. Now we turn to some qualitative considerations.

Although the labor force will be dominated by the prime age group (twenty-five to fifty-four years), it will be weighted significantly at the younger extreme. For this reason, it will include a substantial number who were less than twenty-five in the middle and late 1960s—the period that Samuel Huntington has well described as the years of the "democratic distemper" (1975, pp. 9-38). This was a period in which the demand for more services from government was soaring at the same time that respect and support for the authority of government were undergoing precipitous decline, mainly as a consequence of an increasingly unpopular war. Another facet of this attitude was the spread of the doctrine, particularly among the young, that one should be exclusively preoccupied with the im-mediate gratification of one's own desires, without thought for the future or concern for others. At one time this doctrine would have been called romantic individualism, but today it goes by other names, such as existen-tialism or just "doing your own thing."

For some this became a kind of rebellion without purpose or cause, a re-jection of obligations to others, a contempt for institutions, organizations, hierarchies, managers, and leaders—almost entirely a negative movement, not even sanctioned by an explicit and consistent ideology beyond a nihilistic outlook toward existing society. To a considerable extent matters have settled down again, but the lack of commitment to work and to the industrial system, and a continuing hostility to "The Establishment," are still readily to be observed.

In consequence, then, management and the unions together will confront a different kind of labor force from that of the 1950s—one that is likely to be more intractable, more impatient, more dissatisfied, and perhaps moved by different interests from the traditional bread-and-butter concerns of earlier days. Given their nature, these sentiments may exert more influence upon contract administration and plant management than in contract negotiations, although they deserve mention here also.

The second main characteristic of the new labor force is its substantial proportion of women, reflecting a female participation rate which now exceeds 50 percent. Women workers have problems and interests of their own which will be felt at both the negotiating and the administrative levels. And here it is to be noted that the labor movement in particular faces some difficult adjustments. Traditionally, unionism, like professional baseball, has been one of the most masculine of institutions, as a glance at the membership of the executive council of the AFL-CIO will readily disclose. But the age of the "ladies' auxiliary" is now beginning to change. The question becomes, "Are we about to enter the age of women as national union presidents, as district directors, and as business agents?" Parallel changes have begun already to occur in the employer hierarchy. We may yet, on occasion, see women acting as bargainers on both sides of the table.

A final point is that the labor force continues to become more highly educated. By 1985 it is expected that 20 percent of the overall labor force will have college degrees. Probably most of this group will enter government and the information trades. However, because there is reason to expect the supply of college graduates in the coming years to exceed the demand for them, some will turn up in manufacturing, on the blue-collar side as well as in the office. Here, then, would be a source of articulate, energetic, and relatively sophisticated new leaders for unionism, particularly in the locals. One is tempted to look for a revitalization of union democracy if this development should come to pass, along with a potential source of upheaval in some of the more highly centralized unions in industry.

In what ways might the agenda for collective bargaining undergo change in the years immediately ahead? Given the nature of the work force, I would expect to see more localization of negotiating issues, particularly under deflationary conditions. I base this expectation upon the likelihood that the major national unions will have to become much more sensitive to local plant conditions—the age, location, and efficiency of the operation in particular. Management resistance to patterns of uniformity in large-scale contracts will vary and could be intense in many situations, with the latent threat of plant closure or removal frequently visible in the background.

For the national union, the logical response to these fundamental changes would be a shift to local issues. Here there may still remain some possibility of winning gains for a membership that will be more restive and impatient, both because of its changed composition and because large money settlements may be simply out of the question. Some of the types of demands we might expect from the union side are

1. Increased job security. This could include interplant transfers according to seniority, the four-day week with unemployment compensation entitlement for the fifth day, and a revival of the familiar attrition schemes that began to emerge with the slump in steel in the early sixties.
2. Enlargement of compensation structure. Barbash, who coined this term (1977, pp. 60-61), suggests new or expanded income protections against unemployment, old age, death, illness, and pregnancy, and beyond this, employer-financed aids for education, training, and apprenticeship. In addition, this would include an increase in paid leisure days during the work year—for example, the new thirteen-day provision recently won by the UAW could become the basis for a four-day week at five days' pay within a relatively few years.
3. Incorporation of OSHA, ERISA, and EEOC rights and protections as part of the collective agreement, reducing dependence of complaining workers upon government regulation or court actions.
4. Joint committees to deal with issues that have increasingly come to be viewed as feasible forms of labor participation in management. They would deal with matters of job redesign and restructuring, productivity-sharing schemes, transfer of maintenance functions to production groups, and search for cost-saving changes.
5. Possible enlargement of collective agreements to include certain "constitutional" rights at the workplace: freedom of criticism of management and freedom of expression regarding products, practices, ethical issues; provision for ombudsmen, perhaps as a new element in grievance procedure; and protection of "the right to be different" in matters of belief and dress (Westin, 1978).

On the management side, the central problem would seem to be how to enable particular plants to survive when markets are shrinking or are stagnant. This, of course, is a problem of costs and factor productivities. Therefore, I would look for the following posture for management at the bargaining table:

1. Greatly increased resistance to proposals that would significantly raise labor costs, and a counterpart interest in ideas that offer prospects for

relief. Plant closures or removals will probably become frequent events rather than the conventional idle threat to be served up in bargaining.

2. Determined efforts to obtain relaxation of work rules that have proved onerous and costly: for example, manning requirements, strict work-separation rules, inflexible assignment regulations.

3. Greater willingness to explore through joint committee ways in which productivity can be improved, and efforts to tie increased wages and benefits to such improvements. The time of the Scanlon Plan may finally have arrived.

4. Particularly for marginal plants or companies, determined efforts to escape from wage and benefit "patterns" and "orbits" that are seen as incompatible with long-run survival of the business.

5. Much more recourse to the strategy of taking the initiative in bargaining, particularly through demands that, if won, would have a significant impact upon costs, even unto "give backs" or retrievals of earlier costly concessions.

Perhaps it should be reiterated that for both sides these patterns of demands would be strongly influenced by the advent of general deflation. However, even if the general rate of price inflation should hold at 6 to 8 percent, the manufacturing sector may still display deflationary tendencies of the sort indicated. Manufacturing as a whole is no longer the cutting edge of economic growth in this country. During the years of its dominance from 1905 to 1955, it found its principal locations and concentrations within and around the older cities and metropolitan areas of the Northeast and the East North Central regions. With high taxes, old plants, and old unionization, and with the shift in the distribution of the consuming population, many of these plants have become increasingly uneconomic. At the same time, and partly for the same reasons, they have become increasingly vulnerable to imports.

Thus, although the BLS projections foresee continued growth of output and employment in manufacturing as a whole, this growth is really far from certain. On the contrary, manufacturing may possibly be entering a period of absolute contraction, even within the context of a continuing inflationary economy. But suppose, instead, that the sector does experience slow growth in an environment of continuing general inflation. The import problem will still compel many firms to engage in the bargaining tactics indicated above, to which will be added a continuing migration of industry to newer regions, West and South, with all of the problems that these developments would imply for the unions—in short, the same prognosis.

Changes in the Process of Negotiation

In my judgment, modern collective bargaining in the United States manifests a continuing dialectic between two contradictory themes, centralization versus decentralization of bargaining. One theme is rooted in the idea of worker participation, not in the European sense of a full share in the management of the enterprise, but in the making and administering of the labor agreement. The union local is a vital cell for worker democracy in the formulation of negotiating demands, in the development of negotiating strategy, in the ultimate ratification of the new agreement, and in the daily administration of the agreement through the work of the stewards, the grievance procedure, and arbitration.

The alternative doctrine puts its stress upon the ideas of uniformity and stability, and as derivatives, the domination of negotiations by the national office, with the long-term contract as the embodiment of the outcome of this bargaining. Here the contention is that the national leadership alone has the time and the expertise to give consideration to the interests of the entire industry and its whole work force, and thus makes sure that each agreement is sound and compatible within such a framework. In this view, rank-and-file activism is likely to prove a disturbing element rather than a source of fresh ideas. For example, it is argued that debates over ratification of proposed new contracts provide opportunity for disruptions to break out, for leadership to be undermined, and for impractical demands to be voiced that can either cause rejection of a hard-won agreement or divisions of damaging consequences to the union itself.

What is the outlook in these matters for the next few years?

There is no obvious answer, of course. However, one could guess that the years immediately ahead may well include increasing challenges to the traditional highly centralized and highly institutionalized systems of union representation typical of much of manufacturing in recent times. As discussed above, issues are likely to become more localized and less capable of standardization. It is also my impression that there is a growing impatience generally with representative forms of democracy, however skeptical one may be about the feasibility and even desirability of the "town meeting" model for popular decision-making.

More than this, the new work force, with its restiveness about all institutions, its impatience with status differentiations and orders, and its intense concern about the rights and interests of the individual, may well begin to demand greater participation all along the line, from initial demands to final approval of the agreement. In turn this new spirit may lead to demands for the abrogation of nonstrike clauses, for the replacement of arbitration by the right to strike, and for some version of the initiative, referendum, and recall as regards local union governance. The same impulse may also push the unions further into areas of traditional managerial prerogative than has been considered normal in the past. Finally, if these developments should come to pass, it is entirely possible that some of our sturdiest national unions of the past forty years may experience rebellion of the sort that reduced the governance of the Mine Workers to the low state it reached in 1978.

If the future is as stormy for industrial relations as these speculations suggest, then we might experience more lengthy and difficult strikes, more rejections of proposed contracts by the membership, and more resort to wildcat strikes as well. Several of our apparently strongest unions today have either an active underground opposition already or at least a membership that shows signs of being ready to march to new drums. If the problems of industrial relations follow the patterns discussed above, organizational unrest will very likely be the outcome.

Prospects Regarding the Administration of Collective Bargaining

Rights under the Agreement: The Old View and the New

In the earlier history of collective bargaining, the dominant view was that "the contracting parties" were the employer and the union. The employee in the bargaining unit stood in the position of a third-party beneficiary of the agreement. The union bargained to gain employee rights, and it also protected its employees in the breach or observance of these rights. At the apex of the relationship were the grievance procedure and arbitration, with arbitration as the terminal step in which decision by a neutral, after a proceeding between the parties in which the union represented the grievant, brought the issue to a final determination.

In this view of the matter, the contract embodied a private agreement between the two parties prescribing the law of the plant as regards the employment relationship. It was *their* agreement. They controlled the process by which it was negotiated. They administered its provisions. And finally, they controlled the grievance procedure as well as (for the most part) the arbitration process. The arbitrator could be a stickler for the rules of evidence; he could insist upon an orderly proceeding, and he could go some distance in protecting the grievant when his representative proved to be inexperienced or incompetent. But even here, the parties selected the arbitrator. In consequence, their joint expectations and desires exerted a large influence upon the kind of arbitrator that would be chosen to serve under their agreement.

Since the enactment of the Taft-Hartley Act in 1947 and the Landrum-Griffin Act in 1959, there has gradually emerged a new body of law, however, that prescribes new rights and obligations, and in some instances provides procedures under which employees and others may bring com-

plaints against both employers and unions. The obvious examples are the
Civil Rights Act of 1964, the Occupational Safety and Health Act (OSHA),
and the Employee Retirement Income and Security Act (ERISA). In addition to these statutes, and partly because of them, there has also been
rapidly building up a large body of case law that is replete with changes like
the statutes themselves and is adverse to the traditional doctrine of the
privacy of the parties' agreement and of their contractual relationship.

This is not the place in which to explore the impacts of these
developments extensively. Our immediate concern lies with prospective
changes in the administration of labor agreements in the manufacturing sector. However, within this context, it can be asserted that the evolution of
statutory and case law in these matters over the past thirty years has acquired singular importance because it has brought into being a whole collection of rights belonging to the individual person—rights that extend beyond
those established for him or her in the traditional labor agreement. To illustrate with a single example: under Title VII of the Civil Rights Act, an
employer and/or a union stand in violation if they engage in categorical
discrimination against an employee as regards hiring, promotion, or other
conditions of work, whatever may be the rights of the two principal parties
under their own labor agreement.

In what follows, I propose to examine some of these matters from the
standpoint of the relationship, and on occasion, conflict between individual
rights and the administration of collective agreements.

The Right of Fair Representation in
Grievance Proceedings and Arbitration

As Benjamin Aaron says (1977, p. 8), fair representation is a "judicial invention" that emerged in *Steel* v. *Louisville & Nashville R.R.* in 1944 (323
U.S. 192). In that case, the Court held that because the union had been
granted statutory power to represent employees in the bargaining unit, it
owed them the duty to see that this power was exercised "fairly, impartially,
and in good faith." By 1956, the Court had extended the principle to the
NLRA, although it was not until 1962, in *Miranda Fuel Co.* (326 F. 2d 1972
[2d Cir. 1963]), that the National Labor Relations Board determined that a
breach of this duty constituted an unfair labor practice, on the basis that
Section 7 of the act protects the employee from unfair, irrelevant, or invidious treatment by the union in matters of employment; that Section
8(b)(1)(a) thereby proscribes such actions; also, that Section 8(b)(2) is
violated when a union attempts to have the employer injure the status of an
employee in these respects. Likewise, the employer who discriminates
against an employee in any of these matters violates Section 8(a)(1) and (3)
(Aaron, 1977, p. 10).

In *Vaca* v. *Sipes*, 386 U.S. 171 (1967), an employee who was discharged for reasons of health sued his union for failure to take his grievance to arbitration. Eventually he lost in the Supreme Court but only on a finding that the evidence failed to prove the union had acted arbitrarily or in bad faith. At the same time, the Court also held that the employee did have standing in the state court before which he had taken his complaint; that, indeed, he could bring an action for breach of the bargaining agreement although as a defense the employer invokes failure to exhaust contractual remedies, if the complainant can prove that the union breached its duty of fair representation. Collaterally, this decision means that the NLRB does not have exclusive jurisdiction over these matters.

In 1976 the Supreme Court decided *Hines* v. *Anchor Motor Freight, Inc.*, 91 LRRM 2481. In this case some employees sued their employer under Section 301 of NLRA because he had discharged them for alleged dishonesty. This suit had had its origin in an arbitration which the complainants had lost. The first charge in this suit was accompanied by a second, alleging that the union had breached its duty of fair representation.

Although the district court had dismissed the charge against the employer, it denied the union's motion for summary judgment on the claim of breach of duty. This denial was made on the basis of new evidence showing that the complainants had not been guilty of inflating their motel bills, and that the real culprit was the motel clerk. To the court, this did not show breach of duty but "at most bad judgment" by the union, in its failure to follow up with the matter. By contrast, the court of appeals found that the evidence demonstrated bad faith on the part of the local union, wherefore the petitioners should have been granted opportunity to prove their charges. However, in the upshot the court of appeals found for the employer and the international union, holding that "the finality provision of collective-bargaining contracts" must be upheld, absent any showing of misconduct by the employer or a conspiracy between the union and the employee.

After reviewing the history of the doctrine of fair representation, both in law and in prior cases, the Supreme Court went on to hold, despite *Vaca*, that where a breach of duty by the union is proved, the grievant is relieved of the obligation to seek his remedy through the grievance procedure rather than in court. By its breach of duty, in other words, the union both undermines the integrity of the contractual arbitral process and removes the bar of the finality provision against relitigation of the issue. Here the Court is careful to distinguish situations resting merely upon "error" from arbitration decisions in which the union "has been dishonest, in bad faith, or discriminatory." In consequence, it found the court of appeals in error in its final dismissal of the petitioners' court action against the employer.

It would seem from all this that if the integrity of the process of arbitration is beyond assault in any one case, then its finality stands protected as well. However, this depends upon whether a breach of duty is claimed, and upon the judicial tests of determination that a breach has occurred. In *Steele*, as Aaron points out, the test is whether the union's representation function is exercised "fairly, impartially, and in good faith." With *Vaca*, the test becomes disjunctive: Was the conduct of the union "arbitrary, discriminatory, or in bad faith?" By contrast, in *Holodnak* v. *Avoc Corp. and UAW Local 1010* (423 U.S. 892 [1975]), the Supreme Court rested its findings for the plaintiff on the grounds that the union attorney had overlooked some obvious legal arguments and had not been "sufficiently aggressive" in protecting the grievant from improper questions from the arbitrator (Aaron, 1977, p. 20).

To conclude, the Supreme Court has never squarely addressed the question of an appropriate test of breach of duty, which leaves the matter in confusion—so much so that mere negligence, inexperience, simple incompetence, and bad judgment have on occasion been accepted as criteria together with others of far greater weight.

For purposes of contract administration, the importance of all this would appear to be two-fold. First, there will be a significant increase in the number of grievances taken to arbitration, simply because the unions, inspired by prudence and caution, will lean over backward to avoid risking charges of breaching their duty of fair representation as that concept is now badly interpreted. In consequence, more dubious or even worthless claims will be litigated, while for the same reason it will become more difficult to dispose of, settle, or compromise complaints at the final step of the grievance procedure.

Second, given the elasticity of scope to the judicial meaning of breach of duty in these matters, we should expect some increase in the number of issues taken to court on such charges. Perhaps this tendency can be contained, particularly if the Supreme Court eventually gives precision to the meaning of a breach in this context. If not, we shall probably then see a resurgence of court decisions on the merits of arbitral issues, which would do the cause of arbitration no good in the long run.

The Emergence of Multiple Avenues of Relief for
Adjudication of Claims Based upon Individual Rights

In tradition, voluntary arbitration ultimately acquired the joint characteristics of finality and of exclusivity, once the Trilogy decisions had come down (assuming the integrity of the process and/or the arbitrator was not brought into question). As early as 1955 the NLRB decided in *Spielberg Manufacturing Co.*, 112 NLRB 1080, that it would honor an award in arbitration if the parties had agreed to honor it; if the hearing procedure were fair; and if the award were not repugnant to the act (Updegraff, p. 28). And again, in *Collyer Insulated Wire*, 192 NLRB 837, the board held in a divided decision that it would defer action on complaints brought before it until such issues had been tried in arbitration and the arbitrator had handed down his award.

Taken together, *Spielberg* and *Collyer* showed a desire on the part of the board not to impair the arbitration process and its advance toward finality, and not to open up a competing forum for complainants, absent, of course, any question of the integrity and fairness of the arbitration proceeding itself.

This long period of self-restraint on the part of the board toward voluntary arbitration disintegrated in 1977, in a three-way division in *General American Transportation Corp.* v. *Perry Soape, Jr.*, 228 NLRB 808. In this case, the company claimed that Soape had been laid off for lack of work, while the general counsel of the board found that, by his layoff, Soape had been discriminated against for union activity.

In the hearing before the administrative law judge, the company invoked *Collyer* as grounds for allowing the matter to be resolved through private arbitration. Partly because Soape was unwilling to go to arbitration, although that remedy was open to him, and because the general counsel was opposed to deferral, the administrative law judge denied the company's request. Accordingly, no arbitration was held, and instead the issue went before the board itself.

As part of the majority, Members Fanning and Jenkins took occasion once more to announce their "longstanding opposition" to the *Collyer* doctrine, holding that

> the Board has a statutory duty to hear and to dispose of unfair labor practices and that the Board cannot abdicate or avoid its duty by seeking to cede its jurisdiction to private tribunals. (228 NLRB 808)

Warming to this theme, they went on to assert that the vindication of statutory rights was not to be made "a plaything of private treaty and interpretation." What is at stake here, they affirmed, was the protection of employees from on-the-job discrimination, a protection that "is clearly an individual, as contrasted with a union or group, right." In this view, private arbitration concerns group as distinguished from individual rights, a distinction that entitles an aggrieved employee who is reluctant to arbitrate a claim the right to go straight to the board for relief, without deferral.

In concurring, Chairman Betty Southard Murphy adopted a similar position. Although she does not wholly reject *Collyer* as her majority colleagues do, the chairman would invoke deferral

> only in those situations where the dispute is essentially between the
> contracting paties and where there is no alleged interference with individual
> employees' basic rights under Section 7 of the Act . . . the arbitration
> process [is not] suited for resolving employee complaints of discrimination
> under Section 7. (228 NLRB 810)

Elsewhere the chairman emphasizes her agreement with the *Spielberg* doctrine, but not where an unwilling party is charging violation of his rights
under Section 7. In consequence, she would "defer to arbitration those
cases involving only contract interpretation issues. . . ."

What seems to be emerging here is a distinction between group and individual rights, along with the principle that the board should not defer to
arbitration whenever the charging party is claiming a violation of his/her
rights under Section 7 and is unwilling to proceed to arbitration of the issue.
If this majority view should crystallize, then voluntary arbitration would
lose its exclusivity for a whole class of cases, regardless of its essential
soundness and integrity. At the same time, the board would be thrust into
an activist role to serve as an independent forum for this class of cases. One
wonders what would be the destinies of *Spielberg, Collyer,* and *Gardner-
Denver* if this thinking were to become established dicta. Even more, what
import does it have for voluntary arbitration and the administration of
agreements? External statutory law is being brought to bear in the service of
a theory that, in essence, would substitute agency proceedings for private
proceedings. In this transformation, voluntary private arbitration loses
both its exclusivity and its standing as the terminal step of the grievance procedure for a whole class of cases. Irrespective of the merits of the majority
position, the implications are weighty and deserving of close scrutiny.

Other Problems Related to Government Intervention

In enacting the Civil Rights Act of 1964, Congress provided in the measure
itself for an Equal Employment Opportunities Commission (EEOC). The
EEOC was empowered both to receive and to initiate complaints arising
from allegations of violations of rights created by Title VII of the act. In
turn, the EEOC was authorized to attempt conciliation and settlement between the complainant or complainants and the employer and/or the union.
If such efforts proved to be unproductive, then the commission could enter
suit in federal court on behalf of the complainant.

As far as contract administration is concerned, an employee charging
racial discrimination against either an employer or a union, or both, now
has two additional forums in which to have a grievance ventilated besides
the private contractual procedure for grievances and arbitration: the EEOC
itself, and the district court if necessary. Again, therefore, both the exclu-

sivity and the finality of voluntary arbitration have been weakened, this time for a very large class of cases. A labor agreement, then, is no longer sufficient ground upon which management can control its working forces. It must act in accordance with the requirements of law, and it must be prepared to defend itself before agencies of the government in many of the actions it may take. This can be an episode fraught with inconsistency, as explained below.

For manufacturing industry, unionism is typically of the "nonreferral" type: the employer is free to hire whomever it wishes, while the union enters the picture only after the new employee has completed the probation period. As far as Title VII is concerned, its points of impact in the manufacturing sector ordinarily involve (1) the various labor flows internal to the plant (promotions, demotions, transfers, layoffs, and discharges), and (2) the numerical composition of the work force as regards officially recognized ethnic and racial minorities. More than this, of course, rates of pay and benefits, and designation of work groups must be free of any taint of categorical discrimination.

The most troublesome problem under the act undoubtedly arises under (2). Once numerical composition becomes a factor in a plant, it is but a single step to preferential quotas for hiring, assignments, and promotions. In point of fact, the EEOC has long since taken that step, through both court proceedings and consent decrees. In fact, at this very time it contemplates an arrangement under which an employer would be rendered supposedly immune from charges of discrimination under the act if he concludes that the racial/ethnic makeup of his force is out of line with the composition of the local population, and if in consequence he adopts preferential hiring according to race, sex, or ethnicity to achieve "balance."

For present purposes, where labor agreements call for completely nondiscriminatory personnel practices, as many already do, the employer who adheres to such obligation in good faith can well run afoul of an EEOC intervention or even a court order directing that he adopt preferential quotas. It is obvious that there is a deep legal and moral conflict between the preferential quota and the principle of equal and nondiscriminatory employment opportunities. One need but examine Section 703(j) of the act to appreciate the point. Similar problems for labor contracts and voluntary arbitration exist also where the firm holds federal contracts and thereby is subject to OFCC intervention which may also involve the union.

The enactment of OSHA and ERISA has created some special problems for management and organized labor. Although some of these questions concern the relationship between the parties rather than their contract as such, they do deserve mention.

It is sometimes forgotten that OSHA deals with the health as well as the safety of employees. More than this, the emphasis is now shifting to health, which is a field of much greater difficulty for both management and the union. The basic reason is that some health problems—for instance, those which are the product of carcinogens—are often very slow in manifesting themselves. There is no taxable event, as in safety matters when one is concerned with lead or asbestos poisoning or black lung disease. Thus the union has every incentive to put pressure on the employer to keep longitudinal records so that it can monitor the evidence. By contrast, the employer's incentive is to require regular physical examinations by the company doctor—something that is a real source of fear for an employee. Yet such a requirement seems only reasonable if the employer is made liable for damages arising from industrial diseases. Related to all this, furthermore, is the nature of the employer's obligation to introduce preventive equipment and devices, particularly when medical knowledge is incomplete and uncertain.

Turning to ERISA, distinction is commonly made between "defined benefits" (DB) and "defined contributions" (DC) pension plans. The employer's incentive is to establish DC plans simply to avoid the statutory requirements of full funding and actuarial soundness. By contrast, employees tend to favor DB plans, which then bring in the ERISA regulations. Obviously the new law will make bargaining more difficult in the pension field for this reason alone.

Other problems concern funding of liabilities. One of these involves multiemployer pension plans. Here an individual concern has the right to drop out at any time. Although it may be sued for its own share, it has no obligation for the total unfunded liabilities of the group.

A related problem involves the employer whose plan has large unfunded liabilities, and finds it an advantage to drop the plan. At this point the federal government may intervene through the new Pension Benefit Guarantee Corporation, which may sue the employer for up to 30 percent of his/her net worth. If his/her unfunded liabilities under the plan are in excess of this limit, obviously it will pay the employer to accept the suit, while the employees are the prospective losers.

In any event, it would seem that OSHA and ERISA legislation and regulations are certain to become more elaborate, in the process complicating life even further for both management and the unions.

Summary

Doubtless there is much more to be said about the negotiation and administration of labor-management agreements than I have been able to set forth here. However, in summing up, we have nonetheless encountered some rather large themes.

1. The stagnation and perhaps even decline of manufacturing unionism and the relative decline of the sector as part of the American economy.
2. The disappointing breaks in trend in real wages, productivity, and unit labor costs.
3. The changing nature of the labor force.
4. The disruptive role of chronic inflation for unions, managements, and employees themselves.
5. The gradual but marked erosion of the finality and exclusivity of voluntary grievance aribtration.
6. Vastly expanded government regulation in labor-management affairs.

In the presence of these massive changes, one can predict with safety only that the years ahead are certain to be difficult for industrial relations. Perhaps they may prove to be creative ones as well.

References

Aaron, Benjamin. "The Duty of Fair Representation: An Overview." In *The Duty of Fair Representation*, edited by Jean T. McKelvey. Ithaca, N.Y.: New York State School of Industrial and Labor Relations, Cornell University, 1977.

Barbash, Jack. "Forces Working to Reshape Collective Bargaining." *Monthly Labor Review* 100 (February 1977):60-61.

Bednarzik, Robert W., and Klein, Deborah P. "Labor Force Trends: A Synthesis and Analysis." *Monthly Labor Review* 100 (October 1977):3-12.

Daily Labor Report, "Union Membership in U.S. Falls Four Percent During 1974-76." 172 (September 2, 1977):B-14—B-17.

Douty, H.M. "The Slowdown of Real Wages: A Postwar Perspective." *Monthly Labor Review* 100 (August 1977):7-12.

Eckstein, Otto, and Wilson, Thomas A. "The Determination of Money Wages in American Industry." *Quarterly Journal of Economics* 76 (August 1962):379-414.

Executive Offices of the President. Office of Management and Budget, Statistical Policy Division. *Standard Industrial Classification Manual, 1972*. Washington, D.C.: GPO, n.d.

Freeman, R.B., and MeDoff, J.L. "New Estimates of Private Sector Unionism in the United States." *Industrial and Labor Relations Review* 32 (January 1979):143-174.

Fullerton, Howard N., Jr., and Flaim, Paul O. "New Labor Force Projections to 1990." *Monthly Labor Review* 99 (December 1976):3-13.

Huntington, Samuel P. "The Democratic Distemper." *Public Interest* 41 (Fall 1975):9-38.

Kutscher, Ronald E. "Revised BLS Projections to 1980 and 1985: An Over-
    view." *Monthly Labor Review* 99 (March 1976):3-8.
Kutscher, Ronald E.; Mark, Jerome A.; and Norsworthy, John R. "The
    Productivity Slowdown and the Outlook to 1985." *Monthly Labor
    Review* 100 (May 1977):3-8.
Monthly Labor Review, 98 (December 1975):84-85.
Norsworthy, J.R., and Fulco, L.J. "Productivity and Costs in the Private
    Economy in 1976." *Monthly Labor Review* 100 (September 1977):3-8.
Silk, Leonard. "Study for Congress: Slower Growth Ahead." *New York
    Times,* February 9, 1978.
Steele v. Louisville & Nashville R.R., 323 U.S. 192 (1944).
Updegraff, Clarence M. *Arbitration and Labor Relations*, 3rd ed. Wash-
    ington, D.C.: Bureau of National Affairs, 1970.
U.S. Department of Labor, Bureau of Labor Statistics. "Characteristics of
    Major Collective Bargaining Agreements, July 1, 1975." *Bulletin* 1957.
    Washington, D.C.: GPO, 1977.
U.S. Congress (95th), Joint Economic Committee, *U.S. Long-Term
    Economic Growth Prospects: Entering a New Era.* Washington, D.C.:
    GPO, 1978.
Wall Street Journal, March 14, 1978.
Westin, Alan F. "A New Move toward Employee Rights." *New York
    Times,* April 23, 1978.

Comment

Clifford Hathway

In this discussion, I will chance a few observations and perhaps offer slightly different perspectives on some parts of Professor Hildebrand's chapter.

The preliminary statistical and factual information concerning union and bargaining unit structures, degree of unionization, and specific forms of bargaining and contract relationship needs no embellishment. It provides useful background to any student of the subject, and is also worthy of review by experienced practitioners before attempting prognostication or future planning.

I found it significant and completely logical that Professor Hildebrand would launch his excursion into collective bargaining of the 1980s with a discussion of "Inflation as a Continuing Factor in the Negotiating Environment." The chapter does not grant complete absolution to unions and management for their contributions to aggravating inflation, nor should it. Unions are understandably trying to make real wage and benefit gains. However, a tougher management stance at the bargaining table would undoubtedly slow the rate of inflation. Neither party acts responsibly when it indulges in self-justification while blaming the other party or the government, even though the government may well be the more infamous villain in causing inflation.

I would underscore, perhaps more strongly than Professor Hildebrand, that deflation (or prolonged "stagflation") may more sorely tax the abilities of union and company negotiators than have recent levels of inflation. The cure, in this case, is bound to be painful—particularly for workers. The pressures they can be expected to exert for protection of jobs, maintenance of income, avoidance of plant closures, and limitations on subcontracting will be strongly felt at the bargaining table. Under deflation, management will have difficulty buying its way out of grass root issues.

In his projections about labor supply and demand, Hildebrand shows some concern about the educational preparation and work ethic of new entrants into the manufacturing work force. It seems to me that the manufacturing industry would be able to utilize its higher total compensation to recruit the best of what is available, in order to ameliorate this problem; EEO considerations, of course, will tend to complicate matters. The newer work force utilizing newer technology will naturally create a need for more in-house training.

As to the shape of bargaining structure, like Hildebrand I fail to see the ingredients for any significant change. I anticipate some movement toward centralization in the case of multiplant employers but find little to support a growth in the multiemployer coalition or association approaches.

I also agree with him on the likely future bargaining agenda. Issues related to job security will be high on the unions' priority list. The shorter work schedule is already being strongly pursued both here and in Europe. Whether in the form of a four-day week, more holidays, or longer vacations, reduced work schedules have serious implications regarding the use of plant and equipment. To some extent those problems may be solved by unique scheduling arrangements. However, the design of special daily and weekly schedules will run into considerable resistance from employees who disdain so-called unsocial hours (weekends, midnight shifts, and the like). Problems will also arise in regard to useful patterns set in some sectors which may not be easily transferable to other enterprises. In addition, employers must confront the different scheduling needs of certain types of office and service activities as contrasted with those on the factory floor.

The unions' pursuit of alleged solutions to the unemployment problem through shorter work time also finds expression in demands for increasingly liberal early retirement provisions. Here stronger resistance is bound to surface as employers discover the significant cost of funding these plans, often a staggering future obligation for an enterprise. Of course, we have yet to see the impact of recent changes in the federal age discrimination law on negotiated retirement plans.

In the area of increased job security, we should anticipate union demands for a voice in make-or-buy and subcontracting decisions, as well as in the issue of plant closures and interplant transfers. These are not entirely new issues, but under the aegis of job security, and perhaps as impacted by deflation, they may take on new importance and make unions less willing to be bought out with wage or benefit sweeteners. As a corollary, and again particulary if deflation should occur, employers will find themselves less able to afford these demands or the alternative buy-out stratgegy.

Professor Hildebrand devotes considerable attention to the impact of recent court decisions and government intervention through regulations under EEO, OSHA, ERISA, and the like. I, too, see this having considerable impact upon future bargaining. The grievance procedure is central to the stability offered by the long-term labor agreement. It is seriously threatened by these alternative avenues of redress for certain alleged wrongs. International unions are acutely aware of this threat to the perceived value and importance of their representation role. It seems inevitable that they will seek to negotiate modifications or alternative devices to strengthen the union's role as the advocate most likely to be chosen by employees in claims against management. One direction almost certain to be suggested is greater freedom of strike action during the term of the contract. Any relaxation of existing no-strike pledges would, of course, seriously weaken the attractiveness of long-term agreements. Greater freedom to strike, and expansion of the issues over which legitimate strikes can be called during the life of an agreement, would certainly disrupt stability at the work place and impact on productivity.

When all these are rolled together, the bargaining climate of the next ten years will not particularly encourage joint committees and employer-union cooperative initiatives in new areas of the relationship. While I favor keeping the door open, I am inclined to dismiss expansion of joint union-management cooperative efforts as an area of significant growth in the years immediately ahead.

A lot has been written lately about the so-called "new breed" of workers. Some of this literature has questioned management's ability to cope with the changed values and attitudes presumably characterizing this group. I feel that much of this is too extreme. Change in values, standards, and the work ethic is probably on a regular continuum. A snapshot of the work force I entered in 1935 would show a considerably different picture from one of the work force of 1955, 1965, or 1978. Change has been going on, and it continues at a relatively steady rate, notwithstanding a few blips here and there. Alongside that continuum is one representing change in the skills of managing and supervising. Accordingly, if I look at the work force in general, and if I look at managers in general, I am not particulary skeptical of our ability to cope—the change we will confront is more evolutionary than revolutionary.

Still, there is an element within this new breed that gives me great concern. The campus revolts of the 1960s were not all spontaneous reactions to an unpopular war, or whatever other reasons have been given for them. I, for one, am convinced there was some inspiration and direction from political forces whose goal is destruction of the system. In the course of all that was going on, some missionaries were spawned and those missionaries are present in the labor market and work force today. I do not know how significant the numbers may be; I simply know that they are there and that they are quite capable of creating at least local disasters.

I make these remarks on the basis of personal experience, which has been repeated in a significant number of other cases in the past few years. My own experience had to do with a fifteen-week strike at our San Leandro, California, plant in 1977. We were confronted with the virtual takeover of the local union by a relatively small number of our employees who openly identified themselves with one or more extreme leftist organizations, under an umbrella organization called United Workers Organization. This handful of people managed to capture key positions of local union responsibility. Then they completely dominated and controlled contract negotiations so that it was virtually impossible for the voice of employees to be heard, for any management logic to be considered, or for an agreement to be reached. Their control was only overcome when the International union stepped in, struck an expensive bargain with the company, and submitted that agreement for membership ratification using a carefully supervised secret ballot.

Ours is only one such experience. At approximately the same time a similar event took place between the Hussman Company and a Steelworkers local in the St. Louis area. In 1978 there were situations at Harnischfeger and at Controls Corporations in Milwaukee which appear to have the same characteristics.

One might ask, "Why would you hire avowed Communists?" Obviously, we didn't know that they were, and they were clever enough not to identify themselves until well after their probationary period was completed. These people came to us with excellent credentials, in all respects appearing to be good employee prospects. Why do we keep them? Because we do not have reasons defensible under the contract and the law to discharge them. They are intelligent, high-performance workers who stay at their work stations.

The major international unions are not in danger of being taken over by radicals of this kind. The unions with which I deal are aware of the problem and concerned about it, attempting to take what safeguards they can to prevent the sort of action my company experienced. The fact remains that there is abroad in the land a number of highly dedicated, highly motivated, well-trained individuals of extreme leftist leaning. I am convinced that they pick targets, deliberately set about infiltrating the work force in those target plants, and proceed into concerted activities to bring about the demise of the enterprise. My own guess is that we will experience more of this, in manufacturing industries particularly. Unfortunately a climate of concern about job security and high unemployment, a thrust for democratization at the work place and in the union, and some degree of either overeducated or underutilized workers tend to provide fertile ground for such leftist tactics.

Apart from these different perspectives on the issues, I find little to disagree with in Hildebrand's excellent effort.

Comment

John C. Zancanaro

I see bargaining structure, as it moves into the 1980s, becoming more fragmented and less characterized by existing pattern-setting relationships. Already there are indications that employer associations are beginning to break up. The San Francisco Employers Association and the California Metal Trades Association are gradually losing members. Individual employers are leaving these associations in order to obtain separate collective bargaining agreements. At one time there were approximately 2,300 employers in the California Metal Trades Group; now there may be half as many.

Along with the break-up of association bargaining has been a general decline in the dominance of large pattern relationships. Agreements which have traditionally been written by rubber-stamping pattern-setting negotiations are now beginning to break away from that mold. As Professor Hildebrand indicated, we saw this recently in the nonferrous fabrication industry during negotiations that included a strike at Anaconda Brass. Smaller, more narrowly defined patterns by industry or geographic area are emerging.

There may be many reasons for the breaking up of associations and pattern-following relationships, but economic pressures are undoubtedly the dominant cause. Continued acceptance of old patterns would probably result in the firm's going out of business. Increased foreign competition in manufacturing has probably added to the impetus for change.

These forces were evident in the actions of employers in the electronics industry, which broke with the aerospace industry pattern in 1975. In this case the economics of the electronics industry was different from the economics of the aerospace industry. In another example, Timken Roller Bearing purchased Latrobe Steel but refused to accept the steel industry contract without obtaining twenty or thirty deviations from that pattern. Latrobe said it was willing to close the plant and walk away from it if denied these deviations.

This changing structure of bargaining has an effect on unions. As patterns fragment and associations lose members, the number of bargaining units increases. Unions must therefore staff more positions and service more locals separately, usually with less experienced people. Since the individual employer now manages labor relations more closely and more directly, there is a growing prospect for increased industrial relations problems on an individual employer basis.

Other changes will take place in the process of collective bargaining. Unions will find the labor-management committee to be politically expedient.

Joint committees are a useful way for the union to get rid of frustration: if something cannot be accomplished at the bargaining table, but the rank and file are deeply concerned about the matter, the joint committee permits the union leader to say, "We accomplished something in this area."

The joint committee approach, however, is not without significant drawbacks. If we come to rely too heavily on joint committees, they may become a depository for seething difficulties. Although they are created in crisis situations, the joint committees, in my experience, are really not constructive. The history of these committees is that they do not go anywhere.

Collective bargaining in the 1980s will also find the unions in a defensive posture at the bargaining table. Unions are going to be put in the position of having to defend what they have won. Already there are indications of aggressive behavior by management in the exercise of collective bargaining rights, and in the creation of new bargaining agreements. Management seems to be forcing issues to impasse, and taking strikes as well. This contrasts sharply with the old notion of the union's causing a strike in order to achieve its ends. Most strikes today are caused by management demands. This of course applies to the big strikes—the nasty ones—I have observed as a practicing mediator.

The new aggressiveness of employers is not limited to paycheck issues. Working conditions, work rules, staffing, tenure, restrictive seniority, and job assignments have been the subjects of several thorny negotiations.

The new posture by management also has its roots in economics. In the past, the firm could pass through almost anything agreed to at the bargaining table. Companies are finding that the competitive edge is so sharp, it is necessary to get back from the union an increased ability to operate efficiently. This drive for so-called "give-backs" is especially significant in labor-intensive industries.

As we look into the 1980s, we can see an increased stiffening of managerial resistance and a greater concern for the employer's credibility at the bargaining table. It has gotten to the point where management is playing a numbers game. That is to say, one commonly hears, "We have made twenty-two demands and we intend to come out of here with fourteen of them in order to establish credibility for management's demands in the future. We don't really care which fourteen we get."

One other trend is related to trade unionism's defensive posture. The Industrial Union Department (AFL-CIO) has not created new committees or coalitions to engage in collective bargaining.

In sum, based on my experience, I foresee important changes taking place in the structure and process of bargaining. These will continue into the next decade.

5 Quality of Worklife and Participation as Bargaining Issues

George Strauss

Students today often ask about so-called Quality of Worklife (QWL) issues. Many are familiar with *Work in America* (1973). They have heard a great deal about the "revolt against work," and they are also at least vaguely aware of job redesign experiments at Volvo, Gaines Dog Food, and elsewhere. Often they view job redesign and increased workers' participation as solutions, not just to workplace discontent, but also to low productivity. Consequently, they ask why unions and companies do not take up workplace reforms with greater enthusiasm, when these are so obviously in the interest of labor, management, and the general public.

European visitors ask these questions and others, too. Impressed by the development of codetermination in Germany, the passage of new laws promoting participation in Sweden, and the elevation of industrial democracy to a major political and economic issue in Britain, these visitors wonder why the American labor movement, which some view as the strongest in the world, does not also seek to share in management control. They are sure this should be the next development in this country.

These are good questions, and in this chapter I seek to deal with them (see also Strauss, 1976, 1977a). First I look at the central issue: to what extent is there job dissatisfaction and a demand for more challenging, participative work in this country? In other words, to what extent is there a rank-and-file demand for QWL change? Second, I look at several forms of QWL changes and seek to indicate the problems these create for unions and bargaining. A brief third section suggests that issues such as flex-time and occupational health may represent more urgent collective bargaining concerns than more narrowly defined QWL issues. Finally, I present a few hesitant conjectures as to why QWL and participation have become more central to industrial relations in Europe than they are likely to become here.

Is There a Demand for More Challenging Work?

It is easy to argue that workers should now be demanding more challenging work. Among the developments are the following.

First, in 1948 the average semiskilled worker had 9.1 years of education; by 1977 this figure had climbed to 12.1 years. Better-educated workers presumably have more skills and stronger expectations than they will be called upon to use.

Second, women and minorities are assuming more important roles in the work force. Neither group is as willing to accept "crummy jobs" as they once were.

Third, the proportion of younger workers has increased, a product of the postwar baby boom. Younger workers traditionally are more dissatisfied than their elders, but this particular generation, raised according to permissive standards and affected by the unrest of the 1960s, presumably has learned to reject conventional values of authority or hard work for its own sake.

Finally, despite recent setbacks, the standard of living and economic security of the average American worker has risen considerably over the long run. Both economic and psychological theory predict that under such circumstances workers should be giving relatively greater weight to nonpecuniary rewards. According to economic theory, as jobs become better rewarded and more secure, the marginal utility of additional income declines and the relative marginal utility of noneconomic benefits (such as job challenge) increases (Flanagan, Strauss, and Ulman, 1974). This hypothesis is, of course, consistent with Maslow's psychological theory that as lower-level (primarily economic) needs are satisfied, higher level needs become more important.

Assuming that these developments in fact are occurring, the case for a radical reconstruction of work would seem to be made. However plausible the above hypotheses may sound (especially to professors, who generally place high value on challenging work), the evidence for them is mixed. There are isolated reports of revolt against work, at Lordstown, for example, but often these reports can be explained by factors other than increased unwillingness to accept routine work.

Growing Dissatisfaction?

There are numerous anecdotal accounts of widespread dissatisfaction (Terkel, 1974). But what do systematic studies of satisfaction tell us? The question comes at an inopportune time, since behavioral scientists are in the midst of a debate as to the meaning and appropriateness of various job satisfaction measures (Wanous and Lawler, 1972; Salancik and Pfeffer, 1977). Critics argue that the kinds of answers workers give to job satisfaction questions are so sensitive to the context in which the questions are asked that the answers cannot be accepted at face value. For example, if it becomes socially more attractive to report oneself dissatisfied, one is more likely to do so, regardless of any real change in one's job. Further, satisfaction depends on expectations and goals. Reported satisfaction may mean resignation (the acceptance of one's lot) or merely face-saving.

To add to the confusion, recent job satisfaction reports are somewhat inconsistent. The proportion reporting themselves either "satisfied" or "very satisfied" with work (a so-called single-question measure) rose until the early 1960s and has remained above 80 percent since then, with little difference among occupational groups (Quinn, Staines, and McCullough, 1974; Quinn and Staines, 1978).

Tables 5-1 and 5-2 present data from the last three University of Michigan Quality of Employment Surveys. Table 5-1 deals with global ("facet-free") attitudes toward the job as a whole. Table 5-2 reports attitudes toward specific ("facet-specific") aspects of the job. Note that according to table 5-1 the proportion who are "somewhat satisfied" actually increased from 85 percent in 1969 to 89 percent in 1977. On the other hand, every one of the twenty-four facet-specific items (only eight of which are presented in table 5-2) asked over the eight-year period declined, some quite substantially.

In addition, the National Longitudinal Survey (Andrisani et al. 1977) indicates declines in the percent reporting themselves "highly satisfied"

Table 5-1
Selected Facet-Free Job Satisfaction Questions

Question	Response Category	Percent Responding		
		1969	1973	1977
All in all, how satisfied	Very satisfied	46	52	47
would you say you are	Somewhat satisfied	39	38	42
with your job?	Not too satisfied	11	8	9
	Not at all satisfied	3	2	3
Knowing what you know	Decide without hesitation			
now, if you had to decide	to take *same* job	64	71	64
all over again whether to				
take the job you have,	Have some second thoughts	27	24	28
what would you decide?				
	Decide definitely *not* to			
	take the job	9	6	8
In general, how well	Very much like job worker			
would you say that your	wanted	63	58	53
job measures up to the				
sort of job you wanted	Somewhat like job worker			
when you took it?	wanted	24	34	36
	Not very much like job			
	worker wanted	13	9	12

Source: Robert P. Quinn and Graham Staines, *1977 Quality of Employment Survey* (Ann Arbor: Institute of Social Research, University of Michigan, 1978), table 13.1. Percentages rounded. Reprinted with permission.

Table 5-2
Selected Facet-Specific Job Satisfaction Questions

Question: "How true . . . is this of your job?"	Percent Answering "Very True"		
	1969	1973	1977
The pay is good	40	41	27
The job security is good	55	53	42
My fringe benefits are good	42	44	33
The hours are good	57	51	43
The work is interesting	63	61	53
I am given a chance to do the things I can do best	45	41	31
I am not asked to do excessive amounts of work	43	34	28
My supervisor is very concerned about the welfare of those under (him/her)	45	41	34

Source: Robert P. Quinn and Graham Staines, *1977 Quality of Employment Survey* (Ann Arbor: Institute of Social Research, University of Michigan, 1978), table 13.1. Percentages rounded. Reprinted with permission.

among most age, sex, occupational, and industrial groupings. Finally, a careful longitudinal study of a large nationwide sales organization reports a significant ten-year drop in satisfaction (using a multi-question measure) (Smith, Roberts, and Hulin, 1976).

What do these contradictory figures mean? The stability in the proportion reporting themselves satisfied may merely reflect a convention. The fact that 80 percent of the working population reports itself satisfied may be no more significant than the fact that over 80 percent of the population, when asked "How are you today?" respond politely, "Fine, thanks, and you?" (as Stanley Seashore once pointed out to me). One answers otherwise only if one wants to launch a specific complaint. Put another way, an 80 percent satisfaction reading of psychological health may be much like a 98.6 degrees thermometer reading of physical health. Although an abnormal reading almost always indicates that something is wrong, a normal reading is no guarantee of health.

A decline in facet-specific items may mean that something is changing; the stability in global satisfaction may mean that for the moment workers are still able to adjust to their lot without too much complaint. Indeed, table 5-2 indicates that many more workers believe their "work is interesting" than find their "pay is good." Even if there is growing dissatisfaction, the evidence hardly suggests a revolt, particularly not a revolt against work itself.

Behavioral Measures

For the economist (but not for the psychologist or mental health expert), job satisfaction itself is relatively unimportant. What is important is the behavior which job satisfaction presumably causes. If real job satisfaction were decreasing, behavioral measures such as quit rates might also be affected. However, the limited available evidence suggests that fluctuations in indexes of quit rates, absenteeism, strikes, and accidents can be largely explained by standard economic variables, such as changes in hours of work, unemployment, and the occupational and demographic composition of the work force. Once the impact of these variables was filtered through regression analysis (at least as of 1974) there was no consistent, significant trend over time, which suggests an attitudinal variable at work (Ulman, Flanagan, and Strauss, 1974).

Greater Demand for Job Challenge

Ignoring dubious measures of job satisfaction, is there any evidence that demand for nonpecuniary benefits (especially job challenge) has increased relative to demand for pecuniary benefits (including pay and job security)? Again the evidence is slim. All during the 1940s and 1950s, employees generally ranked job security as the most important thing they wanted from their jobs (Herzberg et al., 1957). By 1969, job security had dropped to eighth place among the work population as a whole (Quinn et al., 1974). Further, there was some evidence that the shift in preference from extrinsic (pay) to intrinsic factors (the nature of the job) continued during the late sixties and early seventies (Andrisani et al., 1977).

On the other hand, there were some important differences in ranking between blue- and white-collar workers (see table 5-3). Among blue-collar workers, pay and security still ranked high, while among white-collar workers interesting work was the clear favorite. These data may be suspect for methodological and conceptual problems already discussed, such as the need of white-collar workers to feel they should place a high value on "interesting work." Nevertheless, these data provide some support for the view that white-collar workers may be more receptive to QWL changes than are blue-collar workers (a view consistent with the relatively greater weight given to QWL demands by professional unions, for example, teachers' demands to be consulted in textbook selection).

On the other hand, one should note that in absolute terms, the differences in percentages of those rating these various factors as "very important" (figures in parentheses) is not great. Sixty-eight percent of the blue-collar workers think interesting work is very important, and good pay is certainly not sneered at by white-collar workers.

Table 5-3
Importance of Selected Job Factors by Occupation

	Rankings of and Percent Reporting Selected Job Factors as Very Important	
	Blue-collar Workers	White-collar Workers
Pay is good	1 (73)	10 (57)
Job security is good	3 (72)	12 (54)
Help and equipment to get jobs done	2 (72)	5 (65)
Interesting work	5 (68)	1 (79)
Opportunity to develop abilities	12 (57)	2 (69)

Source: Robert P. Quinn, Graham Staines, and Margaret McCullough, "Job Satisfaction: Is there a Trend?" U.S. Department of Labor, Management Research Monograph No. 30, 1974.

Even though white-collar workers may give higher priority to interesting work than do blue-collar workers, there is little evidence that either group places high priority on making interesting work a union goal. Regardless of whether union members want intrinsic goals, table 5-4 suggests that only a minority see the union as a means of obtaining these goals (for a similar study, see Giles and Holley, 1978)—and that white-collar workers place less emphasis on this than do blue-collar workers.

To conclude, the polls indicate no strong increased demand, at least among blue-collar workers, for giving high priority to QWL issues. However, this does not mean that if some future UAW leader, for example, made his or her bargaining objective "Jobs Fit for Grown Men and Women to Work At!" this demand would not win rank-and-file support. Attitudes are easily mobilized and the UAW in particular has a long history of articulating what were originally only the semiconscious demands of its members for such things as supplemental unemployment benefits (SUB) and adequate retirement benefits. The 68 percent of blue-collar workers who think "interesting work" very important are hardly an insignificant group.

I suspect that, for most blue-collar workers, good wages and job security come first and that "interesting work" (or job challenge) is something of a luxury. But like most luxuries, it is something they would enjoy and could easily come to expect on a regular basis.

Quality of Worklife Changes

Hard evidence of a revolt against work is difficult to find, but at least in the literature there has been a great deal of concern with what has come to be

Table 5-4
Priorities of Union Members for Their Union

Question: "How much effort do you think your (union/employees' associa- tion) should be putting into. . . ."	Percentage answering, "A lot of effort." White Collar	Blue Collar
Extrinsic		
Getting better fringe benefits	61	65
Getting better wages	62	54
Improving health and safety on the job	40	51
Improving job security	53	55
Intrinsic		
Getting workers a say in how they do their jobs	27	32
Helping to make jobs more interesting	24	33
Getting workers a say in how their employer runs the business or organization	24	26

Source: Robert P. Quinn and Graham Staines, *1977 Quality of Employment Survey* (Ann Arbor: Institute of Social Research, University of Michigan, 1978), table 11.9 Percentages rounded. Reprinted with permission.

known as "Quality of Worklife." This title was selected for the types of programs to be discussed here only after either labor or management had shot down as too controversial other suggested names, many of which contained the suspect term "productivity." Deliberately ambiguous, Quality of Worklife acquires meaning in the eyes of the beholder (Suttle, 1977).

Under the category "Quality of Worklife," Walton (1974) includes such diverse concepts as "fair compensation," "development of human capacities," and socially responsible behavior on the part of the employing organization. In practice, however, QWL literature has dealt chiefly with various attempts to redesign workers' jobs so as to provide greater meaning and challenge, to permit workers to participate in determining either how their own jobs are done or how the larger organization is run, and some combination of both. The nearest European equivalent to QWL, "work humanization," also includes environmental issues, especially occupational health and work place cleanliness.

For convenience, my discussion in the pages which follow proceeds under three headings: (1) job design changes generally; (2) QWL experiments sponsored by what is now called the American Center for Quality of Work Life; and (3) the Scanlon Plan. The first, which is most common in nonunion plants, is normally not tied to an incentive system. The second involves close collaboration with unions, but typically no monetary incentives. The third combines both unions and incentives.

Job Redesign

Recent years have seen considerable interest in job redesign, a generic term covering efforts to restructure jobs in order to increase the workers' sense of challenge, responsibility, and autonomy, all with the purpose of reducing dissatisfaction and raising productivity. These efforts have been most widespread in Europe, where job redesign experiments at Saab, Volvo, Fiat, and Philips have been widely publicized. In the United States, the best-known work has been done at such firms as General Foods, Texas Instruments, AT&T, Donnelly Mirrors, and Non-Linear Systems. Significantly, most of these changes occurred either in nonunion situations (Goodman and Lawler, 1977) or were introduced with little union consultation. Unpublicized examples of job redesign appear especially common among small new nonunion manufacturing plants in such states as Oklahoma.

On the other hand, GM and UAW have been actively experimenting for some time with job changes at a number of various plants, although to date there have been only fragmentary reports as to their success (Dowling, 1975; Walfish, 1977).

Terminology in this area is rather imprecise; nevertheless, the main job redesign efforts have involved one or more of the following activities. *Job rotation* permits workers to switch jobs without necessarily changing the character of these jobs. This most simple of reforms provides the worker more variety in his/her work and perhaps also in social relations. *Job enlargement* adds elements to the job "horizontally," typically lengthening the work cycle, requiring additional skills, and providing a greater sense of accomplishment and task identity. *Job enrichment* adds "vertical," quasi-managerial job components, especially those of planning, supply, and inspection.

The most publicized form of job redesign, the *self-managing work team* (sometimes called the "autonomous work group"), involves a group form of job enrichment. Typically such groups meet periodically to determine job assignments, schedule work breaks, and decide the rate of output. As Dowling (1973, p. 59) has observed at Volvo, "the production team, a group of 5 to 12 men with a common assignment, elects its own chargehand, schedules its own output within standards set by higher management, distributes work among its members, and is responsible for quality control." At the Topeka General Foods dog food plant, production groups participated in hiring, firing, and wage-setting decisions. At the Tarrytown GM plant, "business teams," which include production workers as well as supervisors, are reported to set production goals and develop solutions to production problems. Groups at other plants have been given the responsibility of developing relations with vendors, determining which operations can be handled individually and which by the group as a whole, training new employees, and, at Non-Linear, even keeping financial records.

Taken as a whole, these projects introduce variety, autonomy, feedback, and task identity, all of which have been identified as contributing to motivation and satisfaction (Hackman, 1977). It should be carefully noted, however, that these changes do more than provide what Herzberg (1966) calls "motivators."

In the first place, the changes also involve alterations in workflow and especially reduction in the number of friction-causing interfaces. Reported productivity increases may be more the result of better material flow than of harder work. Second, the best publicized have been accompanied by important changes in the job environment (what Herzberg would call "hygienes") and in workers' status position. These changes have begun to reduce what UAW Vice President Bluestone (1974, p. 47) describes as

> the double standard that exists between workers and management. . . . Workers challenge the symbols of elitism traditionally taken for granted, such as salary payment vs. hourly payment; time clocks for blue-collar workers; well-decorated dining rooms for white-collar workers versus plain, Spartan-like cafeterias for blue-collar workers.

At the Topeka dog food plant, for example, there are no reserved parking lots, no time clocks, and no differentiation in decor between management offices and worker lounges. Most important, perhaps, workers are given ample opportunity to break the monotony of the job and even, in one department, to make phone calls on company time.

Wider Organizational Impacts

Job redesign is difficult to introduce, and when introduced it is likely to fizzle out unless accompanied by wider organizational change. Although intended to increase workers' sense of participation, job redesign is often imposed by nonparticipative methods. Indeed, for the change to "take," substantial changes in managerial philosophy and behavior may be needed. Fewer supervisors may be required, and those that remain must learn to let subordinates make decisions for themselves. According to rumor, one large company found that job redesign reduced its need for supervisors, but it retained these in order to keep essential services going in case of strike. Predictably, these supervisors resisted further spread of job redesign, which they saw as already eroding their authority. Schrank (1978, p. 221) reports that management at Philips Eindoven in the Netherlands feared that an extension of job enrichment might lead their unionized foremen to strike.

Further, it is difficult to introduce changes in one department without affecting others. Even if workflow relations are not disrupted, workers in other departments may want equal freedoms.

Especially important, as workers take on more responsible jobs, they normally expect higher pay. By contrast, many companies seem to feel that increased satisfaction and more interesting work should be reward enough. This has been a sore point, particularly in unionized situations. Even at Topeka, where promotions (and therefore wages) were determined by peer evaluation, the pay issue was a potent cause of interpersonal differences. "The match in the gasoline," one worker said, "is pay" (Walton, 1977, p. 428). Job redesign does not banish economic issues.

Union Attitudes toward QWL

Another wider impact of job redesign is on union-management relations. Union leaders find it difficult to deal with QWL issues (in this they are no different than are members of management). Insofar as there is a union position today, it is one of caution. I suspect that most of the relatively few leaders who have given the matter much thought still have an open mind.

Top Leadership Attitudes. The *American Federationist* has published three articles (Brooks, 1972; Gomberg, 1973; Barbash, 1977) which are generally negative to the QWL movement. Interestingly, the first is by a freelance writer and the other two are by professors. Their general position is, as Barbash (pp. 12-13) puts it, that QWL is

> ideologically and institutionally hostile to trade unionism and collective bargaining . . . a putdown of the union's high evaluation of economic benefits and job security. . . . The psychological assumptions of the humanization movement . . . are mainly based on the needs of middle-class managers for participation and self actualization. The advocates seem incapable of understanding that the economic calculation is the prism through which other values are filtered. . . . [T]he humanization movement [is] really aimed at increasing productivity without appropriate payouts.

Similarly William Winpisinger of the IAM has called job enrichment nothing more than "'time and motion study' in sheep's clothing" (1974), but his objection (as I understand it) is to job enrichment in a context which excludes collective bargaining.

By contrast Leonard Woodcock and Irving Bluestone of the UAW have been generally sympathetic to what Bluestone calls "introducing democracy at the workplace." The 1973 auto agreements established joint union-management committees to sponsor research in this area and "commits both sides to seek joint answers to the difficult questions of job enrichment" (United Automobile Workers, 1973). Bluestone cautiously concludes (1977, p. 10):

Unions express concern that such programmes are wolves in sheeps' clothing, a gimmick to decoy the workers away from their loyalty to the union and make them even more pliant to the will of management. In the author's judgement, circumstances will cause this resistance to diminish in time. Through their unions the workers have already drastically reduced the traditional, autocratic type of managerial control over the worker and the workplace. The concept of workers' rights in the decision-making process has taken root. It will flower.

In the United States the thrust to improve the quality of working life will manifest itself in direct participation by workers in managing their jobs. Perhaps, in later years, it will spread to participation in managing the enterprise. The incontrovertible fact is that the democratic values of society—based on participation in the decision-making process—will be extended to the place of work. Democratising work is an idea whose time has come.

According to a 1975 sample of top union officers, 69 percent agreed with the statement that "job enrichment is a promising strategy for improving productivity" and 97 percent agreed that "it is possible for union and management to cooperate on specific programs which will improve productivity" (Katzell and Yankelovich, 1975). Taken as a whole, the study does not suggest ideological commitment against QWL changes; neither does it indicate enthusiastic support.

Local Level Leadership. Table 5-5, adopted from a survey of union activists in upstate New York (Kochan, Lipsky, and Dyer, 1975), provides some indication of local level attitudes.

Several interesting conclusions emerge from this study. As expected, basic economic issues are ranked most important. Yet substantial numbers also rate as "very important" such QWL issues as safety, control of work (described as "having more to say about how the work is done"), adequate resources (described as "improving conditions that interfere with getting the job done"), and interesting work. Both productivity and work load receive reasonably low votes. In sum, QWL is a secondary but still important issue for these activists.

The second column contains some surprises. With the exception of safety, a majority of these activists do not believe that their company and union wish to accomplish the same thing in these areas. Even "adequate resources" was viewed as being a distributive (rather than integrative) issue. The final column suggests considerable union support for joint programs in these areas, especially since other data (not reported above) indicate that they were felt not to be effectively handled through collective bargaining (for confirming evidence, see Ponak and Fraser, 1979).

To conclude, although union leaders are concerned about QWL conditions, they are somewhat uncertain as to how to handle these issues within a collective bargaining context, particularly since economic issues are still of

Table 5-5
Attitudes of Union Officers Toward Selected Issues
(percent)

	Issue Very Important[a]	Issue Integrative[b]	Issue Appropriate for Joint Program[c]
Earnings	92	26	6
Fringe benefits	79	48	4
Safety	75	68	41
Job security	68	44	12
Control of work	47	34	54
Adequate resources	46	46	61
Interesting work	41	39	68
Productivity	30	30	51
Work Load	22	29	44

Source: Thomas Kochan, David Lipsky, and Lee Dyer, "Collective Bargaining and Quality of Work Life: The Views of Union Activists," *Proceedings*, Industrial Relations Research Association, 27th Annual Meeting, 1975. Reprinted with permission.

[a]Percent rating issue "very important."

[b]Percent reporting that with regard to given issue "my union and company want to accomplish completely the same thing" or "my company and union want to accomplish somewhat the same thing."

[c]Percent feeling that the "best way" to deal with issue is to "set up a joint program with management outside collective bargaining."

primary concern. Thus, if properly approached, unions will be supportive of QWL reforms; on the other hand, like management, they will have to feel their way into this terra incognito. Among the main problems are that (1) QWL issues are difficult to handle within the traditional adversary context, (2) the issues of productivity and reward are difficult to solve, and (3) changes in jobs also involve changes in traditional work rules.

The Adversary Relationship. QWL issues are difficult to fit in the normal union-management adversary mold. As Nat Goldfinger of the AFL-CIO put it, "a union demand is a negotiable demand which, if not satisfied, can be met by a strike. How do you talk about these [QWL] questions in terms of a negotiable demand and a possible strike?" (Jenkins, 1977, p. 317). In general, unions have resisted making management decisions, particularly when this requires invidious choices among members. Further, there is a fear that QWL issues will "coopt" the union and that it will either be diverted from its true mission or actually begin to accept management's point of view.

These comments may exaggerate the problem, however. In the first place, unions frequently participate in making hard decisions in favor of one group of members over another, for example, whenever they negotiate new seniority rules or agree to a contract which provides greater benefits for skilled tradesmen. Second, experienced negotiators are able to live in "mixed motive" situations, to use Walton and McKersie's (1965) terminology, in which "distributive" bargaining (where one party can gain only at the cost of the other) exists side by side with "integrative" bargaining (where the solution can provide gains for both parties). QWL is an integrative issue par excellence. Actually, unions have a long history of dealing with integrative problems from plant picnics to job evaluation through the establishment of joint union-management committees which function separately from mainstream, distributive bargaining.

Productivity and Compensation. For management people, productivity is an unquestioned good. Union leaders are less sure. While there is a general recognition that companies must be profitable if they are to pay decent wages, the term "productivity" is often associated with the speed-up and loss of jobs. Note that, of the local union sample discussed above, 70 percent viewed productivity as an issue about which the union's interest would be likely to diverge from that of management.

Thus union leaders are hardly likely to be enthusiastic about QWL changes sold in the name of productivity unless higher productivity is clearly needed to save jobs, or higher productivity will be compensated by higher wages, as in the Scanlon Plan. Fortunately, however, there are numerous other issues, besides productivity, around which QWL changes can be focused.

Traditional Work Rules. Regardless of how they are introduced, QWL programs will have an impact on a number of collectively bargained policies. The thrust of collective bargaining has been to rigidify and codify managerial practices, for example, to define job classifications ever more strictly and to insist that no one work outside his/her job classification. Job enrichment requires movement in the opposite direction: the combination of some jobs, the blurring of boundaries between others, and even the blending of worker and supervisory functions. New career patterns disturb established promotional ladders. Reforms of pay systems involve the heart of bargaining agreements. Collective bargaining leads to what the Webbs called the "common rule," in which all workers are treated alike. The QWL movement is part of what Kerr has named the "multi-option society," in which diversity flourishes (Kerr and Rosow, 1979).

Some unions may adopt the policy of "no backward step" and refuse to make concessions of any kind. However, this is unlikely to be the norm.

Once unions' suspicions are allayed, exceptions and changes may be permitted, subject of course to carefully negotiated safeguards. After all, difficult problems like those mentioned are constantly being resolved through bargaining; for example, in many plants work rules are the subject of constant renegotiation. Once union leaders discern a clear mandate for QWL changes from their members, job redesign problems may well be solvable within this work-rule context.

To put the preceding discussion in perspective, unions are unlikely to initiate demands for job redesign in the near future. Union leaders see little demand for this from the rank and file. They themselves give it low priority. They are in no way prepared to trade off concrete gains such as wage increases for anything as nebulous as greater freedom to make work decisions. In addition, these leaders find it difficult to fit QWL issues into the adversary relationship with which they are comfortable. Management, for its part, fears that permitting unions to consult about work methods will threaten its managerial prerogative to "direct the work force" (Osterman, 1975). Thus a company publicity barrage suggesting that job redesign is a totally new policy may well lead to strenuous opposition. On the other hand, a management policy of gradually increasing worker responsibility is unlikely to meet union resistance, especially if management is willing to negotiate appropriate wage adjustments.

But is it possible that QWL changes can be made by union and management jointly? The following section describes some innovative attempts to introduce changes jointly and in a nontraditional manner.

**Formal Joint Labor-Management
Quality of Worklife Experiments**

Formal QWL experiments are the well-publicized union-management programs sponsored by the American Center for Quality of Work Life, which frequently have been partly funded by the Ford Foundation and/or the Department of Commerce. Among the common characteristics of these experiments are the following:

1. For each organization there is a steering committee including top local representatives of union and management; usually this committee spawns several tiers of subordinate "working committees" or "task forces" consisting of those directly involved in the change program.

2. The steering committee selects an outside consultant, usually an individual or firm with a strong background in organizational development. Often a number of prospects are interviewed before a decision is made.

3. Separate independent outside researchers observe the change process, conduct attitude surveys at various stages before, during, and after the

experiment, and also collect "objective" data on productivity, costs, turn-over, and so on. Since experiments normally are confined to one part of a larger organization, attempts are also made to obtain comparable data from "control" groups in the same organization. Thus an effort is made to maintain scientific experimental rigor, with the purpose being both to learn whether experimental change makes a difference and how to introduce change effectively.

4. Union and management sign "shelter" agreements allowing each side to withdraw from the experiment on short notice. It is understood that the collective bargaining agreement is not to be superseded except by specific, joint consent. All decisions of the various committees are to be by consensus, and no worker will lose work or pay as a result of the project.

So far joint union-management programs of this sort have been in-troduced into more than a dozen settings. Some projects lasted only a short time and others are still in the preliminary stages (Drexler and Lawler, 1977; Nadler, 1978). Reports are available on only three projects: an engineering department at TVA (Tennessee Valley Authority, 1976); Harmon, an auto parts factory in Bolivar, Tennessee (Duckels, Duckels, and Maccoby, 1977; Lelyveld, 1977); and Rushton, a coal mine in Pennsylvania (Trist, Susman, and Brown, 1977). Other projects are (or were) underway at Mt. Sinai Hospital, New York (Nadler, 1978), at a governmental agency, and in several manufacturing firms around the country (Lawler and Drexler, 1978).

Nature of QWL Changes

The nature of the changes (and the methods by which they were introduced) varied considerably among the experiments, depending in part on the con-sultants' philosophies. On the basis of a consultant's recommendation, Rushton introduced an autonomous work team which planned its own work, freeing the nominal foreman to work on safety and long-range plan-ning. At TVA and Bolivar, joint groups identified problems and initiated changes on their own. The engineers at TVA proposed changes in (1) workflow, including the elimination of unnecessary engineering draw-ings and the centralization of environmental matters in a newly created divi-sion, and (2) personnel practices, for example, a new performance evaluation procedure, the introduction of special awards for outstanding service, and a ten-hour, four-day week for employees whose jobs required them to spend many nights away from home. Initial work suggestions at Bolivar related chiefly to what Herzberg would call hygienes, for example, air conditioning and the absence of Gatorade in the coin-operated dispensing machine. Later, after an incentive was introduced—in the form of allowing workers to go home after their day's work quota—other changes were made, including, in one department, the rotation of the foreman's role among members of the work force.

Problems

The TVA, Rushton, and Bolivar experiences suggest problems which may be common to plans of this sort.

1. Workers are unequally interested in making work decisions. As might be expected, involvement appeared greatest among professionals (engineers at TVA), next among skilled tradesmen (The Rushton miners), and least among the semiskilled (at Bolivar).

2. The programs require that managers listen to workers' suggestions and that union leaders suspend their adversary roles. Neither is easy.

3. A successful QWL program requires the development of a new network of interpersonal relations which center around the whole set of novel institutions. Establishing new relationships is difficult enough, but these are superimposed on (and partly in conflict with) older relationships, both within and between union and management. Plans have developed trouble, for example, because of jealousies between the various tiers of new committee structure, and particularly because middle-level managers and union leaders feel bypassed.

4. The success of the program at each site was heavily dependent on its environment. TVA has been traditionally hospitable to experiments in participation (Patchin, 1965). Worsening nationwide labor-management relations in coal helped doom the Rushton program. The Bolivar experiment owed its existence to the enthusiastic support of Sidney Harmon, the company president; once Harmon sold the company to Beatrice Foods, the program's continuance was in doubt.

5. Pay was a problem throughout. As production increased, workers wanted to share the gains. At Bolivar, productivity was rewarded by allowing workers to quit early when they finished their day's work quota. At Rushton participating workers moved to the top of their pay scale. In practice, neither solution was a completely happy one.

6. Consultants believe that programs should be introduced slowly and experimentally, on a department-by-department basis. At Bolivar and Rushton the intial experiments were confined to several departments. However, differences in treatment, privileges, and compensation led to serious friction between the experimental groups and the rest of the organization; there was a rush to extend the experiment before the consultants felt the other groups were ready. On a more general level, unions find it difficult to support programs which do not involve all employees

equally. (For a fascinating discussion of how this concern helped destroy the New York State productivity program, see Osterman, 1975.) On the other hand, a requirement of uniform treatment is inconsistent with the spirit of group self-determination inherent in the QWL philosophy.

7. None of the programs was generated by the workers and local managers involved. In each, external stimulus was required. While the TVA program continued after the consultants left (they were later recalled, with the parties paying their expenses), the Bolivar program seemed to have become completely dependent on the consultants for whatever momentum it had. Each of the programs was supposed to be a demonstration project which presumably would lead other organizations to copy it, but this did not happen. Indeed, the entire QWL program appears largely dependent on expensive externally financed consultants. One wonders what will be left when the financing expires.

Results

Efforts were made to introduce QWL programs at a number of sites; reports are available from only the three programs discussed above. In all three there was considerable short-run success, including improved productivity. In each case the atmosphere of union-management relations improved. For example, in the face of outside competition, the union at Bolivar cooperated with management in a study which led to standard production rates being raised; nevertheless, according to latest reports, the Bolivar project seems to have run out of steam. In the Rushton experiment, the union voted to terminate the formal aspects of the program by a close 79-75 vote.

Perhaps the most significant product of these projects has been the testing of organization development (OD) techniques in the context of labor-management relations. OD consultants have acquired an impressive array of skills for dealing with intraorganizational problems generally, but until recently the OD approach has been often felt to be inappropriate for labor relations (Strauss, 1977b). The QWL program shows that third-party consultants can induce cooperative activity in circumstances where the parties might not have developed these without external assistance.

Another new form of OD applied to industrial relations is the relationships-by-objectives (RBO) program of the Federal Mediation and Conciliation Service. Other OD-like programs designed to improve QWL, labor relations, and/or productivity have been started on a communitywide basis (as in Jamestown, New York) and on a plant or company basis (as at Heinz, Rockwell, and GM).

Two problems highlighted by the QWL experience so far have been that

quality of worklife as a goal is rather vague, and that none of the programs
has fairly faced the questions of productivity and reward. One program
which is not ambiguous in its goals and which does attempt to deal directly
with productivity through monetary rewards is the so-called Scanlon Plan.
In the next section we look at some problems and opportunities associated
with it.

The Scanlon Plan

Joint union-management efforts to raise productivity are not unknown in
the United States. Such programs existed in the B&O Railroad, at Pequot
Mills, and in other places prior to World War II, and during the war there
were numerous joint production committees. Of all these, the Scanlon Plan
is the most carefully designed. It has a forty-year history, and it is the
closest American equivalent to the European ideal of workers' participation
in management. (Of course, we have a small number of worker-owned
plants, and in some cases the workers have retained their union membership: Bellas, 1972; Whyte, 1977; Perry, 1978.) Further, there have been few
participation experiments involving groups of more than thirty people; the
Scanlon Plan has been successful in organizations of up to 500, thus, for the
first time, extending cooperation beyond the face-to-face group.

Like jointly run QWL programs, the Scanlon Plan provides a committee structure, including departmental production committees, which meet
periodically to discuss suggestions from individual employees and to formulate plans for improving productivity, and a plantwide screening committee which considers suggestions affecting the organization as a whole.
The plan's unique characteristic is a wage formula designed to distribute the
gains of increased productivity proportionally among the employees involved, in the form of a monetary bonus when earned. Thus increasing productivity becomes a goal which has a payoff for both parties, and this goal
provides a focus for the participative efforts of those involved. Meeting the
goal offers a form of satisfaction which goes beyond the pecuniary value of
the associated bonuses. And a successful program gives ample opportunities
for individuals and group participation in decision-making. Though better
QWL and higher satisfaction are not the direct goals here, they are almost
inevitable by-products. (For critical analyses of Scanlon Plans, see Driscoll,
1977; Kochan and Dyer, 1976; Ruh, Wallace, and Frost, 1973; White, 1979;
Strauss and Sayles, 1957.)

Given the plan's many merits, why have only 200 to 300 companies
adopted it?

Plan success appears related to managerial philosophy (Ruh et al.,
1973). Traditional company prerogatives must be forgotten. Foremen,

superintendents, and even company presidents must learn to consult with subordinates and be willing to listen to sharp criticism. Lower levels of management, who frequently feel bypassed, understandably at times sabotage the plan.

In addition, equally difficult adjustments are required within the union. The relationship between the traditional distributive bargaining function and the integrative bargaining behaviors required in the Scanlon Plan is never easy. Often grievance committeemen are barred from sitting on Scanlon committees, with only the union president serving in both a cooperative and adversary capacity. By fostering two potentially competitive power structures, the plan makes conflict difficult to avoid.

Moreover, there is the danger that the top union leadership will become so involved with management's problems that it will become less sensitive to the rank and file's concerns. Constant intraorganizational and interorganizational communication is vital.

Also, few successful plans cover more than 500 employees. An experience of mine may illustrate why this is so: I was having lunch in the cafeteria of a Scanlon Plan plant. About twenty minutes after the rest of the workers had begun eating a few stragglers came in. At first people glanced angrily at them, and then began pointing their fingers as they went by. I was told that this was the finishing group, whose ineffective performance was holding up the entire plant's monthly bonus.

Subjected to this much social pressure, the finishing group presumably reacted by working harder. However, suppose the organization as a whole were much larger and social pressure more difficult to exert. The other groups might well say, "Since they're goofing off, why shouldn't we?" Blaming others is easier than working harder. As Olson (1965) suggests, the larger the group, the more difficult it is to mobilize for the collective good.

Finally, there is the constant danger of "plateauing"; the simple problems are solved and everyone loses interest. Alternatively, a mass of problems at one time may easily overwhelm the rather fragile structure of cooperation.

For these and other reasons, one might predict that the plan will be most successful in firms with the following characteristics: small size; stable or expanding product demand; pattern-following rather than pattern-leading in bargaining (so as to reduce the pressures from distributive bargaining); and a fairly flexible technology such as batch production, so that worker suggestions can make some impact. Cumulatively, these are quite restrictive conditions, so the Scanlon Plan is likely to be appropriate in comparatively few locations.

In sum, job design or worker participation projects are difficult to introduce in unionized situations, whether this is done with or without formal union cooperation, and regardless of whether it is tied to monetary reward systems.

Alternate Means of Improving Quality of Worklife

QWL, at least in its broader definitions, involves more than attempts to make work itself more meaningful. QWL changes may include improving the work environment and giving workers greater self-determination over such things as work schedule.

Flex-time and Unconventional Work Schedules

Forms of unconventional schedules range from the ten-hour day, four-day week through various schemes permitting employees to pick their own starting and quitting times, to part-time and shared (two workers on a single job) work.

I suspect that the desire for greater flexibility in work schedules, the freedom to decide when to work and not work, may be stronger than the desire to determine how to work. Certainly flex-time has organized pressure groups behind it; job redesign does not. The demand for change has come largely from women's groups. Flexible starting and quitting times have spread surprisingly rapidly, but they are confined largely to white-collar and professional work, areas which are largely nonunion.

At least initially the union reaction to flex-time has been one of suspicion. The male, full-time, high-status employees who dominate most unions have little interest in flex-time, while the organized women's groups which have fought for this have on occasion bypassed and thus antagonized the union hierarchy. Union leaders at a 1977 conference expressed concern that flex-time might threaten "the long-fought-for eight-hour day" or might "lead to flexible job classifications or other losses to employees" (*Daily Labor Report*, 1977, p. A-8). The AFL-CIO has so far successfully opposed legislation that would permit the federal government to experiment with flexible or compressed work weeks through relaxing the usual rules requiring overtime pay after eight hours work.

Unions have also expressed concern that, since flex-time may result in work being done more efficiently, it will result in the elimination of opportunities to earn the overtime (for working more than forty hours weekly) upon which many workers have come to depend. Further, since flex-time provides no set starting or finishing times, it may be more difficult to enforce the Fair Labor Standards Act (Owen, 1977).

> From a union point of view, it is not enough to argue that workers are happier and better under flextime, and thus a fair tradeoff has been effected. The employer has also gained from the transaction, but has given up nothing. The terms of the bargain need to be adjusted. (*Daily Labor Report* 1978, p. A-7).

It is suggested that flex-time "is already being used as a means of thwarting unions' organizing efforts" (*Daily Labor Report*, 1978, p. A-8). The demand for part-time work runs into opposition from some unions (for example, in the Post Office) which have been trying to eliminate such work altogether. Nevertheless, flex-time meets a definite need, employer experience with it has been generally favorable, and clerical unions in some cases have finally made the cause their own.

Other recent personnel innovations which have increased emplyees' freedom to schedule their work activities include freedom to decline overtime, optional early retirement, and contractual and legal provisions raising the age for compulsory retirement or eliminating it altogether. Unions have fought for the first two rights, but their attitudes toward restricting compulsory retirement have been mixed, particularly where unemployment is high.

"Cafeteria" fringe benefit programs (in which workers have some choice of benefits) also increase worker self-determination and likewise have sometimes met union resistance. Freedom from lie-detector tests, to criticize management, and the right to remain on the job pending final resolution of disciplinary issues are QWL provisions which labor may push in future years. The UAW in 1976 also sought "clean, well lighted 'satellite' areas for rest and relaxation during relief periods with sufficient vending machines . . . clean, well-kept toilet facilities . . . protection against snooping through the use of TV cameras, electronic devices, motion picture cameras, etc." (Bureau of National Affairs, 1976, p. 12:26).

Occupational Safety and Health

Until recently, occupational safety and health received relatively little collective bargaining attention. Unions gave it low priority and felt it was largely a management concern. In some locations the union was more likely to resist safety rules (like requiring that safety shoes be worn) than to seek to identify and eliminate unsafe conditions. Safety rules were often felt to be too restrictive, and they went against the "macho" culture of many work situations.

All this has been changed by the increased consciousness of insidious, delayed-action health hazards (such as those which are associated with cancer), plus the passage of the Occupational Safety and Health Act. Under certain economic conditions union leaders may still occasionally fear that if they push companies too hard, management will shut down a hazardous plant rather than go through the expense of making it safe. In more situations, however, unions are now pushing safety harder than management, and the subject has become an adversary issue, to be handled through bargaining and the grievance procedure rather than in joint safety committees (Kochan, Dyer, and Lipsky, 1977). Unions have been pressing particularly for the right to refuse to work whenever the worker feels a condition is unsafe, regardless of what the supervisor (or the arbitrator later on) might conclude. Further, unions argue that companies should eliminate the causes of hazard rather than merely provide devices to protect against them (for instance, to reduce noise directly rather than passing out ear plugs).

The European Experience

It may be useful to conjecture about why "work humanization" and "industrial democracy" are so much higher on the European agenda than they are on ours.

Sweden is often held up as the country with the greatest commitment to work humanization. The economic climates in Sweden and the United States, however, are quite different. Swedish interest in work humanization was motivated in part by the desire not to import additional "guest workers" during the labor shortages of the early 1970s. Swedish nationals were shunning the assembly line, absentee rates were high, and equalitarian wage and tax policies made it difficult to make unattractive jobs financially more desirable. QWL changes appeared to be the only viable alternative to importing guest workers. With our relative high unemployment rates, QWL policies are less popular here. In the United States, as in Germany, where support for work humanization declined after unemployment became a problem in the mid-1970s (Jenkins, 1977), job security appears to be a higher order requirement than QWL.

A second difference between us and the Europeans is that real income has increased much faster in Europe since the war than it has in the United States. As mentioned earlier, economic and psychological theory both suggest that as pecuniary income rises, nonpecuniary rewards become relatively more desirable. On the other hand, "expected" standard of living, in pecuniary terms, tends to increase over time (perhaps more slowly than actual income), and this rising expectation may in effect gradually lower the psychic value of any given pecuniary income. Thus Europeans may have enjoyed a substantial surplus above their "expected income" and so felt able to afford such luxuries as improved QWL. Americans, by contrast, had trouble "keeping up with the Joneses."

The European movement may represent an attempt to dethrone the autocratic manager. American cultural patterns, the impact of shop-centered unions, and the cumulative impact of "human relations" teaching in business schools may have already combined to make U.S. managers more democratic than their European counterparts. (According to Tannenbaum et al. [1974], American managers are viewed by their workers as being less autocratic and more participative than Italian and Austrian managers and even [on some dimensions] those of the Israeli kibbutz and Yugoslav worker-managed factories. In addition, the discrepancy between desired and actual control and participation is somewhat less in the United States than in the other countries studied, suggesting that participation is a less critical issue here [Haire, Ghiselli, and Porter, 1966].)

There may also be some difference in cultural attitudes toward conflict. U.S. autoworkers sent to Saab on a Ford Foundation-sponsored project and longshoremen similarly sent to Rotterdam both found the European work atmosphere too sterile and paternalistic for their tastes. Most of these workers were union activists, and they missed the vigorous work-level give-and-take characteristic of labor relations in this country.

Another factor may be that European collective bargaining is typically conducted on an industry-wide level and the scope of bargaining is relatively narrow. To some extent the European demand for industrial democracy represents an attempt to strengthen plant-level bargaining and to extend its scope to cover the broad range of subjects standard in the United States. However, European demands go beyond American practice, since European unions seek to be consulted regarding layoff decisions, investment policy, and the rate of technological change, while U.S. unions are satisfied to bargain over the impact of such decisions on their members. European unions want codetermination, not redesign. Indeed for many European unionists, shop-level job redesign is small potatoes, since it ignores the critical questions of power and control.

Finally, workers' participation serves a variety of ideological meanings, depending on the country (Strauss and Rosenstein, 1970). Some European unions look upon it as a means of reducing class differences. With almost equal ideological fervor U.S. unions suspect it as blurring the distinction between labor and management (Kirkland, 1978). In effect, U.S. unions wish to preserve the present system; European unions wish to change it. To put it another way, in Europe workers' participation is viewed as strengthening unions; in the United States it is feared as weakening them. A cynic might say that the advocacy of participation permits continental European unions to reconcile their pro-forma socialism with the reality of their support for wage restraint. Or that the motivation for participation

has been that of reconciling ideological contradictions in a symbolic fashion than that of solving practical on-the-job problems. In general, the impetus for participation has come more from intellectual propagandists, and politicians . . . than it has from the rank-and-file workers who were supposed to be doing the participating. (Strauss and Rosenstein, 1970, p. 199)

Conclusion

History may prove me grievously wrong, but I predict that in this country neither job redesign nor workers' participation in management will rank high as bargaining issues during the 1980s. Flexible work schedules and occupational health will receive greater attention, although, once ground rules are laid down, the former may prove relatively noncontroversial.

Management may well lengthen job cycles, especially in new plants, and work assignments may encourage the development of natural work teams. Furthermore, skilled foremen may continue to seek informal employee participation in work decisions, just as they have in the past. To the extent that the new jobs require greater skills and responsibilities, pay adjustments will be made through bargaining, as they have always been. Increasingly, we may see pay determined by personal skill rather than job assignment, but this is already the practice in some plants.

I do not anticipate the spread of formal schemes for workers' participation in this country. We lack Europe's recent history of full employment and rapid economic growth; more important, our unions have different ideological traditions. Thus there is little likelihood of an interest in European-style participation developing here.

Plant-level participation, of either the QWL-experiment or the Scanlon-Plan variety, presents great difficulties, as we have seen. Aside from ideological doubts, both sides give QWL low priority. Management is interested in productivity, and unions, in pay, and neither is willing to give up bargaining chips to win participation. QWL lacks the constituency which flex-time enjoys.

Management fears that once it agrees to consult with the union about productivity and work methods it will lose its prerogatives to "direct the work force" and receive nothing in return. The union fear, of course, is that participation will weaken work rules.

Beyond this is the unresolved question of gain-sharing. Job redesign and formal QWL programs are supposedly not concerned with productivity; the Scanlon Plan is. In either case, if the program is successful productivity will increase and workers will want their share. If the productivity gain is shared only by the work groups directly involved, friction will arise between those groups and others not similarly favored; at times the other groups may combine to contain and destroy the experiment. However, if the gains are equally shared among all members of the larger organization (and in the New York productivity agreement this larger organization comprised thousands of workers), the incentives and social pressures necessary to maintain motivation will be lost. This fact alone tends to confine participation to small units. (For other conditions, see Kochan and Dyer, 1976.)

Thus job redesign and informal participation may well flourish, but neither will be an explicit bargaining issue. Except in special cases (small organizations, national emergencies, or threats of plant shutdown), formal joint participation on job design issues will be confined chiefly to relatively inconsequential matters. I make this prediction somewhat reluctantly because the evidence suggests that under many circumstances labor and management can work together to redesign work and increase productivity—and do so in a manner which will provide lowered costs and increased profits for management, and higher satisfaction through their unions, when workers participate through their unions on the basis of an equality which is lacking in nonunion situations. I would be very happy were union-management QWL experiments to spread. However, this dream is not likely to be realized soon.

References

Andrisani, Paul; Appelbaum, Eileen; Keppel, Rose; and Miljus, Robert. *Work Attitudes and Labor Market Experience*. Philadelphia: Center for Labor and Human Resources Studies, Temple University, 1977.

Barbash, Jack. "Humanizing Work—A New Ideology." *AFL-CIO American Federationist* 84 (July 1977):8-15. Reprinted by permission of the publisher.

Bellas, Carl J. *Industrial Democracy and the Worker Owned Firm*. New York: Praeger, 1972.

Bluestone, Irving. "Comments on Job Enrichment." *Organizational Dynamics* 2 (Winter 1974):46-47. Reprinted by permission of the publisher, © by AMACOM, a division of American Management Associations. All rights reserved.

―――― . "Creating a New World of Work." *International Labour Review* 115 (January 1977):1-10.

Brooks, Thomas R. "Job Satisfaction: An Elusive Goal." *AFL-CIO American Federationist* 79 (October 1972):1-8.

Bureau of National Affairs. *Collective Bargaining Negotiations and Contracts*, no. 805 (April 4, 1976).

Daily Labor Report, March 24, 1977, p. A-8; June 20, 1978, pp. A-7-A-10.

Dowling, W.F., Jr. "Job Redesign on the Assembly Line." *Organizational Dynamics* 2 (Autumn 1973):51-67.

―――― . "At GM: System 4 Builds Performance and Profits." *Organizational Dynamics* 3 (1975):23-38.

Drexler, John A., and Lawler, Edward E., III. "A Union-Management Project to Improve the Quality of Work Life." *Journal of Applied Behavioral Science* 13 (July 1977):373-386.

Driscoll, James W. "Problems of Union-Management Cooperation and the Scanlon Plan Approach." Unpublished manuscript, 1977.

Duckles, Margaret; Duckles, Robert; and Maccoby, Michael. "The Process of Change at Bolivar." *Journal of Applied Behavioral Science* 13 (July 1977):387-399.

Dyer, Lee. "Implications of New Theories of Work for the Design of Compensation Systems." *Proceedings*, 28th Annual Meeting, Industrial Relations Research Association, 1976, pp. 160-167.

Flanagan, Robert; Strauss, George; and Ulman, Lloyd. "Worker Discontent and Work Place Behavior." *Industrial Relations* 12 (May 1974):1-23.

Giles, William F., and Holley, William H. "Job Enrichment Versus Traditional Issues: What Members Want." *Academy of Management Journal* 21 (December 1978):725-730.

Gomberg, William. "Job Satisfaction: Sorting Out the Nonsense." *AFL-CIO American Federationist* 80 (June 1973):14-20.

Goodman, Paul, and Lawler, Edward E., III. *New Forms of Work Organization in the United States*. Geneva: International Labor Organization, 1977.

Hackman, J. Richard. "Work Design." In *Improving Life at Work*, edited by J. Richard Hackman and Lloyd Suttle. Santa Monica, Calif.:Goodyear, 1977.

Haire, Mason; Ghiselli, Edwin E.; and Porter, Lyman W. *Managerial Thinking: An International Study*. New York: John Wiley & Sons, Inc., 1966.

Herzberg, Fredrick. *Work and the Nature of Man*. Cleveland, Ohio: World Publishing, 1966.

Herzberg, Fredrick; Mausner, Bernard; Peterson, R.; and Capwell, Dora. *Job Attitudes: A Review of Research and Opinion*. Pittsburgh: Psychological Service of Pittsburgh, 1957.

Jenkins, David. "The West German Humanization of Work Program." Unpublished manuscript, 1977.

Katzell, Raymond A., and Yankelovich, Daniel. *Work, Productivity, and Job Satisfaction*. New York: Psychological Corporation, 1975.

Kerr, Clark. "Introduction." In *Work in America—The Decade Ahead*, edited by Clark Kerr and Jerome M. Rosow. New York: Van Nostrand Reinhold Company, 1979.

Kirkland, Lane. Quoted in *Daily Labor Report*, May 30, 1978, p. D-2.

Kochan, Thomas; Lipsky, David; and Dyer, Lee. "Collective Bargaining and Quality of Work Life; The Views of Union Activists." *Proceedings*, 27th Annual Meeting, Industrial Relations Research Association, 1975, pp. 150-162.

Kochan, Thomas A., and Dyer, Lee. "A Model for Organizational Change in the Context of Labor-Management Relations." *Journal of Applied Behavioral Science* 12 (January 1976):59-78.

Kochan, Thomas; Dyer, Lee, and Lipsky, David. *The Effectiveness of Union and Management Safety and Health Committees*. Kalamazoo, Mich.: Upjohn Institute, 1977.

Lawler, Edward E., III, and Drexler, John A. "Dynamics of Establishing Cooperative Quality-of-Worklife Projects." *Monthly Labor Review* 101 (March 1978):23-28.

Lelyveld, Joseph. "The Gone Fishing Syndrome." *New York Times Magazine*, May 29, 1977, p. 62.

Nadler, David. "Hospitals, Organized Labor and Quality of Work: An Intervention Case Study." *Journal of Applied Behavioral Science* 14 (September 1978):366-381.

Olson, Mancor. *The Logic of Collective Action.* Cambridge, Mass.: Harvard University Press, 1965.

Osterman, Melvin H. "Productivity Bargaining in New York." *Occasional Paper*, No. 8, New York State School of Industrial and Labor Relations, Cornell University, Ithaca, New York, 1975.

Owen, John D. "Flextime: Some Problems and Solutions." *Industrial and Labor Relations Review* 30 (January 1977):152-160.

Patchin, Martin. "Labor-Management Consultation at TVA: Its Impact on Employees." *Administrative Science Quarterly* 10 (June 1965):149-174.

Patten, Thomas H. "Job Evaluation and Job Enrichment: A Collision Course?" *Human Resources Management* 6 (Winter 1977):2-8.

Perry, Steward. *San Francisco Scavengers: Dirty Work and Pride in Ownership.* Berkeley: University of California Press, 1978.

Ponak, Allan M., and Fraser, C.R.P. "Union Activists' Support for Joint Programs." *Industrial Relations* 18 (Spring 1979):197-209.

Quinn, Robert P.; Staines, Graham L.; and McCullough, Margaret. "Job Satisfaction: Is There a Trend?" U.S. Department of Labor, Manpower Research Monograph No. 30, 1974.

Quinn, Robert P., and Staines, Graham. *The 1977 Quality of Employment Survey.* Ann Arbor: Survey Research Center, University of Michigan, 1978.

Ruh, R.A.; Wallace, R.L.; and Frost, C.F. "Management Attitudes and the Scanlon Plan." *Industrial Relations* 12 (October 1973):282-288.

Salancik, Gerald R., and Pfeffer, Jeffrey. "An Examination of Need-Satisfaction Modes of Job Attitudes." *Administrative Science Quarterly* 22 (September 1977):427-456.

Schrank, Robert. *Ten Thousand Working Days.* Cambridge, Mass.: MIT Press, 1978.

Smith, Frank; Roberts, Karlene; and Hulin, Charles L. "Ten Year Job Satisfaction Trends in a Stable Organization." *Academy of Management Journal* 19 (September 1976):462-468.

Strauss, George. "Job Satisfaction, Motivation, and Job Redesign." In *Organizational Behavior: Research and Issues*, edited by George Strauss et al. Belmont, Calif.: Wadsworth Publishing Co., Inc., 1976.

_____ . "Managerial Practices." In *Improving Life at Work*, edited by J.R. Hackman and Lloyd Suttle. Santa Monica, Calif.: Goodyear Publishing Co., Inc., 1977a.

_____ . "The Study of Conflict: Hope for a New Synthesis between Industrial Relations and Organizational Behavior?" *Proceedings*, 29th Annual Meeting, Industrial Relations Research Association, Madison, Wisconsin, 1977b, pp. 329-337.

Strauss, George, and Sayles, Leonard R. "The Scanlon Plan: Some Organizational Problems." *Human Organization* 16 (Fall 1957):15-22.

Strauss, George, and Rosenstein, Eliezer. "Workers Participation: A Critical View." *Industrial Relations* 9 (February 1970):197-214.

Suttle, J. Lloyd. "Improving Life at Work—Problems and Prospects." In *Improving Life at Work*, edited by J.R. Hackman and J.L. Suttle. Santa Monica, Calif.: Goodyear Publishing Co., Inc., 1977.

Tannenbaum, Arnold; Kavčič, Bogdan; Rosner, Menachem; Vianello, Mino; and Wieser, George. *Hierarchy in Organizations*. San Francisco: Jossey-Bass, Inc., Publishers, 1974.

Tennessee Valley Authority. *The Quality of Work Experiment* 1 (1976).

Terkel, Studs. *Working*. New York: Random House, 1974.

Trist, Eric; Susman, Gerald; and Brown, Grant R. "An Experiment in Autonomous Working in an American Underground Coal Mine." *Human Relations* 30 (1977):201-236.

Ulman, Lloyd; Flanagan, Robert J.; and Strauss, George. *Worker Discontent: Where Is the Problem?* Report to the Ford Foundation, February 1974.

United Automobile Workers. "Summary of Agreement with Ford Motor Company." *Daily Labor Report*, November 5, 1973.

Walfish, Beatrice. "QWL Project at GM Plant Cited as Key to Labor-Management Accord." *World of Work Report* 2 (December 1977):133, 139-140.

Walton, Richard. "Improving the Quality of Work Life." In *The Worker and the Job*, edited by J.M. Rosow. Englewood Cliffs, N.J.: Prentice-Hall, Inc., 1974.

_____ . "Work Innovation at Topeka: After Six Years." *Journal of Applied Behavioral Science* 13 (July 1977):422-433.

Walton, R.D., and McKersie, R.B. *A Behavioral Theory of Labor Negotiations*. New York: McGraw-Hill, 1965.

Wanous, John P., and Lawler, Edward E., III. "Measurement and Meaning of Job Satisfaction." *Journal of Applied Psychology* 56 (April 1972):95-105.

White, J. Kenneth. "The Scanlon Plan: Causes and Correlates to Success." *Academy of Management Journal* 22 (June 1979):292-312.

Whyte, William F. "The Emergence of Employee-Owned Firms in the U.S." *Executive*, Spring 1977.

Winpisinger, William. "The Job Satisfaction Debate—What's Relevant to Labor." Remarks to a conference sponsored by the Institute of Industrial Relations, University of California, Berkeley, 1974.

Work in America. Report of a Special Task Force to the Secretary of Health, Education and Welfare. Cambridge, Mass.: MIT Press, 1973.

Part IV
Labor Relations in Foreign-Owned Firms

The Labor Practices of Foreign-Owned Manufacturing Companies in the United States

6

Michael Jay Jedel

The Characteristics and Impacts of Foreign Investment

Foreign direct investment (defined as direct or indirect ownership of 10 percent of the voting securities of an incorporated business, or an equivalent interest in an unincorporated business) in the United States has grown substantially in the past two decades. Department of Commerce "benchmark" surveys show that the level of investment had quadrupled to $26.5 billion in 1974 from $6.6 billion in 1959 (U.S. Department of Commerce, 1976a, p. 11). Moreover, during the three-year period 1974-1976, the Department of Commerce has informally estimted that foreign investors added $4.4 billion in acquisitions, mergers, and equity increases in U.S. firms (*U.S. Department of Commerce, 1977,* p. 5). In 1977, it is estimated that new capital inflows totaled about $2 billion, and there was every indication that this high and increasing level of foreign investment activity would continue into the 1980s (Ibrakin, 1978).

The 1974 benchmark survey also gives us the following additional characteristics of foreign-owned U.S. subsidiaries:

1. Employment totaled 1,083,000, with about half in manufacturing. Approximately 95 percent of all employees were U.S. citizens (U.S. Department of Commerce, 1976a, p. 20).

2. Overall employment was concentrated in four states: New York, 146,642, or 13.5 percent; California, 104,373, or 9.6 percent; New Jersey, 79,388, or 7.3 percent; and Illinois, 71,380, or 6.6 percent. Manufacturing employment was more diffuse, however. The twelve states in the Southeast accounted for 28.8 percent, the Mid-Atlantic states represented 24.9 percent of the total, and 19.5 percent of the total was found in the Great Lakes area.

3. Total assets of all U.S. affiliates were $174.3 billion (U.S. Department of Commerce, 1976a, p. 19).

4. Nearly one-third of foreign direct investment in the United States was in manufacturing; one-fourth was in petroleum; one-fourth was in finance, insurance, and real estate; and one-sixth was in wholesale trade (U.S.

Department of Commerce, 1976a, p. 21). Interestingly, the relative share of the manufacturing sector two years later was 47.4 percent) U.S. Department of Commerce, 1977, p. 10).

5. The United Kingdom, Canada, and the Netherlands, with about equal shares, accounted for approximately 60 percent of total foreign direct investment in the United States (U.S. Department of Commerce, 1976a, p. 18). Commerce Department data for 1976 reveal that the principal foreign direct investments continue to come from the usual leading source countries which include these three plus Switzerland, France, Belgium, and recent additions West Germany and Japan (U.S. Department of Commerce, 1977, p. 7).

6. Sales of U.S. affiliates totaled $146.8 billion (U.S. Department of Commerce, 1976a, p. 20).

7. Exports of U.S. affiliates were 24 percent of total U.S. exports; imports equaled 30 percent of total U.S. imports (U.S. Department of Commerce, 1976a, p. 19).

Admittedly, the size of the foreign holdings in this country are still small compared to the value of direct U.S. investments abroad—at $137 billion by the end of 1976, outward investment was more than four times as large. However, the recent rapid growth in "reverse foreign investment," accompanied by uncertainties about what impact it might have on the U.S. economy, has led to considerable interest in this phenomenon over the past several years. In addition, the aggregate statistics can also hide important relationships which have been transpiring at the micro level.

Public concern about the increasing presence of foreign direct investment has manifested itself in at least three dimensions: competitive effects, political and social dimensions, and labor practices employed at the U.S. subsidiaries.

Competitive Effects

Concern about the effect on competition in the United States of foreign direct investment can be related to the closer tie between a foreign business and its government. As noted in a 1973 speech on the floor of the House of Representatives,

> if, as in the past . . . foreign owned business gets a subsidy from its government, it is not fair and open competition. Able to sustain losses indefinitely, that company can undersell the American company, and eventually, force it to close shop. With the competition out of the way, the foreign owned plant controls the market and can peg the price of its product as high as it wants. (U.S. Congress, 1974)

Managers at U.S.-owned firms also may be concerned about the unique capabilities which could be generated at the parent level because of its greater worldwide resources, and then implemented at the U.S. affiliate. Such a transfer might well be viewed as an unfair competitive edge. In addition, innovations in management and employment practices could tip the scales in favor of the non-U.S.-owned enterprise. A study supported by the National Commission on Productivity on the impact of transplanted Japanese management practices on productivity concluded that, in many instances, Japanese companies in the United States "are outperforming American companies in the same industries" (Johnson and Ouchi, 1974, p. 61).

Political and Social Effects

Foreign direct investment has had important political and social consequences. In one case, growing Japanese investment in Hawaii caused local concern. Foreign purchases of Alaskan timberland and other lands on the West Coast were challenged by some as jeopardizing the national interest in controlling inflation, the environment, and employment (Culver, 1974, pp. 157-158). Direct investment by Communist countries, such as Rumania's $50 million joint venture with Occidental Petroleum in Virginia, concerned a large number of Americans (*Wall Street Journal*, July 3, 1975). That this Rumanian investment was to be in a high-grade coal mine, a portion of the output of which was to be used by Rumania for steel production, certainly underscored the potential significance and political sensitivity of the venture. Also, investment in the United States by Arab countries aroused considerable attention, and in some quarters outright opposition. This, of course, was in response to the Arab countries' blacklisting of firms doing business in Israel (*Wall Street Journal*, June 25, 1976), and discrimination against Jewish managers and other employees in Arab-owned subsidiaries (*Wall Street Journal*, March 5, 1975).

Labor Practices

Numerous concerns about the kinds of management, employment, and industrial relations practices foreign investors might bring with them also surfaced in the early 1970s. Hearings in 1974 of the House Committee on Foreign Affairs, Subcommittee on Foreign Economic Policy, revealed

> concern that foreign management will not adapt to U.S. labor practices
> and needs and might be more likely [than a U.S.-owned firm] to close shop
> if business becomes bad. (U.S. Congress, July 7, 1974)

Similarly, the director of the U.S. Federal Mediation and Conciliation Service reportedly questioned whether foreign investors will insist on bringing their own management practices—forged under entirely different labor-management climates—to U.S. bargaining tables and whether American managements of foreign-owned plants will be influenced by the industrial relations policies of the owner's home country. (*Business Week*, September 29, 1973)

Indications were that foreign management practices would affect the spectrum of U.S. union-management relations. For example, it was claimed that the Georgetown Steel Company in South Carolina, a subsidiary of German Korf Industries, had "embarked on a bitter campaign to resist union organization." In another instance, Sony Corporation had stated that there would be no layoffs at its U.S. plant in San Diego, a practice not uncommon in the Japanese home of the parent, but atypical of the industrial experience in the United States. According to another report, the International Association of Machinists and Aerospace Workers was "upset by Japanese plants . . . in California, because the Americans [employed there] are getting lesser skilled work while the Japanese retain the skilled jobs at home." In addition, there was concern that Japanese nationals in managerial positions at the U.S. subsidiaries might prefer grievances to be presented as group charges because of Japanese interest in face-saving, which is not the usual way grievances are administered in the United States (*Business Week*, September 29, 1973). Finally, the United Steelworkers was concerned about possible employment consequences after Imetal, a French company, purchased a controlling interest in Copperweld Corporation. At its 1975 convention, the AFL-CIO reacted to these events by adopting a resolution which expressed the Federation's strong disapproval of the "unregulated takeover of the United States firms by foreign interests" (AFL-CIO, 1976).

The U.S. Government's Reaction

Congress, too, was concerned with the growing presence of foreign investment. A number of bills were introduced which were intended to regulate the incidence or operations of direct foreign investors. One 1975 bill would have required thirty days' advance notice to the U.S. government by any prospective foreign investor which sought 5 percent or more of the stock of an American corporation, and would have limited foreign ownership to 5 percent if the investor participated in the Arab boycott (*Wall Street Journal*, March 5, 1975). During hearings on this and the other foreign investment bills by the House Committee on Foreign Affairs, Subcommittee on Foreign Economic Policy, it became apparent that there was not a great deal known about the actual operations and practices of foreign investors in the United States. To remedy this deficiency and preclude the dangers of either enacting inappropriate public policies, or not responding with proper political initiative, the Foreign Investment Study Act of 1974 was passed by the Congress. It directed

> the Executive to undertake a comprehensive survey and analysis of foreign investment in the United States and to report the findings and recommendations to the Congress. (U.S. Congress, July 7, 1974, p. v).

As might be evident from the earlier discussion, the management and labor practices of foreign direct investors, which had been a major area of interest to Congress, became the subject of this study.

Initial Studies of Labor Relations Practices, 1974-1978

Cited below are findings from two studies of labor relations in foreign-owned firms: one, a study of 100 foreign-owned firms conducted on behalf of the Department of Commerce in 1975-1976; the other, a study of ninety-one firms in 1974 (which I conducted with Duane Kujawa as reported in Jedel and Kujawa, 1974, 1976, 1977, and hereafter cited as J-K, 197-). Readers are referred to the original studies for descriptions of the samples with respect to the nationality of the parent company, geographic location, unionized status, industrial identification, and size. It should be noted here that 38 percent of the firms in the Commerce Department study and 64 percent of the firms in the J-K study was unionized. In another section, findings from more recent studies are reviewed.

"Labor practices," as they were examined in these studies, fall into four areas: union recognition, collective bargaining negotiations, labor contract administration, and personnel administration practices.

Union Recognition

Three aspects of union recognition are of interest: the extent to which recognition of a labor union affects the firm's location in the United States; whether foreign or domestic personnel determine the U.S. subsidiary's response to the possibility of unionization; and the practices which the firm adopts toward union organizing.

The likelihood that part or all of the work force will be unionized has not been a major factor in foreign investors' location decisions. In fact, of greater significance, Canadian and European parent managers are generally indifferent to unionism. Although attitudes of foreign-owned subsidiary managers reveal a preference to operate without a union, the strength of this response was found to be no different from that expressed by managers at U.S.-owned firms (J-K, 1977, p. 74). The decision to undertake direct investment in the United States is one of long-term strategic importance, made only after a detailed, careful analysis of market potential, economic conditions and trends, and political environment. In this context, labor relations is viewed as a subject for accomodation rather than as one of strategic significance.

Japanese investors tend to place importance on remaining nonunion if possible, since they feel unionization might impede their greater interest in adapting traditionally successful home country employment practices to their U.S. operations. In at least two known instances, Japanese investors considered the likelihood of avoiding unionization a major factor in their location decision (J-K, 1976, p. 35).

Overall, however, the prospect of a firm's having to recognize and bargain collectively with a labor union is not a major determinant of location. In fact, in a great majority of cases where the foreign investor entered the U.S. market by acquiring a firm, the acquisition was undertaken with full acceptance that some or all of the work force was already represented by a labor union. Similarly, the presence or absence of state "right-to-work" laws is not an active independent variable in the firm's location decision, despite the continuing claims by proponents of such laws that they are (J-K, 1976, p. 14).

Once the specific geographical location for the foreign-owned firm's manufacturing operations has been determined, managers from the subsidiary assume responsibility for responding to the prospects of unionization. Parent company involvement, it was found, was minimal, irrespective of nationality. Foreign investors recognize the uniqueness of the U.S. industrial relations system and leave to subsidiary management the formulation of the appropriate action. Where a foreign national heads up the "industrial relations" function, it is most likely to be in a nonunion firm not faced with possible unionization. As unionization becomes a prospect for these companies, the labor relations response will probably be turned over to an in-house U.S. national, or contracted out. Thus, for example, when one Japanese-owned firm, which desired to remain nonunion and whose industrial relations was headed by a Japanese national, was faced with a union organizing drive, local management decided to retain the services of a law firm especially skilled and renowned in opposing such union campaigns (J-K, 1976, p. 35).

In certain circumstances, foreign nationals at the U.S. subsidiary do get involved in the question of union recognition. This is particularly true in Japanese firms for reasons already noted and also because of the greater incidence of Japanese nationals among the top management of the U.S. subsidiary. Also, in smaller firms, foreign nationals at the subsidiary level may influence the firm's response to union recognition; this is especially true where the foreign national in a line position is called upon to play an expanded industrial relations role in the absence of any formal industrial relations position.

In one smaller company, for example, Japanese nationals at the subsidiary level were asked to play a more substantial role in the future, despite the apparent success of a U.S. employee in directing the company's response to a union organizing campaign. According to a Japanese employee of the firm,

> originally we tried to get Americanized here. . .in personnel and in all other aspects. . . . We might have been too sensitive about U.S. personnel practices originally. Now, since the second union attempt, we feel we have found people the same regardless of nationality. . .what we believe right can be effective. . . . We felt uncomfortable in adopting [the parent company's] personnel practices because they were Japanese, not American. . .but now we have more confidence. . .we viewed American practice as very business-like. . .you meet that requirement or that's the end. . .not important for the supervisor to know the worker and his family. . . . We hesitated emphasizing the need to get to know people better to improve performance. Now we have more confidence that the family concept is the right thing to do. . . . We expect it will take some time. . . . We just launched a recreation committee. . .to come up with a comprehensive recreational activity package to cover everyone in the company. . . . This is a major attempt to increase ties to the company and avoid unionization. (Jedel, 1975)

Finally, there is the conduct of the foreign investors when faced with union organizing campaigns. Here the evidence is clear that the approach of U.S. nationals in the subsidiary is comparable to that which the union would find at a U.S.-owned firm in the same industry and geographical location. Management seeks to remain nonunion, if legally possible, but prefers to adhere to applicable U.S. labor laws rather than take the stance of avoiding unions at all costs. Similarly, there is little likelihood that the firm will demonstrate favored treatment to a "more desirable" union (J-K, 1976, p. 15). Thus with respect to the union recognition practices and policy, the initial studies show almost no importation of alien labor practices.

Collective Bargaining Negotiations

Once a union has been certified, responsibility for the conduct of collective bargaining negotiations resides with management of the subsidiary. The parent does not influence the firm's decision on whether to join an employer association, does not determine the negotiating team, has not been found to express any interest in whether multiplant subsidiaries negotiate particular issues locally or at the national company level, does not normally require the subsidiary to report the union's initial demand, or the management's responses, and offers no research support in preparation for or the handling of contract negotiations (J-K, 1976, pp. 35-38).

The foreign owner generally is alerted when a strike is threatened so that it may take notice of possible financial and operational impacts. Parent management does not participate in resolving the dispute.

It has been suggested that foreign-owned firms have a greater ability to withstand a strike. To the contrary, these companies had a low potential for switching production for the strike's duration from the struck U.S. subsidiary to another subsidiary of the foreign parent (J-K, 1976, p. 39). Furthermore, because foreign-owned U.S. subsidiaries are on average more intensive exporters than U.S.-owned companies (U.S. Department of Commerce, 1976a, p. 19), unions derive additional leverage from the fact that a strike at the U.S. subsidiary can impact negatively upon the multinational's performance in other markets also (Kujawa, 1977, p. 17). Almost half of the foreign-owned firms examined in one study (J-K, 1977, p. 59) received supplies, components, or subassemblies from units outside the United States.

Turning to the conduct of collective bargaining by U.S. subsidiaries, the pattern uncovered appears indistinguishable from what would be found in a similar set of U.S.-owned firms matched by factors such as size, plant location, industrial classification, age of operation, and nature and incidence of unionization. Thus, where firms in a particular industry and geographical setting practice employer association bargaining, the foreign-owned firm adheres to that pattern. Where the size of the firm suggests independence from an employer association, the firm in its preparations for bargaining follows closely the industry pattern established by the association of larger employers. Decisions by multiplant foreign-owned subsidiaries about national and/or local issue bargaining also are made at the U.S. subsidiary level based on individual situations, not nationality of ownership (J-K, 1976, p. 17).

The composition of the bargaining team also follows a pattern more customary in the United States than in Europe. Thus, in the United States, in a single plant facility, one would expect to find the company's chief labor relations offical charged with principal responsibility, while local labor relations officers and plant managers handle this chore in multiplant operations. This pattern is consistent irrespective of nationality of foreign parent (see also J-K, 1977, pp. 54-79).

Labor Contract Administration

An early examination of typical contract clauses in the collective bargaining agreements of the U.S. subsidiaries of foreign-owned manufacturing firms compared to those of U.S.-owned manufacturing firms showed the subjects cited [namely, seniority, grievance process, dues checkoff, management rights, overtime, union security, discipline, subcontracting] generally appear at least as frequently in the union contracts of the foreign-owned U.S. firms as they do in domestic companies. Because arbitration of rights is primarily a U.S. phenomenon, the disparity with respect to its inclusion is not surprising. Grievance arbitration simply may not yet have been introduced in these foreign-owned firms.

Also of interest is the relative frequency with which the no strike-no lockout and grievance arbitration clauses appear in the same contract. In U.S. industrial relations practices, they are well-established quid pro quos. Not so in foreign-owned firms. In only twenty-two of the thirty-five contracts (62.9%) did both clauses appear. The relative labor peace to which U.S. firms have become accustomed while contracts are in effect may not be as widespread in these foreign-owned firms. It is likely, however, that the U.S. industrial relations approach will predominate and the relative frequency of these two clauses in contracts soon will conform to the American experience. (J-K, 1977, p. 62)

Subsequently it was found that the incidence of arbitration and no strike/no lockout clauses in the contracts of foreign-owned firms did indeed conform to the U.S. pattern regardless of nationality of ownership.

Contract language on disciplinary practices, incidence of work rules, and layoff procedures were comparable in foreign-owned and domestic firms except for the Japanese-owned companies. Unionized firms have written disciplinary practices, work rules, and layoff procedures in a codified form. Almost all unionized firms, which have layoff procedures set forth in their collective bargaining agreements, rely on seniority as the basis for deciding among production workers.

Overall, management in the foreign-owned firm wishes to eliminate the need for layoffs to forestall this requirement. Workers at these firms also have been found to recognize this, as they feel at least as secure, or in many cases even more job secure, at their foreign-owned employer than they did when the same firm was owned by U.S. interests, or when they worked at some other U.S.-owned company. Employees at Japanese-owned companies hold these feelings the most strongly (J-K, 1976, p. 56). However, when conditions finally warrant, the foreign-owned firm will resort to layoffs (whether unionized or not). Any expectation that a more paternalistic attitude by European or Japanese investors might result in fewer layoffs in the United States is not borne out by the facts (J-K, 1976, p. 21). Only among Japanese-owned firms might it seem that this judgment bears additional scrutiny. Thus, with respect to the area of contract administration, the labor practices of the foreign-owned manufacturer parallel those of the U.S. employer.

Personnel Administration Practices

The last area of inquiry concerns employment and personnel practices of the foreign owner. Here again it has been found that "management and employment practices of foreign investors in the United States [are] more similar to traditional U.S. practices thatn dissimilar. . . ." Where there are differences, the most important area is that of the level of benefits, "where foreign-ownership coincide(s) with improved employee benefits in over one-fourth of the [cases examined]. . ." (J-K, 1976, p. iii). Thus, hiring policies and procedures are comparable to U.S. practices for firms of similar size. Smaller firms with limited personnel resources entrust a more active role to line managers. Larger, multiplant operations have more extensive functions, and plant personnel assist line managers. Single-plant operations near a headquarters personnel department utilize the corporate officials. This pattern holds irrespective of nationality or industry (J-K, 1976, pp. 31-32). Similarly, wage and salary levels and payment methods are determined by examining the same local market competitive factors as that of a U.S. firm, and are at least competitive (J-K, 1976, pp. 24-25).

Employee benefits, however, are worthy of note. It has been suggested that certain foreign investors would be more receptive to innovations than other foreign or U.S.-owned companies, that the nature of innovation in benefits may vary with nationality of the foreign investor, and that some investors may be quite innovative indeed (J-K, 1974, pp. 13, 15). Innovations in benefits appear to be associated with one or more of three attributes: transference of liberal practices from the home country to the U.S. subsidiary (to attain worldwide consistency, for example); greater financial stability of the U.S.-owned firm after acquisition by a foreign investor; and the presence of a U.S. national serving as the personnel manager who senses a greater willingness by the non-U.S. owners to accept improved or innovative benefits (J-K, 1976, pp. 28-29).

Innovations in benefits tend to be positive improvements beneficial to the employees. This probably stems from the need of foreign owners to compete successfully in the mature U.S. market as a precondition to success elsewhere, as Graham and others have explained. A loyal, motivated work force is necessary for that success. When combined with the more heightened social concerns of foreign owners (especially those from Britain, France, Germany, Holland, Japan, and Sweden) and the wealth of foreign investors, it is understandable how employee benefits in foreign-owned companies are at least as substantial as the average for all U.S. companies.

More Recent Findings

In one study, Ricks and Campagna (1978) examined employment levels and layoff patterns of foreign-owned firms in the United States during a recent economic recession. More than 80 percent of their respondents were in manufacturing. Their principal findings were that in durables and nondurables as well as in all major manufacturing sectors (chemicals, primary and fabricated metals, industrial and electrical machinery) the employment levels and layoff rates of foreign-owned firms were similar to the U.S. average. This finding, they believe, runs counter to the rather popularly held belief that foreign firms in the United States have a more stable employment record.

Overall, Ricks and Campagna conclude that there is growing evidence that foreign-owned firms in the United States behave much like their local counterparts and seem as willing as the rest of the firms to lay off employees during both good and bad economic times (Ricks and Campagna, 1978, p. 79).

In another study, Ryan (1978) examined certain managerial and employment practices in detail at the three largest Japanese-owned manufacturing firms in the United States. Ryan's findings given broad support to earlier findings of Jedel and Kujawa regarding Japanese firms. The control of the parent organization over the subsidiary is judged to be relatively loose, but still provides for substantial influence. Among the unionized Japanese-owned firms, Ryan found that managers would rather not have to deal with unions. In the study, Japanese firms also were reluctant to lay off employees during periods of economic downturn. This,he believes, is evidence of a stronger commitment than found earlier to achieve Japanese-style job security for workers in these foreign-owned plants. Finally, Ryan found no evidence that Japanese subsidiaries in the U.S. introduced Japanese-type reward systems across the board; however, elements of the Japanese system crept in here and there.

Also of note are the conclusions of another recently published study (1977) undertaken for the Organization for Economic Co-operation and Development (OECD), conducted to examine the industrial relations and related employment impacts of foreign multinationals in seven industrialized nations, including the United States. The study concludes in its relevant part:

> There is a trend to much greater conformity to national situations by these enterprises than in the past. There are, of course, different degrees in this conformity and this is influenced by the extent to which a host country imposes legal obligations concerning labour-management relations. Where these are based more on customs than legislation, the possibility is open to these enterprises to introduce their own policies and practices largely inspired by home-country systems. This is also true of their affiliation. . .to employer associations and corresponding conformity to the level of collective bargaining customary within a particular country. Thus, there is less variation in their behaviors as compared with that of domestic enterprises in those countries where there is detailed legislation covering industrial relations. . . . On the question of comparability of wages and salaries with those paid by domestic employers, it would appear that multinational enterprises tend to adapt to the local situation, but sometimes offer better

remuneration. As regards working conditions, these appear to be similar to
or sometimes more favourable than those of local employers. (Morgan and
Blanpain, 1977, pp. 39-40)

Discernible Trends

What direction will the labor practices of foreign-owned manufacturing
companies in the United States in the 1980s be likely to take? And what
developments will prove to be the most significant causal factors?

At the time of this writing the more important events likely to shape the
future are developments in the legal area and in the employment sphere.
The increasing importance of legal parameters in U.S. labor-management
relations, even if labor law reform is ultimately thwarted, and the costs of
noncompliance with the law of job discrimination, safety and health, or
pensions and retirement plans should reinforce the reliance of foreign
owners on U.S. nationals for subsidiary management in labor relations matters.

Even more likely to occur is an increased concern in the workplace on
issues such as employment and income security. The reasons are clear.
Evidence is mounting that projected labor force growth in the 1980s will
greatly outstrip the increases in employment opportunities, leading to what
one top AFL-CIO researcher has referred to as "zero employment growth"
(Jager, 1978). With the U.S. Department of Labor recently revising upward
its estimates on average annual growth in the U.S. labor force, but without
corresponding upward revisions in anticipated job opportunities, one can
expect the already employed to voice their security fears clearly. The growing movement by key union leaders to make the shortened work week a major bargaining issue in 1979 as a way to open up more jobs is additional
evidence of this concern (Townsend, 1978).

Management also is being urged in some quarters to explore what for
U.S. labor-management relations would be largely new relationships. Thus
a top official of a prestigious management consulting firm wrote, in a
publication read widely by corporate heads and other decision-makers, that
U.S. management must now begin to learn from the experience of European managers that new forms of labor-management cooperation are essential for future success. He urges U.S. managers seriously to explore
guaranteed employment security for all employees, experiments in
employee-management cooperation, and labor involvement in resolving
problems related to broad national employment issues (McIsaac, 1977).

If employees will indeed desire more security, then in the 1980s one
might expect to find more attention to innovative personnel practices by
U.S. and foreign-owned firms alike. Accordingly, there would be ever
greater similarity in style, with differences explainable more and more by
characteristics such as size, location, age of enterprise, industry, profit

ability, and the like, and less and less by whether the enterprise were foreign-owned or U.S.-owned.

In conclusion, the labor practices of foreign-owned manufacturers in the United States are expected to come even more like those of U.S.-owned firms. Where union-management matters are involved, the unique U.S. industrial relations system and the substantial, perhaps ever increasing, need to understand the legal parameters, require indigenous leadership. With respect to employment and personnel practices more generally, the evidence seems to suggest a growing recognition on the part of U.S. firms that they might also adopt some of the more innovative practices foreign investors have brought into the United States. Only Japanese-owned firms seem to have unique practices attributable primarily to parent nationality (*Atlanta Constitution*, January 15, 1978). There, too, though, it may simply be a matter of a longer time dimension before convergence occurs. If, as has been suggested (*Wall Street Journal*, December 21, 1977), economic conditions in Japan cause unique labor and employment traditions to fade in the homeland, it is likely that they also will be transferred to their subsidiaries less and less over time.

References

AFL-CIO, *AFL-CIO Platform Proposals*. Washington, D.C.: AFL-CIO, 1976. p. 31.

Arpan, Jeffrey S. "Foreign Manufacturing Firms in the U.S.: A Study of Their Impact on Three Small Southern Communities." *Atlanta Economic Review* 24 (March-April 1974).

Culver, John C. "Foreign Investment in the United States." *Foreign Policy*, 16 (Fall 1974):157.

"Economic Woes Spur Firms in Japan to Alter Lifetime Job Security." *Wall Street Journal* (Eastern Edition), December 21, 1977.

"Foreign Capital, a Key to Rise of Early U.S., Now Stirs Misgivings." *Wall Street Journal* (Eastern Edition), March 5, 1975.

"How Arab Countries Are Trying to Punish Firms Helping Israel." *Wall Street Journal* (Eastern Edition), June 25, 1976.

Ibrakin, Youssef M. "The Foreign Invasion of the U.S. Economy." *New York Times* National and Economic Survey, January 8, 1978.

Jager, Elizabeth. Telephone conversation. Washington, D.C.: Research Department, AFL-CIO, June 5, 1978.

Jedel, Michael Jay. Unpublished interview with Japanese national in U.S.-owned firm, 1975.

Jedel, Michael Jay, and Kujawa, Duane. "Industrial Relations Profiles of Foreign-Owned Manufacturers in the United States." In *Multinationals, Unions, and Labor Relations in Industrialized Countries,* edited by Robert F. Banks and Jack Stieber. Ithaca, N.Y.: Cornell University, New York State School of Industrial and Labor Relations, Publications Division, 1977.

_____ . "Innovations in Industrial Relations of Foreign Direct Investors in the U.S.: An Empirical Study of the Manufacturing Sector." Paper presented at the Annual Meeting of Academy of International Business, San Francisco, December 29, 1974.

_____ . "Management and Employment Practices of Foreign Direct Investors in the United States." In U.S. Department of Commerce, *Foreign Direct Investment in the United States: Report to the Congress*, vol. 5, Appendix 1. Washington, D.C.: U.S. Government Printing Office, 1976.

Johnson, Richard Tanner, and William G. Ouchi. "Made in America (under Japanese Management)." *Harvard Business Review* 52 (September-October 1974).

Kujawa, Duane. "The Labor Relations of U.S. Multinationals Abroad: Comparative and Prospective Views." Paper presented at the Conference on Contemporary International Labor Problems, Madison, Wisconsin, December 1-2, 1977.

McIsaac, George S. "What's Coming in Labor Relations?" *Harvard Business Review* 55 (September-October 1977).

Morgan, Alun, and Blanpain, Roger. *The Industrial Relations and Employment Impacts of Multinational Enterprises: An Inquiry into the Issues*. Paris: Organisation for Economic Co-Operation and Development, 1977.

"New Labor Force Projections to 1990." *Monthly Labor Review*, December 1976.

"New Plans to Monitor Foreign Investment in U.S. Are Outlined by Administration." *Wall Street Journal* (Eastern Edition), March 5, 1975.

"Occidental Sets a Coal Venture with Rumania." *Wall Street Journal* (Eastern Edition), July 3, 1975.

Ricks, David A., and Campagna, Anthony. "Job Security in the Foreign-Owned Firm." *Business Horizons*, February 1978.

"Rising Sun." *Atlanta Constitution*, January 15, 1978.

Ryan, Robert J. "The Great Japanese Factory Controversy—The American Box Score." U.S. Department of State Executive Seminar in National and International Affairs, Twentieth Session, 1977-1978.

Townsend, Ed. "Unions Ready to Push for Four-Day Workweek." *Atlanta Journal and Constitution*, May 14, 1978.

U.S. Congress, House of Representatives, Committee on Foreign Affairs. *Direct Foreign Investment in the United States*. A Report of the Subcommittee on Foreign Economic Policy, 93d Congress, 2nd session, July 7, 1974.

U.S. Congress, House of Representatives, Committee on Foreign Affairs. *Foreign Investment in the United States*. Hearings before the Subcommittee on Foreign Economic Policy, 93d Congress, 2nd session, 1974.

U.S. Department of Commerce. *Foreign Direct Investment in the United States, Vol. 2, Report of the Secretary of Commerce: Benchmark Survey, 1974*, April 1976a.

U.S. Department of Commerce. *Foreign Direct Investment in the United States, Vol. 1, Report of the Secretary of Commerce to the Congress*, April 1976b.

U.S. Department of Commerce, Office of Foreign Investment in the United States. *Foreign Direct Investment in the United States: 1976 Transactions—All Forms; 1974-76 Acquisitions, Mergers and Equity Increases*, December 1977.

U.S. Department of Labor. "The U.S. Labor Force: Projections to 1990." Special Labor Force Report 156, U.S. Department of Labor Bureau of Labor Statistics, July 1973.

"Wary About Importing Foreign Work Rules." *Business Week*. Reprinted from the September 29, 1973 issue of *Business Week* by special permission, © 1973 by McGraw-Hill, Inc., New York, N.Y. 10020. All rights reserved.

Comment

Joseph A. Tierney

There is not a great deal to say in disagreement with Mike Jedel's chapter. It may be interesting, though, to look at some of Jedel's conclusions in light of the experiences of one foreign-owned company—Michelin.

With regard to the role of unionization as a factor in geographic location, Michelin is an exception, along with some Japanese companies cited in Jedel's chapter. Michelin is nonunion and wishes to remain so. We are firmly convinced that unions have nothing to offer either the company or its employees. We view the adversary nature of union-management relations as not only unnecessary but destructive to the teamwork so important to the building of radial tires according to the stringent quality standards required for success. Thus to some extent the location of Michelin plants in the South does reflect its position. We are also impressed with the industriousness and independent attitude of the southern worker. The atmosphere of nondependence on unions and teamwork, the ability to take or give criticism constructively without rancor, and the willingness to work as expressed by right-to-work laws in southern states are all definitely factors in our decision to locate in the South.

Jedel also sought to determine whether the parent sets policy with respect to union recognition. Again I would say that Michelin is an exception to the weight of the statistics. While the owners do not set out in writing "thou shalt" or "shalt not," the "Michelin Spirit of Excellence" precludes accepting a work force divided into adversary camps of union and management. This Michelin spirit and its emphasis on human dignity comes through in our work orientation programs, our grievance procedure, and our uncommon nonhierarchical organizational structure. In terms of labor relations attitudes, I was born and raised in the United States, but I have learned to understand the Michelin approach and have come to believe in it. The study of and participation in this system have caused me to accept and internalize these values.

As a result of Michelin's being unique relative to the pattern of attitudes toward unionization Jedel describes, we have a different layoff policy as well. According to Jedel, foreign-owned companies will lay off just as quickly as their domestically-owned counterparts in the same industry under the same circumstances. There are very few American or European companies of Michelin's size who can claim, as we can, a record of virtually no layoffs since World War II and probably even before then. The only layoffs at Michelin of which I am aware have been in the United Kingdom, and those for short periods in limited instances due to the direct impact of wildcat strikes. The very suggestion of a layoff is repugnant to Michelin, because we believe in the concept of teamwork and the traditional employee-stockholder partnerships. Layoffs are to be avoided in every way possible.

The maintenance of a productive, goal-oriented work force is essential to this no-layoff philosophy. Such a work force permits us to react quickly in case of emergencies, sudden market shifts, possible changes in product requirements, and to do so in the most fair and equitable fashion for all concerned. A union and the resulting adversary relationship, we feel, would seriously jeopardize if not destroy our capability to make that no-layoff policy a reality.

On the economic side, a no-layoff philosophy is good business. It maintains economic stability, cuts training costs arising out of turnover, and increases the experience of the work force. We also feel that it increases the capabilities of the work force to adjust to change.

So while I find little with which to disagree in Jedel's chapter, I do feel that it is useful to point out how the Michelin experience is unique relative to the picture he paints.

**Part V
The Search for
New Leverage**

7 Unions and Politics

Michael J. Piore

In recent years American unions have tended to appeal to their constituencies in the workplace on the basis of the constituents' narrow and particularistic interests. In the political process, the unions' appeal to their constituents and likely political allies has been equally narrow and particularistic. In this, they seem to be operating as "business unions" as that term is understood by the Wisconsin School of labor relations and its successors (including the bulk of American industrial relations professionals). This chapter takes issue with that approach. It attempts to argue that particularism or business unionism is not in the long-run interests of the American labor movement and its constituents. It probably does not succeed in sustaining the strongest version of that argument, but it does show that, as a strategic approach to the problem of labor in American society, business unionism has major drawbacks which scholars of American labor relations have failed to recognize. These drawbacks call for a serious reevaluation of the political tradition and current strategy of organized labor in the United States.

For the argument which follows, the essential characteristic of business unionism is the effort to appeal to workers on narrow, particularistic grounds, eschewing any claim to represent interests outside immediate work needs. As such, business unionism is distinguished from more general appeals to workers as consumers, citizens, members of a broader social class, or members of an ethnic or racial grouping. The distinction between the narrow and particular on the one hand and the broad and the general on the other, as well as the notion that the two appeals are necessarily competitive alternatives, are themselves characteristic of business unionism as a way of thinking about worker organization.

A second characteristic of business unionism is a sharp distinction between "economic" and "political" activity. By economic activity is meant the exercise of economic pressure upon employers through direct job action at the workplace. This is generally contrasted to the pursuit of goals through pressures upon governmental bodies. The way in which this distinction is drawn makes it possible in principle to pursue different strategies in the economic and the political spheres, but, as will be argued below, the American labor movement has tended to take an equally narrow and particularistic approach to both types of activity. This is undoubtedly no accident and indeed the political strategy is as explicit in the writings of Commons, Gompers, and Perlman as the economic strategy.

Two other characteristics of business unions are relevant to the analysis, although not central to the argument. The first is a tendency for business unionism to define itself in opposition to philosophies and ideologies, such as socialism or communism, in which issues of work and the economy are seen in terms of a transformative vision of the socioeconomic system. The second aspect of business unionism which is relevant is an extreme distrust of "intellectuals." Sometimes this is an extension of the opposition to communism and socialism, but often it seems to border on generalized anti-intellectualism.

The Strategic Problems of American Labor

In the post-World War II period, business unionism's political strategy has been a relationship between organized labor and other groups built upon tactical alliances for specific issues of common interest, leaving the members of these alliances still free to disagree on other issues. For example, the unions have allied themselves with black organizations on issues of national economic policy but opposed these same organizations on certain aspects of equal employment opportunity legislation and on leadership issues within the Democratic party. In this process, organized labor has defined itself and presented itself to the world as a special interest group. I mean to use that term in a neutral sense, but its pejorative connotations are symptomatic of the difficulties which the strategy creates for labor in the political process. By presenting itself as a special interest group, labor invites other parties to react toward itself solely in terms of their own special interests. Additionally, this special interest strategy motivates other special interests to ally themselves with the labor movement in the most narrow and particularistic terms. It is not clear, however, that all of these narrowly defined issues of interest to the labor movement are capable of pulling together a majority coalition. In some of the most critical political battles which labor faces, only a more broadly based coalition is likely to prevail.

The Politics of Union Rights

The union's approach to politics is perhaps most obvious in terms of the political protection of the right to organize. A particularistic appeal made sense prior to the 1930s when the American labor movement was dominated by craft unions which survived through reliance upon the natural skill monopoly of the membership. Organization and bargaining under these circumstances depended almost exclusively upon the ability of the union to convince the workers directly involved that it was in their interest to act together. The philosophy of business unionism within the labor movement and the academic foundations of that philosophy in the universities date from this relatively early period of American labor history.

Since the 1930s, however, the labor movement has come increasingly to be composed of industrial unions whose existence and survival are predicated upon governmental protection. That protection is provided through specific legislation supplemented by a network of administration and judicial regulation. The resultant protective framework has not eliminated the need for unions to win the adherence of the members of the bargaining unit through appeal to particularistic work-oriented issues, but an appeal to the constituency in the shop is no longer enough. Unions must also make an appeal to an electorate at large which is broad enough to protect the legislative framework from amendment or repeal, and to sustain it as it is molded by administrative and judicial interpretation. The danger is that if unions appeal too narrowly in organizing and bargaining to the immediate and particularistic interests of their membership (actual or potential), they will not provide a justification which is broad enough to attract and maintain the larger political consensus upon which their continued existence depends.

The political problem is not a simple one. It is not always necessary to appeal to a majority of the electorate. To the extent that it is possible for one or another interest group to win out through the concentration of electoral strength and financial resources upon particular candidates because an issue did not arouse broad interest, the maintenance of political support may be quite compatible with a narrow appeal to the union's immediate constituency. On the other hand, the judicial bodies, which are the ultimate arbitrators of any legislative framework, very often make their decisions in terms of some notion of the public interest which may be much wider than that which was mobilized when the legislation was passed in the first place.

While it is not obvious that the particularistic appeal of the American labor movement has been an unsuccessful political strategy, even for industrial unionism, one can be concerned about the future viability of that appeal. The current legislative framework is a product of that period (the 1930s) when the American electorate tended to identify with the working class and to see a harmony of interest between workers and American society. It was also a period in which the appeal of the labor movement, phrased in terms of worker solidarity, was attractive beyond the worksites being organized.

However, the legislative protection obtained in the 1930s has gradually been eroded in subsequent years by Taft-Hartley, Landrum-Griffin, and a series of court decisions (McAdams, 1964). The success of the particularistic strategy in formulating legislation in the 1930s led to its continual use in protecting the legislative framework against erosion through efforts to abolish or amend it.

The weakness of this strategy was most apparent in the battle over Landrum-Griffin. The momentum for that legislation was generated by a series of public hearings which produced a widespread popular reaction so strong that it made antiunion legislation inevitable at the very time when union strength was larger than at any time in the post-war period, if judged by the number of congressmen indebted to the labor movement for campaign and electoral support. The legislation which ultimately emerged was nowhere near as bad as the leaders had feared in the heat of the battle, and the particularistic strategy was no doubt responsible for that fact. However, this should not be allowed to obscure the fact that there was indeed legislation.

The episode clearly illustrated the vulnerability of the particularistic strategy to an attack mounted on more general moral, political, and ideological grounds (in the best sense of these terms). It also indicated just how widespread among the American electorate is the belief that unions are in conflict with the general interest. Certainly one could question after Landrum-Griffin whether the particularistic strategy has been a more successful defense of the legislative framework than a broader ideological appeal would have been. And if the efficacy of the particularistic appeal as a defense strategy is questioned, it clearly can claim little success in extending legislative protection. Witness the defeat of the situs picketing legislation in 1977, or the fact that more comprehensive labor law reform legislation experienced a similar fate in 1978.

The Politics of Substantive Legislation

In addition to its concerns with the legislation governing the procedures of union organization and collective bargaining, organized labor has had a number of substantive political concerns as well. These have ranged from broad economic policy to narrower issues such as minimum wage, equal employment opportunity, and environmental and consumer protection.

On substantive legislation, it can be argued the labor movement tended to operate for much of the postwar period in a somewhat less particularistic fashion. Its leaders sometimes have seen themselves as the spokesmen for a broad and fairly permanent alliance of progressive, democratic forces in American society. They articulated a philosophy and supported positions in the national arena which made labor the leading force, not only for legislation in the narrowest interests of its immediate constituency, but also for the civil rights and employment opportunities of blacks, for consumer protection, for health and safety on the job, and government-supported medical care.

However, as these issues became the focal point for independent political organization outside the labor movement, it was evident that many of the legislative provisions and administrative protections which were consistent with the Movement's philosophy, conflicted with the narrow interests of workers on the shop floor; organized labor found itself in conflict with groups for whom one or another piece of legislation constituted the primary political goal. The Movement has tended to handle such conflicts through direct opposition in the Congress or in the courts. Thus it has opposed blacks and women's groups on equal employment opportunity legislation when this conflicted with the freedom of collective bargaining—most notably, the right to negotiate seniority rights. The Movement has similarly tended to oppose environmental and consumer regulations where these seemed to threaten existing jobs or job expansion. Even on the issues of worker health and safety, organized labor has been suspicious of new regulations when they seemed to be the outgrowth of spontaneous grass roots movements which did not respect traditional organization structures and which threatened to conflict with existing contract provisions.

The labor movement has done all of this while continuing to ally with some of these same groups on such issues as the minimum wage or full employment. What has thus emerged is a strategy of shifting temporary alliances around particular issues. Such a strategy is very similar to the particularistic approach to organizing and collective bargaining and to the kind of political strategy unions had pursued on procedural legislation as well.

The record on substantive issues is mixed. There appear to be short-run strategic victories and short-run defeats. For example, in the battle over the minimum wage legislation in 1977, organized labor favored a $3.00 minimum which would increase automatically with the cost of living. However, the legislation which was finally enacted raised the wage to only $2.65 and included no escalator. In terms of labor's announced position, the legislation appeared to represent a defeat. But George Meany was able to argue that politics, like collective bargaining, is a process of compromise. Thus, when the official position was viewed as a bargaining stance, the actual outcome was a substantial victory, much closer to labor's goals than to those of its opponents. The credibility of this interpretation was enhanced by the fact that labor had successfully resisted an effort to create a special, subminimum wage for youth.

An example of a short-run defeat which stands out especially is the image of a high AFL-CIO official standing on a public platform bitterly waving a bottle containing a pickled snail-darter, a kind of. minnow, on whose account an environmentalist had waged a successful battle to halt construction of a major federal dam. Another strategic defeat was the nomination of George McGovern at the 1972 Democratic Convention by a coalition of all the environmentalists, consumerists, women, blacks, and minorities whom organized labor had taken on individually on particular issues. In my mind, at least, a question arises as to what would have been the outcome on union rights issues and substantive issues if the unions had been less particularistic. An argument is made in subsequent sections.

Evangelical Politics

The difficulties organized labor has had with radical reform movements in the last decade are not labor's problem alone. Since the late 1960s, American politics has taken on a particularly evangelical flavor.

Political Movements

The political landscape has been swept repeatedly by movements which, while concerned with relatively narrow issues and directed at limited legislative goals, have made an unusually emotional and moralistic appeal. I would tend to include among them the consumer and environmental campaigns, as well as campaigns by groups such as the Gray Panthers. These movements have managed to mobilize significant electoral and financial strength for relatively short periods of time. And they have been so successful so quickly that their staying power has never been fully tested. This "new" politics seems to date from the antiwar and the civil rights movements, from which the subsequent campaigns have borrowed tactics, personnel and many rank-and-file supporters. The major characteristic of these movements is that they are narrowly defined in purpose and arise suddenly, without warning, like an emotional wave that overwhelms the political landscape as it swiftly rushes over it.

Politics of this kind has several unfortunate consequences. First, the issues are never seen in relation to the structure of the socioeconomic system in which they arise. New "causes" emerge so quickly that no one has time to figure out what their costs are. Moreover, the single-issue focus of each campaign obscures the interdependencies which make up a social system. As a result, the effect of the proposed reforms on other social goals is neither understood nor anticipated. Even the supporters of the initial reforms do not perceive what the costs will be on their other interests, costs which they themselves will ultimately be forced to bear. The second consequence of the evangelical politics is that everything happens so quickly that even if the true costs were perceived in advance, the opposition would have no time to organize and enter into the political debate or the legislative contest. Any potential opponents, who have nothing to gain from the reform, are unaware of what is happening until a new law is already on the books and in operation.

However, the legislation at which the movements are initially directed is only the beginning of a lengthy, complex process. Once this legislation is passed, the administrative agencies responsible for its implementation start to work out a set of regulations. Generally these regulations are conceived in a political climate still dominated by the mood in which the legislation first emerged. Often the agencies draw their staff from the reform lobby itself. As the regulations appear, however, the individuals and industries involved begin to work out the implications in terms of their own operations. The true costs gradually become apparent, and a lengthy process of bargaining begins among the agency, its erstwhile supporters in the reform movement, and opponents in the impacted sectors of the economy. Sometimes the initial regulations are amended; sometimes—as in automobile safety and emission controls—the legislation is actually changed. Whatever the outcome of the regulatory skirmishes, all parties have recourse to the courts for further interpretation and compromise.

All of this occurs in an evolving political climate in which the debate always threatens to activate new constituencies, either spontaneously or by the design of one of the affected parties. It also tends to involve genuine learning by all concerned. The things which happen are all the things which used to occur in congressional hearings when major social reforms were discussed and debated over a period of years. But now, while views are fluid, the regulations are not, and people are responsible for adhering to the rules, even though it is clear that the rules are in the process of changing.

Effect on Economics

Since the targets of the reform movements are embedded in the economy, the political process tends to affect economic processes. This is independent of the economic impact of the specific regulations which have emerged through the political process. The most salient of these effects is an increase in the uncertainty and instability of the climate in which business decisions are made. Businessmen in newly regulated areas know that the regulations are likely to be changed once their impact is felt. However, the magnitude of those changes cannot be foreseen, because it is likely to be the outcome of a bargaining process in which even the major contestors are at the outset unclear.

Most of these areas involve major long-term capital investment. This is most true of energy, where the environmental and safety impact of alternative energy sources is interwoven with the uncertainties of foreign policy and with the energy "crisis." But it is also the case in a number of other environmental, health and safety, and consumer protection issues, as the snail-darter case illustrates. In the face of these uncertainties, it is easiest for businessmen simply to postpone long-term investment decisions. This may be an important factor in the failure of anticipated long-term capital investment to materialize in the 1970s.

The Challenge

It is my opinion that labor is one of the few institutions in American society capable of channeling the forces generating these reform movements in a different way. Even when conceived in the narrow terms of business unionism, the interests of organized labor should be broad enough to encompass all of the issues around which reform movements have grown up, and to force these reform movements to see issues in terms of an interdependent socioeconomic system. Organized labor is, moreover, a continuing entity, presumably interested in the consequences of reform over the long as well as the short run. It has the financial resources to support a research staff capable of identifying conflicts among various social goals, and the political and economic leverage to get government and industry to engage in similar research. Finally, historically in the United States and even more consistently in Europe, organized labor has been able to assert itself ideologically and politically as the leader of a progressive coalition, possessing a broad program for reform. Labor also has experience in resolving internal conflicts through negotiation and compromise. Had it been willing to play this leadership role—were it even to try to do so today—unions might be able to pursue a more systematic, measured reform strategy.

I believe that labor has failed to play this role because it has misread contemporary history. It has persisted in interpreting the current waves of reform in terms of the ideological battles of the 1930s and 1940s. It perceives the reform leaders (first the leaders of the antiwar movement and then the leaders of the various post-Vietnam protests) as being like the Communists and Socialists. However, if our argument is correct, the difficulty for the labor movement (and for American society more generally) with the "new" politics is precisely the opposite of the difficulty unions had with the "old" left: a complete inability to see beyond smaller issues to a larger social system. If the old Communists were willing to sacrifice everything for broad systemic change, the "new" left seems at times willing to make any petty annoyance into a cause, independent of any other issues on the social agenda and isolated from all its consequences. If the "new" politics has any historical antecedents, it is not the ideologies of the 1930s but the American evangelical tradition of the nineteenth century. In my view, the policy organized labor needs to assert in dealing with the new politics is not that which differentiated it from its adversaries in more recent history, but precisely that sense of a social system it shares with them. The leaders of the "new" politics are already committed to the strategy of incremental reform through electoral and judicial processes which distinguishes contemporary labor leaders from their more radical adversaries of the past.

The evangelical analogy is suggestive in another respect as well. Such movements have inevitably presented a brief challenge to established religious organizations until institutional links to rival organizations could be fashioned and converts channeled into established churches. American labor might be well advised, this suggests, to see in Ralph Nader not Nikolai Lenin but Billy Graham. Or, to push the metaphor in another direction, imagine how organized religion would have fared in American society if it had mistaken Billy Graham for Oliver Cromwell.

The Requirements of a New Vision

If organized labor is to assert a commanding claim as leader of a broad, progressive coalition and assume an effective role as mediator and ultimately arbitrator of the conflicts of interest which arise among coalition members, it must develop an underatanding that leads it to be seen and to see itself in this role. To achieve this, labor needs an ideology, a philosophy, and a kind of scientific understanding—a vision or a paradigm of action (Kuhne, 1970). Such a vision serves at once to define and link together in a unique combination a particular set of means and ends, and to express the felt needs of the various groups and individuals involved. The concept of business unionism as articulated by the Wisconsin School has served as this kind of paradigm for labor's current strategy, and has constituted the basis for labor's claim to existence as a legitimate organizational entity in American society. What is required for a different political role is a substitute for business unionism. If, in fact, I had such a substitute to offer, I would have written a very different kind of paper for this conference.

However, I do think that once one poses the question in these terms, it becomes clear that the issue is not basically one of political strategy but of the weakness of the paradigm in which that strategy is conceived (namely business unionism). And if one cannot identify as yet a clear alternative, one can at least identify the characteristics which that alternative must possess to be effective.

The Philosophy of Individualism

The basic philosophical difficulty which organized labor faces in this country is that Americans conceive of themselves and their society in highly individualistic terms. The commitment to individualism is both a normative commitment to the integrity of the individual as a moral standard against which the evolution of social policy is to be judged, and a positive commitment to the notion that atomistic individuals are the basic unit of analysis. Any understanding of society must arise through the aggregation of these units. The preeminent expression of this conception is neoclassical economic theory, with its dual claim as a scientific understanding of the way in which the economy operates and its normative prescriptions for atomistic competition as a means of preserving individual freedom and maximizing economic welfare.

The analogue to this mode of discourse in political theory has been democratic pluralism. The problem for organized labor is that unions are built around cohesive social groups and their behavior is predicated upon a notion of group action which contradicts and appears to violate the central tenets of individualism. The basic task of a philosophy of organized labor is to overcome these contradictions and create "space" within the individualistic self-conception of Americans for such a group. Again, this is true in both the normative sense of "legitimizing" the existence of such groups and in the "positive" sense of explaining how such groups operate and when group behavior is likely to prevail over individual behavior. How does business unionism perform this task?

The basic asset of those who undertake this task is that the very groups which individualism denies are in fact organic to the functioning of industrial society and politics even in the pursuit of individualistic goals. As long as individualistic politics tries to resolve real social problems, it cannot escape the incipient need for an alternative mode of understanding which recognizes such groups and accords them a place in its analytical scheme and moral discourse.

In recent years, this need has come to the fore in the area of race relations and civil rights. Our individualistic ideals lead us to abhor a system which treats blacks as members of a racial grouping. And yet, not only do we have a society which obviously operates upon that principle, but, in the attempt to change society, we rely upon a set of racially defined targets and quotas which seem to institutionalize the very behavioral principles which we are seeking to eliminate. The individualistic conception of society leaves us completely unable to understand, let alone cope with, this dilemma.

Because we do not understand why society treats individuals as members of a group, we are incapable of fashioning workable remedies, except on a blind trial-and-error basis. We have fallen back upon quotas as seemingly the most direct way to eliminate what we do not like and are unable to circumvent. However, since we don't really understand what it is we have, let alone why we have it, we are incapable of distinguishing clearly in our minds between quotas as the problem and quotas as the remedy; indeed, we really do not know whether the quotas are making things better or worse. It is this confusion in the face of society's most pressing social problem which creates the space for an alternative paradigm.

I think one can argue that, historically, unions have posed a very similar dilemma for American society, and that they continue to do so today, although that dilemma is not presently as pressing as it has been in the past.

I will not attempt to develop that argument in detail here. The central point is that to a very large extent American acceptance of trade unions has been pragmatic rather than philosophical: workers organized into unions, and the attempt to break up these organizations was so disruptive to industrial peace and social stability at critical junctures (most notably the Depression and World War II) that industrialists have been forced to accept their existence and deal with them through collective bargaining. That kind of pragmatic acceptance is certainly the central theme of the preamble of the Wagner Act, and it remains the only convincing justification in the business school classroom. The difficulty is that having recognized trade unions on this basis, Congress and the courts continue to be troubled by the conflict between such organizations and the individualistic terms in which they understand and evaluate the social structure. The law has thus been molded by the courts and Congress in an attempt to reassert the values which union recognition appears to compromise.

In a sense, all of the central issues of labor-individual rights, the duty of fair representation, union democracy, the closed shop, the secondary boycott, union monopoly, situs picketing, and so on—can be seen as an attempt to abridge the notion of group cohesion. The result in most of these areas has been a law which is of dubious efficacy at best (the attempt to bar a closed shop in construction), and which is at worst an incredible confusion (secondary boycott provisions or the duty of fair representation [Feller, 1973]). The confusion arises because the attempts to assert individual rights through labor law constitute fundamental contradictions. They are contradictions not in the sense that they are wrong or misguided, but in the sense that they conflict with the group cohesion upon which the existence and behavior of the union is predicated. That cohesion seems to be a basic fact of human existence, and it is that fact which leads to the recognition of the union in the first place. Most basically, then, the attempt to assert individual rights through such provisions in the law is contradictory in the sense that the logic from which it springs points to the outlawing of the very trade unions which the law is designed to recognize in the first place. Thus such provisions are always a threat to organized labor: a threat in the small because they insert into its midst a set of antagonistic behavioral principles, and a threat in the large because they assert a logic which implies the total suppression of the organization.

The philosophy of business unionism has not been very successful in helping society resolve these contradictions. In terms of American individualism, it is comprehensible only as an expression of pluralism, a temporary alliance of individuals to pursue particular ends, one among the multitude of shifting alliances which characterize democratic politics. We have already discussed the weakness of a political strategy which is grounded in this understanding. The more basic weakness of this understanding of business unionism, however, is in its economic implications: in a sense, it can be said to provide no true economic foundation for trade union behavior at all. To the extent that the economic analogue to pluralism in the political sphere is neoclassical economics, the optimal world is one of atomistic competition in which there is simply no room for trade unions.

The Role of Countervailing Power

There is a secondary current in American thought which attempts to formulate a theory of competition in which unions do play a constructive role. The most recent formulation of this view is Galbraith's (1956) notion of countervailing powers. Essentially the same notion was formulated earlier by John R. Commons (1935). It is also articulated by Oliver Wendell Holmes, in *Vegelehn* v. *Guntner*, where he grounds the idea in Social Darwinism and calls it "free struggle for life" (Cox and Bok, 1962). The notion in Galbraith, Commons, and Holmes is that the social welfare will be preserved not by horizontal competition among individual buyers and sellers in the market, but by the vertical "competition" among large coalitions of buyers and sellers. Thus organized workers are counterposed to organized producers, and organized producers to organized consumers. The UAW, GM, and Ralph Nader become the principal actors in economic analysis.

This notion undoubtedly catches much of economic reality which neoclassical theory neglects, and it certainly accords the union an organic role in both the actual functioning of the economy and the achievement of some set of normative standards. However, it has two principal problems. First, as an intellectual construct, it remains underdeveloped; it has nowhere near the cohesion and rigor of the neoclassical notion of perfect competition. Given the length of time "countervailing power" has been around, one might wonder whether the state of intellectual development does not indicate some more basic weakness, but in and of itself, it does not seem fatal. The second drawback would seem, however, to be much more serious: the notion of countervailing power as applied to unions does not deal with the problem of individualism at all, and because it does not, it provides absolutely no answers to the questions about individual rights, union democracy, the size and scope of the bargaining unit, and the like which preoccupy policymakers in this area and which, because they do so, are the central questions with which a theory of the labor movement must deal.

Of course, neither the American labor movement nor the Wisconsin School had in mind as they formulated the concepts which we now call business unionism a set of ideas which could be reduced either to pluralism or to some notion of countervailing powers. For example, there is no place in the former and very little room in the latter for jurisdictional ideas of the AFL, which must certainly be counted as central to its union philosophy as what has survived today. Indeed, the notion of a "natural" union jurisdiction existing independently of worker choice, prior to an organization and immutable in the face of history, seems to be in direct opposition to the pluralist notion of shifting, particularistic alliances. And the insistence that one cannot be a carpenter and a plumber at the same time would seem to preclude in fact, if it does not in sheer logic, the idea that one could be both a carpenter and a consumer.

Likewise, Perlman's attempt to identify the consciousness of workers and to distinguish their way of thinking from that of other social actors is at odds with the notion of essentially similar individuals with diverse interests which lead them into shifting alliances, upon which the dominant social theory builds (Perlman, 1949). Rather than an expression of American individualism, the organizational concepts of American labor seem to be an attempt to express a felt sense of the work group as a natural, permanent social unit which precedes institutional expression. Indeed, I think that the members of the Wisconsin School must be viewed as true "organic intellectuals," in Gramsci's (1971) sense of the term, attempting to capture these feelings and form them into a coherent set of ideas that would at once articulate the experience of American working men and permit a vision of society that would facilitate the realization in a transformed social order of the aspirations toward which that experience led.

My argument is basically that the Wisconsin School failed in this endeavor. It failed not because its ideas were an expression of pluralism, but because they could be, and have in practice progressively been, reduced to pluralism. As such, they reduce the group to a collection of individuals. They lack the capacity to deal effectively with the group as an organic part of the social order. And because they do not do so, they are unable either to secure the position of unions as organizations within the society or to help the society to think about, let alone resolve, the conflicts between the group and the individual which plague the field of labor policy.

Clearly, if this is true, labor can only secure its position by returning to and redefining in an ideological and philosophical sense—as well as in a positive, scientific sense—the nature of group identity in democratic society. To this extent, it must of necessity deal not only with what labor and labor organization are as a group, but also with the meaning of the other groups, most of whom labor deals with as allies and as protagonists in contemporary politics. It is in this sense that the framework which will resolve the questions left unanswered by the Wisconsin School will provide an alternative political strategy for organized labor, opening up the way for a new stance toward all social groupings.

References

Bernstein, Richard J. *The Restructuring of Social and Political Theory.* New York: Harcourt, Brace, Jovanovich, 1978.

Cammett, John. *Antonio Gramsci and the Origins of Italian Communism.* Stanford, Calif.: Stanford University Press, 1967.

Commons, John, R. "Labor Movement." In *Encyclopedia of the Social Sciences*, Vol. 8, edited by Edwin R.A. Seligman, New York: Macmillan, Inc., 1968.

Cox, Archibald and Bok, Derek. *Cases and Materials on Labor Laws* 5th ed. Brooklyn: The Foundation Press, 1962.

Dorfman, Joseph. "John R. Commons." In *International Encyclopedia of the Social Sciences*, Vol. 3, edited by David L. Sills, New York: Macmillan, Inc., 1968.

Feller, David E. "A General Theory of the Collective Bargaining Agreement." *California Law Review* 61 (May 1973).

Galbraith, John Kenneth. *American Capitalism: The Concept of Countervailing Power.* Boston: Houghton Mifflin, 1956.

Gramsci, Antonio. *Selections from the Prison Notebooks.* New York: International Publishers, 1971.

Greenspan, Allen. "Business Confidence in America." *Economist* 264 (August 6, 1977).

Kuhne, Thomas. *The Structure of Scientific Revolution.* Chicago: University of Chicago Press, 1970.

McAdams, Alan K. *Power and Politics in Labor Legislation.* New York: Columbia University Press, 1964.

Perlman, Selig. *A Theory of the Labor Movement.* New York: Augustus M. Kelly, 1949.

Skinner, Quentin. "The Flight from Positivism." Review of Richard J. Bernstein, *The Restructuring of Social and Political Theory. New York Review of Books*, 25 (June 15, 1978).

Comment

Stanley Ruttenberg

The idealism expressed in Professor Piore's chapter should be encouraged and promoted; however, I hope that it could be tempered a little with a different interpretation of American society as we find it today. And therein, I think, lies the real difference between Professor Piore and myself.

We really agree on the fact that business unionism which predominated before 1930 was not then, and certainly is not now, in the best interests of the American labor movement. Business unionism, as defined in his chapter, held that unions kept their noses to the grindstone and worked on the narrow, particularistic issues of the workplace. That concept as practiced in the early years is certainly not the situation today. Perhaps some people believe that it was in the best interests of the labor movement then, but I do not think so. Certainly it is not now.

Piore and I also agree that during the 1940s and 1950s the American labor movement swung away from this narrow, particularistic concern at the workplace in terms of some of the issues he has cited in his chapter.

However, where he and I disagree is over his claim that the interests of the labor movement during the 1960s and 1970s reverted to the more particularistic, narrow issues of the workplace. He says that unions were articulating issues such as civil rights and employment opportunities for minorities, consumer protection, health, safety, and national health insurance in the 1940s and 1950s, but that they did not really come to the political fore until the 1960s and 1970s. By that time the strategy of the labor movement seems to have shifted back to the workplace in its narrow, particularistic business unionism.

Piore's concept of the 1940s and 1950s seems to make the point that it was the development of the CIO which gave leadership to this broader view of social reform, and by implication, it was the December 1955 merger of the CIO with the AFL from which we may date the attitude shift. At this point, he says, the AFL-CIO reverted to more particularistic interests of the workplace.

The evidence does not support this thesis. If one looks at the 1960s, which was certainly after the merger, it would have been exceedingly difficult for Lyndon Johnson to have put through the civil rights legislation without a coalition of the National Urban League, Clarence Mitchell as a particular individual, and the AFL-CIO's progressive, enthusiastic efforts in Congress for the adoption of civil rights legislation.

Likewise, there would not have been success with President Kennedy's (and later President Johnson's) efforts to pass the Economic Opportunity

187

Act which led to the Office of Economic Opportunity, and the attempt to do something about poverty and low income, disadvantaged individuals, and those with low educational levels and training. This has been an interest on the part of the labor movement that has persisted in the 1960s and 1970s.

Nor do I think that consumer protection legislation would have gotten as far as it has if Piore were correct. Certainly, the creation of consumer effort at the White House through Esther Peterson, an old-line trade unionist from the Amalgamated Clothing Workers, would never have come to fruition had the labor movement not been vigorously behind it. Undoubtedly the Carter administration would not have been as interested in pushing it without labor's support.

I could cite other examples in the area of environmental protection and air pollution; those were items of continued reform and political interest to the labor movement, which persisted during the 1960s and 1970s.

Admittedly, the way in which the American labor movement has followed through on its very firm and aggressive pronouncements of the 1960s and 1970s has not been in as vigorous a public fashion as it might have been. To overstate the case, it is not uncommon for the Federation to have a good solid debate in its policy committees on a resolution which the Federation eventually adopts, and which says almost everything that we would want it to say on a particular issue, and to follow that through by presenting testimony to the appropriate committees of the House and Senate, and to end up saying, "Oh well, now it is up to the Congress to do it." To that extent, the 1960s and 1970s have seen a slight reversion in the labor movement's interest and enthusiasm for pushing and going forward.

There is one comment in Piore's chapter that should be corrected, or at least discussed. He says unions were opposed to providing better employment opportunities for blacks and women. While there was a dispute between Walter Reuther and George Meany on Martin Luther King, Jr.'s, 1963 civil rights march in Washington, at the same time among the marchers was A. Phillip Randolph, black leader of the Sleeping Car Porters, and conscience of the old AFL, with his strong supporter Bayard Rustin, who had organized and helped King put on that civil rights march. Bayard Rustin is now a very trusted and high-level adviser in the ranks of the AFL-CIO.

I do not really believe that the problem of providing opportunities for blacks or women has been minimized in the Federation. Rather, the issue is one of degree. To illustrate, in the mid-1960s, while with the Department of Labor, I helped establish the Outreach Apprenticeship Program. This was designed to assist the building and construction unions in overcoming discrimination against blacks' becoming journeymen in certain occupations. That program was planned, I must admit, without much support from the construction unions but with the support of some AFL-CIO people. Gradually, however, it was totally embraced by the construction unions and became a successful method for increasing the proportion of minorities and blacks among journeymen in those occupations. But progress has not been as rapid as the NAACP and maybe Mike Piore would have liked it to be. Perhaps sensitivity to degree or pace is the source of our disagreement. I do know that the rate of change has been fast enough to have maintained the support of the National Urban League and similar organizations. Interestingly and importantly, the outreach concept is being expanded to include women as well.

Therefore, I think we have a problem as to what constitutes a success, what constitutes a failure, and how much progress has been made. This point is equally relevant to Piore's comments on relations between labor and the environmental protection interest groups, specifically those concerned with the construction of nuclear power plants. Unions are basically very much interested in promoting and pushing ahead the nuclear energy program, primarily to expand job opportunities in their field. This is true not only of construction unions but the utility and manufacturing unions as well.

However, it is wrong to criticize these unions for being business- or growth-oriented on this issue. Although they have not joined with the all-out antinuclear people, neither have they joined with a moderate group of individuals, including the business community and the utility community, which needed more energy for the purpose of building the American economy. The unions want to see progress, but not necessarily of the same kind or at the same pace as the new left or the new politics wants.

I could cite other examples of positive social action not related to particularistic concerns. Certainly it has been the vigorous support of the Americn labor movement working with many other groups that has moved the Equal Rights Amendment as far as it has gone to this point. However, it would be a more expedient use of the space allotted to move on to a consideration of Piore's prescription for change. A few points are called for.

Piore is asking organized labor to challenge and bring together the divergent interest groups of the last decade so that they may form a coherent pattern. Even he is aware that this is something no other group or individual has been able to do.

Clearly, it is possible for labor to work with certain organizations. There have been continued ad hoc coalitions between labor and many groups, and certainly a continuing coalition on almost all issues with the National Urban League and Clarence Mitchell. These alliances deal with topics which range from the business unionism of improving minimum wage to the broader issue of the Humphrey-Hawkins bill and full employment. However, it is not possible to work with all groups. For example, many of the all-out environmental protection organizations whose major concern is that there may be a very serious accident in a nuclear plant really have no interest in the future energy needs of the country. All of this notwithstanding, one gets the impression that Piore wishes there were a labor party which would take the leadership in bringing all these special interest groups together in a coordinated and cohesive approach to social reform. Without actually stating it, he implies that if they only had a labor party, there would be a sense of discipline within that party which would limit dissent as it brought society closer to the party's agenda.

I cannot move from his analysis to this conclusion. Simply because we are a nation so far unable to resolve very fundamental differences among divergent groups, there is no reason to assume that the labor movement has abandoned social reform and returned to business unionism because it has been unsuccessful in leading the progressive forces in a way Piore finds acceptable.

On the contrary, social reform is an evolutionary process which remains the goal of the labor movement. Some, myself included, would like to see this goal pursued a little more vigorously than it has been recently. So, while it is true that social reform in another era, the pre-1930s, was anathema to the old AFL, it is not reasonable to assume that it is now anathema to the current labor movement. The labor movement is going to make more progress in the future by continuing the process it followed during the 1960s and 1970s.

Comment

Lloyd Ulman

Ever since the suggestion was made that casting one's bread upon the waters might turn out to be a good investment, altruism has been periodically defended in terms of its opposite. Piore's chapter is an example of this type of approach, and if I read it correctly, it seems to go like this: if the labor movement had been more altruistic and less special-interest in its priority and approaches, it would have been more successful in protecting those narrow, selfish interests which have been preventing it from taking a more altruistic approach in the first place.

This is not to say that Mike Piore is too sure that the special-interest approach has been a complete washout. Thus Landrum-Griffin, he claims, "ultimately emerged . . . nowhere near as bad as the leaders had feared in the heat of the battle, and the particularistic strategy was no doubt responsible for that fact." Also, he supports the view that the minimum wage legislation of 1977 was much closer to labor's goals than to those of its opponents.

However, he is disturbed by two happenings. The first is the double rejection by the AFL-CIO leadership of McGovern and the snail-darters. The second is the development in the 1960s of a conflict between "many of the legislative provisions and administrative protections which were consistent with the Movement's philosophy" and "the narrow interests of workers on the shop floor."

As a way out, Piore seems to suggest that the organized labor movement deploy its institutional resources to mediate and mitigate the conflicts and the economic costs which he attributes to those haphazard and uncoordinated reform movements which have generated and been generated by specific economic substantive issues. In addition, he almost comes close to blaming the labor movement for the adverse effects on economic performance which have allegedly issued from these movements and measures on the grounds that it failed to prevent the costs while allegedly possessing the capabilities of doing so. (When Mr. Meany reads this chapter he will doubtless know how Mr. Castro must have felt on being informed that he was to blame for the invasion of Zaire because he did nothing to prevent it.)

However (so the argument continues), in order to be able to tackle this task, the labor movement must (1) rid itself of its traditional antiintellectual and antiideological biases, and (2) ultimately redesign the purposes and functions of the trade unions which have thus far comprised its component units. He does not minimize the difficulty of fulfilling either of these conditions and, in my own opinion, he is wise not to do so. The antiintellectual

191

bias in the American trade union movement is stronger than it is in other trade union movements, where investment in the resources of reseach capabilities has generally been more liberal and more politically productive.

On the other hand, this bias is partly rooted in a belief that an important and historic function of the trade union has been to deploy collective strength in defense of substantial numbers of workers with moderate educational and other intellectual endowment against exploitation by those whose intellectual resources are greater. (This belief is, for reasons which are perhaps painfully obvious, not well aired in the literature, but I have found that it surfaces quite readily from the depths of coffee cups and beer mugs.)

Such exploitation of what Sumner Slichter called "the average and subaverage man" contributes to the perceived inequality of bargaining power between managers and unorganized employees in a direct adversary relationship between buyer and seller. Paternalism, of course, can be another form of exploitation; managerial paternalism once furnished Slichter with a powerful argument on behalf of unionism. It can also be practiced by those whose hearts are pure and whose talents are placed at the disposal of a social conscience which impels them to prescribe what is in the best interest of others. In addition, trade unionists, whose specialty is the art of compromise, do tend to regard intellectuals as sadly deficient in this area, often to the point of priggishness. If Mr. Piore could persuade Mr. Meany to pass the stogie of peace to Mr. Nader, could he persuade the latter to try a few puffs?

However, deep-seated as the tendency may be in this country to reject rather than accept what one cannot evaluate, this problem should be diminished in magnitude by the emergence of a younger, better-educated membership. With greater ability to evaluate, distrust and suspicion should abate, and greater appreciation of the usefulness of intellectual expertise should characterize the unions of tomorrow.

Unfortunately, the ideological point remains an obstacle to the political detente which Piore has in mind, but not because the AFL-CIO people can't distinguish between communism and charisma (they can and do), or because they reject them both on separate but equal grounds (they do not). It is primarily because eradication of the conflicts generated between some of the social measures enacted in the postwar period and "the narrow interests of workers on the shop floor" would require redefinition of those interests—that is, a heavier dosage of altruism in the ideological mix. Business unionism is the moniker bestowed (by Hoxie, incidentally, and no Wisconsinite, he) on the institutionalization of proletarian selfishness in this country; however, it was the Webbs (and no Wisconsinites, they) who defined a union anywhere and everywhere as a "continuous association of wage earners for the purpose of maintaining or improving the conditions of *their* working lives" (my italics, but with their permission). Subsequent experience has shown that this is true under socialism as well as capitalism.

This is not to say that the ghost of altruism has been exorcised, even in the nonsocialist, nonutopian American labor movement. The central federations have always regarded themselves as the guardian of that spirit as well as the political representative of the narrow selfish interests of the dues payers. Their spiritual burden has been lightened by their refusal to admit the existence of any distinction between the two, but for the most part even this fallacy has been sincerely maintained. And in practice they have attempted, on specific occasions, either to subordinate the selfish interests of some of their more powerful groups to the selfish interests of weaker groups in their own or the wider community, or to invest "per capita" in projects which did not obviously further the interests of at least the most powerful affiliates.

Central federations have even used the political process to substitute for their own lack of organizational control over affiliates, and even for the affiliates' effective control over their own members at the local level. The existence of employee discrimination—especially in the South—had long inhibited the leadership of many national unions, but the AFL-CIO leadership lent vigorous and decisive support to the passage of the Civil Rights Act, and, in particular, its Title VII. Passage of the Landrum-Griffin law reflected recognition by the central federation of (1) the need for the labor movement publicly to subscribe to some ethical criteria governing the internal political life of its affiliates which would be consistent with those professed by the community at large, and (2) the inability of the federation itself to enforce these criteria. (Of course, it is not implied that outright labor opposition to this legislation would have prevented its enactment.)

Finally, in supporting the ill-fated common situs package, the AFL-CIO and the weak national unions in the building trades tried to have it both ways: while amendment of the picketing provision was advertised as a quid pro quo for acceptance of more effective national union (and public) control over bargaining, in fact the latter was desired in its own right by the national unions (and also by many local leaders) who were well aware of the self-destructive properties of uncoordinated and competitive local bargaining.

However, there are limits to the circumstances under which such political end runs can be played, whether or not they are in the ultimate self-interest of those whose flanks are being turned. Just as, in jurisdictional disputes, the old Federation tended virtuously to support the more powerful and affluent of the two contestants, so in politics the AFL-CIO cannot afford to ride over or run around the narrow self-interests of too many unionists. David Feller likes to recall how the CIO would resoundingly condemn a tax on the sale of colored margarine—surely to the interests of the consuming public—courageously rejecting the objection of the single local union which represented workers who made the containers of do-it-yourself yellow dye that were packaged with the uncolored "workingman's spread." And the CIO, and later the AFL-CIO, remained a staunch champion of free trade as long as the opposition was largely confined to the Textile Workers and the garment trades. But when selfish interests (perceived as important) in too many shop floors are involved, the political arm of the trade union movement cannot long remain in opposition, however commendable that position might be, whether viewed in terms of the general good, the welfare of unprotected and poor minorities, or even the true selfish interests of those who oppose it.

It so happens that the 1960s, when a change in the labor movement's political stance seems to have occurred, was a period in which causes prevailed which the Movement had generally supported, and bore fruit in "an increasing quantity of substantive regulations of the terms and conditions of employment"—the Equal Pay Act, Title VII, OSHA, ERISA. In economists' terms these have appeared as substantial increments to employer costs; in institutional terms, they seem to be constraints on collective bargaining and on the ability of the bargaining arm of the union movement to protect those narrow selfish interests on the job, especially including job security, which are not protected by the legislation itself.

The problem reflects, but does not imply, the relatively great American emphasis on the method of collective bargaining, when judged by international standards. In other countries, where the political arm of the labor movement is relatively longer than in the United States, the contest between collective bargaining and public policy is often more decently cloaked under a mantle known as wage drift. In Sweden the public has long been treated to the spectacle of social democratic members of parliament voting for increased public consumption, and virtuously, for the increased taxes to cover it, and then leaving the solemnity of the Riksdag for the livelier give and take of central bargaining, where they have duly negotiated wage increases to cover the increased taxes. That is but one example, but it should serve to remind us that the Webbs' definition has proven to be generally applicable. It should also remind us that we cannot expect the union movement to play too significant a role as political mediator in a game in which its own members' preferences have cast it, at least to some extent, into an adversary position.

Yet economic adversity may furnish a joint cause for expecting an expanded role for the labor movement. The first is that the impetus to social reform may be sharply decelerating; the result of this could be that ardent proponents of various causes may yet acquire a greater disposition to compromise and trim their sails. The second is that an income's policy may force a reordering in the American labor movement's priorities away from collective bargaining, where the power is closer to the grass roots, and in the direction of political bargaining, much of which takes place in a certain nonindustrial community.

Part VI
Summary of the Conference

8

The Shrinking Perimeter: Unions and Collective Bargaining in Manufacturing

Hervey A. Juris and
Myron Roomkin

There is no question that significant changes have taken place in the industrial relations system in manufacturing. After many years during which manufacturing labor relations passed sequentially through periods of aggressive organizing and power-oriented collective bargaining, unions in this sector are on the defensive, seeking to hold on to their achievements. This conference addressed the question: How strong and long-lived would this era be? The authors looked at union organizing efforts, the structure and administration of unions, the process and substance of collective bargaining, and the role of unions in the political arena. On balance, opinion was divided. The purpose of this chapter is to bring together participant thoughts in each of these areas and to raise some issues which surprisingly escaped discussion.

The Size and Strength of Unions

The number of union members by union and industry is probably the most widely discussed measure of the labor movement's strength and vitality. Thus conference participants were understandably concerned by the continuing paucity of, and lack of adequate detail in, data on unions and union members. Currently, these data are either self-reported by unions or estimated by BLS. Membership statistics within manufacturing are especially troublesome, and as the traditional union jurisdictional boundaries continue to blur, self-reported information on membership may become even less useful. What we need is membership information by SIC code.

We are heavily indebted to a transcript of the open discussion that followed each presented paper and to George Strauss, who provided us with his summary of the conference. The attributions which follow, unless otherwise indicated, refer to the statements of conference participants made during this open discussion. The transcript represented a wealth of interesting views and comments, many of which we were unfortunately unable to use. Likewise, more than one person often shared a particular viewpoint or insight, thereby making it very difficult to identify the true owners of ideas. Since this summary was written after the conference adjourned, we have also been able to draw upon more recent developments in formulating our assessment. For these editorial judgments, our own views and possible errors, we accept full responsibility.

What we have are inferences from self-reports. For example, the International Brotherhood of Electrical Workers, once predominantly a building trades union, probably represents more workers in electrical manufacturing than either the International Union of Electrical, Radio and Machine Workers or the United Electrical Radio and Machine Workers of America, both mainline unions in that industry. We have no way of knowing for sure.

Notwithstanding these limitations, the data on union membership unambiguously document an ebb in the percent of the work force affiliated with manufacturing unions. Various causes of the decline have been identified at the conference and elsewhere, as have speculations about the ability of unions in manufacturing to bring about a reversal in this trend.

Causes of Declining Union Membership

The decline in manufacturing sector membership is a mixture of structural shifts in the economy and qualitative changes in the characteristics of union-management relations.

First, although the level of employment in manufacturing will grow over the next decade, as Preston so clearly documents, the manufacturing labor force will continue to shrink relative to the total labor force. Moreover, where growth in the manufacturing labor force has occurred, it has been in high technology industries where, for a variety of reasons, workers have not yet been highly motivated to join unions. Second, there has been a long-term shift in the occupational composition of the manufacturing labor force. White-collar and technical employees—two groups historically resistant to unions—now account for a much higher proportion of total employment. Third, women, younger workers, and highly educated people now comprise a larger portion of the total labor force. These are also groups long known to be relatively more resistant to unionization.

Finally, the focus of manufacturing employment has shifted geographically. Manufacturing activity has moved to the South and West from the midwestern and eastern states. Other manufacturing jobs have been exported to foreign countries. We do not want to imply that the shift from the heavily unionized snowbelt to the union-resistant sunbelt or foreign nations is based on the union issue alone. The most appealing qualities of the sunbelt have long been an economic environment of lower taxes, lower wages, and cheaper energy. The current need to replace capital equipment and the creation of new industries present opportunities to move. The economic environment of the sunbelt serves as the incentive. All of this notwithstanding, the sunbelt has been touting its workers' and employers' historical resistance to unionization as an additional advantage. Jedel, for example, notes how the southwestern states were vigorously courting foreign investors with descriptions of an attractive economic climate while, at the same time, pressuring some highly organized foreign companies not to accept unionization once they moved here.

Along with these gradually developing structural shifts, unions today face a degree of management resistance in some instances reminiscent of the antiunion hostility of the mass production firms in the 1930s. Although conference participants could agree that management's opposition to unions has become resolute, the causes of this change were not as clear.

One hypothesis often stated is that it is more difficult to organize in already heavily organized industries, since the remaining firms are likely to be the most bitterly antiunion. But if this were true, the signs of stronger employer resistance should have materialized much sooner than they did in manufacturing. Nor does this explanation account for the attempts by firms already heavily organized to operate new facilities on a nonunion basis.

An alternative hypothesis is more plausible: industry may never have fully accepted the legitimacy of unions but was willing to tolerate collective bargaining as long as it was economically feasible or necessitated by environmental realities. By this explanation, rising price levels, increased economic uncertainty, and the knowledge that unions might now be vulnerable allowed antiunion sentiments to resurface. Equally as important may be the increasing competition of foreign producers who have made American employers highly concerned about labor costs, productivity, and prices. Whatever the explanation, a high level of employer resistance to unions currently exists.

Moreover, the practice of union avoidance has become a sophisticated business. Employers have come to communicate more effectively with employees and to understand why workers organize. While it is true that in the past management had some understanding of the reasons behind unions and made some efforts to eliminate the causes of labor unrest, management typically treated this issue in an ad hoc fashion. Today, many employers systematically and continually monitor performance of first-line supervisors, wage levels in the community, and workers' sentiments in order to keep grievances below the critical mass needed for unionization. To help them in this program, companies are turning to law firms and to consulting firms that specialize in personnel matters and union organizing campaigns. These firms have been sufficiently effective to draw the attention of the AFL-CIO Executive Council, which in 1979 promised a drive against those firms whom the Federation viewed as making a science out of preventing unions.

The Role of Public Policy

The mass organizing of the 1930s is associated with the passage of the Wagner Act both as an expression of public policy and in the establishment of orderly procedures for certifying unions. Today public policy grants employers greater freedom to resist unions. The labor movement in 1978 attempted comprehensive labor law reform hoping that a reexpression of the commitment and incidental changes in the procedures would foster a rebirth of the spirit of the 1930s. Rees, however, has shown what many suspected: at the margin the reforms being pushed could have, at best, only a small impact on union membership.

But public policy has affected union organizing in other ways. Job rights and job security, areas in which the unions were once the sole provider of benefits, more recently have been expanded through legislation and court rulings. In a more subtle way, regulatory programs such as Equal Employment Opportunity, Occupational Safety and Health, and Employee Retirement Income Security may also have curtailed union membership by raising operating costs and forcing management to become more sophisticated in its personnel practices.

The Prospects for Change

Six scenarios on the future size and strength of the labor movement have been identified. Five deal with the prospects for new growth, one with accelerated decline.

In the first scenario, Derber reminds us that union membership bursts ahead in economically and/or socially atypical periods such as war, depression, or hyperinflation. Whether the current economic situation of high rates of unemployment and inflation, clearly atypical by postwar standards, will have such an effect remains to be seen. A highly severe recession might also affect organizing success, for as Ulman noted, no union substitute yet designed can completely shield employees from market forces. While Ulman did not forecast such an economic decline, even the rosier economic forecasts reported by Preston foresee only modest growth rates in manufacturing over the next decade.

On the one hand, manufacturing unionism may receive a big boost from a new manufacturing industry. Some people believe that synthetic fuels or chemical alteration of microbes and genes could produce biological manufacturing industries equal to the computer industry in economic significance. Even if such an industry were to emerge, however, it is not clear, as discussed above, that high-technology workers would organize. Moreover, even if a new industry were to develop, it might not benefit manufacturing unionism in the United States. There were once great expectations for employment opportunities in the microelectronics industry, until manufacturers decided that the products could be made less expensively abroad.

A second scenario looks at possible changes in organizing strategies and the quality of the new generation of union leaders. It was generally agreed that unions would continue to target large companies because the need for unions is greater in large establishments, because small units do not contribute enough in dues to justify the expense of servicing them, and because small units are more likely than large ones eventually to decertify. Victories such as the one achieved by the Steelworkers in organizing 19,000 employees of the Newport News Shipbuilding and Dry Dock Company in 1978, or the UAW's victory in GM's Oklahoma City facility in 1979, also serve to give the labor movement considerable publicity and momentum.

A strategic weapon of which much has been made is the use of financial pressure by the Amalgamated Clothing and Textile Workers Union in its battle against the J.P. Stevens Company. In that campaign, the Amalgamated, along with other unions, forced the resignation from the company's board of directors of several bank and insurance executives, by threatening to withdraw funds from their banks and insurance companies (*Wall Street Journal*, September 13, 1978). Whether this practice will become widespread remains to be seen. Whatever success this tactic enjoys, there is a certain sense of déjà vu associated with its use. The potential union abuse of the power associated with large pension and health insurance holdings was a burning issue in the 1950s.

Will leadership make a difference? Even though a new generation of union leaders is emerging, conference participants were divided on whether new leaders will bring about greater organizing success. Oddly enough, except for a few cases in which logical successors have been identified, there is very little known about the training, skills, and interests of the persons likely to assume positions of power within the labor movement during the next decade. However, participants generally agree that the new leaders alone will not make a big difference. The fact is that union leaders follow membership preferences more than they shape them—a relationship that is likely to remain unchanged in our judgment.

A third scenario says that unions in manufacturing could reverse their decline by capitalizing on the growing discontent among white-collar, young professional, and female workers. Female workers are already beginning to show an increased willingness to join unions (Lublin, 1979), thus confirming an earlier finding of Scoville (1971) that men and women have the same propensity for enrolling in unions after adjusting for differences in labor force attachment. In appealing to white-collar workers, unions may be aided by two likely economic developments. First, over the next few years, there will be a growing shortage of persons aged eighteen to twenty-four and a labor market glut of highly educated persons in the twenty-five to forty-four age range, a group expected to comprise 50 percent of the labor force by 1990. The consequences of these developments, as Weber

(1978) has noted, will be greater competition for available jobs and promotions, slower career growth, lower rates of increase in wages for the twenty-five to forty-four age group, and increased wage pressure from those eighteen to twenty-four. Second, we believe that employers have come to treat white-collar workers as variable costs. Whereas in prior recessions white-collar workers were inventoried and blue-collar workers were laid off, more recent experience suggests that white-collar workers are no longer buffered from the vicissitudes of the business cycle. Taken together, these two forces could create the classic concerns of job insecurity and job consciousness among white-collar workers.

A fourth scenario foresees a spillover of prounion sentiment from the public sector into manufacturing. Ruttenberg, for example, believes that the 1978 passage of Proposition 13 in California and the apparent shift toward fiscal conservatism throughout the country will eventually accelerate the rate of public sector union growth, leading to a manufacturing spillover much sooner. Loevy, drawing a different inference from the same data, felt that the tax revolt would likely reduce the appeal of unionism in the public sector, since a wage gain would be more difficult to obtain given reduced employer and voter willingness to pay. Those who support the spillover projections might also want to consider the effect of potential union penetration in the service industries, large banks, and insurance companies.

A fifth scenario is based on a belief that sunbelt workers will become less adverse to unionism over the long term. Piore cites the South's experience in accepting civil rights legislation as demonstrating that the traditional antiunion attitudes of southern workers can also be changed. Ulman points out that industrialization will facilitate attitudinal change. Southern industrialization, says Ulman, will bring about urbanization, the abolition of cheap labor, and, eventually, workers who are less intimidated by employers.

While these five scenarios focus on the prospects for growth in union strength and membership, an equally likely scenario, proposed by George Strauss playing devil's advocate, calls for a substantial weakening and even crumbling of the labor movement. Strauss is not predicting such an outcome, but he asks that we recognize the following omens:

> In the construction industry, long a bedrock of union strength, clients increasingly are hiring open shop firms.

> The Teamsters' master contract is widely violated as employers pay less than the negotiated wage rates.

> Public employee unions in California have lost a number of key strikes, and resistance inspired by Proposition 13 will probably make it much harder for these unions to win future bargaining table victories.

Considering the current widespread use of antiunion consulting firms, it is conceivable that a number of companies will take the offensive against labor during the 1980s, forcing unions into a series of disastrous strikes, leaving some decertified and others reduced to impotence.

Unions in some fields, such as the garment industry, may become so weakened that it would make little difference whether they disband or not. Indeed, unions in these declining industries, because they are wealthy, may be able to survive organizationally, even though their membership may dwindle. They would not, however, be a force in society or the industry.

Between the forecasts of new vitality and precipitous decline is perhaps the most conservative and most likely prediction: union membership in manufacturing as a percentage of all manufacturing employment will continue to decline gradually with reductions in overall manufacturing employment. Since bargaining power is still strongly related to union penetration, we expect a concomitant loss of union strength in this sector.

The Structure and Administration of Unions

Most students of industrial relations believe that unions as organizations adapt to their environment. Accordingly, if the environment were altered, we might expect, over the long term, changes in the structure and internal workings of unions. The open question, given the deep traditions of the American labor movement, is how responsive union structure and administration will be to the different contextual changes we might reasonably anticipate over the next decade.

Barbash, at one extreme, argues that the golden principles of the labor movement have evolved into a rather good fit with American institutions, making further change very unlikely. Some participants believe Barbash's analysis overstated its case. They cite the fact that practice clearly has modified the meaning of such important founding principles as exclusive jurisdiction and voluntarism. Therefore, they argue, we should at least acknowledge the potential for further change. Still other participants believe strongly in the inevitability of change in the structure and administration of unions. They base their reasoning on fluidity in union leadership, the changing composition of the rank and file, and the uncertain environmental climate in which unions would exist. We examine each of these in turn.

The next few years will produce a new and as yet untested cohort of union leaders. For instance, over the next four years six of the highest-ranking officers in the UAW, including President Fraser, will be forced to retire at age sixty-five (Smith, 1979). No one knows for sure whether the new union leaders will share the values or skills of their predecessors, but their training and credentials will surely be different. The founders of the labor movement grounded their authority in charisma and a baptism in earlier labor battles. The new leaders will more likely come with professional degrees and bureaucratic training. It remains to be seen whether the technocratic union leader is more or less vulnerable to (or skilled in dealing with) political challenges from the rank and file than the labor statesman of old.

People who look for change coming from this new leadership often assume that the new leaders will be younger than their predecessors. The age of the leaders may have little to do with things, for, as Barbash reminds us, John L. Lewis and other CIO leaders were middle-aged when they revolutionized the labor movement.

A second source of influence on union structure will be the emerging interests, needs, and goals of the rank and file. Hildebrand referred to them as "Age of Aquarius" workers who have certain expectations about participation on the job and participation in their union, and are less willing to submit to authority. Another likely source of stimulation to change will be females, younger workers, and the newly organized professional employees in manufacturing, the latter being more accustomed to greater job autonomy than blue-collar workers. The intergroup competition among males and females, and older and younger workers, will be heightened by the abolition of mandatory retirement rules which will block channels of promotion, and by equal employment opportunity laws which will decrease the value of seniority.

Further complicating the governance of unions, according to Hathway and Loevy, will be the existence of dissident groups among the rank and file. At present, according to several other conferees, the number of radical union members is small. Nonetheless, as they indicated, only a few are needed to precipitate confrontation within the union or to capitalize on labor-management disputes.

Beyond leadership and rank-and-file considerations, the governance of unions will also be influenced by the environment. Continued high rates of inflation and the labor movement's likely involvement in incomes policies are particularly important. Historically, elected union leaders have been unwilling to moderate wage demands solely to satisfy the conditions of a voluntary antiinflation program. However, Preston argues that if high rates of inflation remain a national problem, unions must become a partner in the formation and administration of incomes policies. Ruttenberg believes such cooperation will come about among enlightened union leaders and Rees, a former government inflation fighter, believes that several union leaders are already cooperating in such an effort. How leaders handle the political aspects of pressure from the rank and file below and the President of the United States above could be a factor in the redistribution of power within unions.

The structure of unions will also continue to be affected by changes in the structure of industry, which itself will be responsive to the changing economic environment. In the 1930s the exclusive jurisdictions of industrial unions made sense in light of the structure of the mass production industries. As firms integrated vertically, unions claimed jurisdiction in these related product lines or forged mergers to achieve the same effect. The era of conglomerate and concentrated enterprise predicted by Preston may necessitate the continued blurring of union jurisdictions and a speedier growth of conglomerate unions. While this prediction seems logical enough given past trends, we should also recognize that coalition bargaining committees, one method for responding to changes in industrial structure, are not becoming more numerous. Nor does the limited empirical research which exists support the hypothesis that such coalitions of unions have been formed to offset the bargaining power advantage achieved through the formation of conglomerates (Hendricks, 1976).

An additional incentive for change in union structure may come as union operating revenues begin to decline. According to Strauss, as long as unions were prosperous, an inappropriate internal organization was not too costly. Now that belt tightening is appropriate, Strauss believes that unions may embark upon efforts to increase organizational effectiveness, which should lead to more centralized administrative structures.

Collective Bargaining

Collective bargaining is discussed under four headings: structure, process and impasse resolution, output, and contract administration.

Structure

In the major oligopolistic manufacturing industries (steel, auto, and farm implements) pattern and association bargaining appear to be stable structures for the next few years. In other industries and regions (for example, the California Metal Trades Association) there are signs that bargaining may become decentralized: employer associations are breaking up, pattern relationships are ending, and union interests in forming coordinated bargaining committees under the auspices of IUD have waned.

As theory would suggest, bargaining structure is in the process of adapting to the economic, political, and social environment. Current tendencies toward the decentralization of bargaining structure are a reaction to the presence of increased foreign competition, an uncertain economic future, and as Hildebrand reminds us, a crisis in capital formation—all of which tend to motivate employers to seek more appropriate and more narrowly defined occupational, interfirm, or geographic wage patterns.

Not all of the conferees believe that bargaining in manufacturing will become less centralized. Drawing inspiration from outside the manufacturing sector, Ruttenberg points to signs of centralization in the generally decentralized construction industry. He cites as one such sign the so-called project agreement under which a contract is written to cover all employers and unions involved in a particular construction project. However, the economics of the construction industry are not the economics of manufacturing. Ruttenberg's observation is more properly seen as supporting the hypothesis that bargaining structure reflects environmental conditions.

Process and Impasse Resolution

The chapters and comments were surprisingly silent on the future of strikes and alternative impasse resolution procedures. Nevertheless, a few things can be said based on conclusions in other areas. Notwithstanding all that has been written about the acceptance of interest arbitration in the steel industry, the strike will remain an integral part of collective bargaining. Indeed, the future is more likely to see an increase than a decrease in industrial strikes. The incentives and opportunities for work stoppages will also increase: as manufacturing moves away from being the dynamic, leading, highly productive sector of the economy; as cutbacks affect job security; as government continues to insert itself in bargaining through EEO and incomes policies; and as bargaining units fragment further. Zancanaro, like Hathway and Loevy, was also concerned with the influence of ideologies in the union movement who might tend to create or prolong industrial disputes, especially as bargaining becomes more centralized.

There does not seem to be as much change as one might expect in the process of collective bargaining per se. Some notice was taken of the use of special study committees for dealing with difficult problems during negotiations. It was recognized that this practice has proved valuable in the past, as in the case of the steel industry's Human Relations Committee. But according to Zancanaro, committees today are being used to sidestep important issues that might interfere with contract settlements. The failure of these committees actually to solve the problems they were created to solve could enhance worker frustrations, feed back into subsequent negotiations, and become a source of future labor-management disputes.

Outputs

Conference participants believe that collective bargaining will continue to deal with the traditional issues of job and income security. The changing economic environment, the changing demographic composition of the work force, and the increasing role of foreign competition all lead to a belief that the bread-and-butter issues will dominate the esoteric issues of quality or worklife and worker participation in management. In fact, the current discussion of productivity bargaining and so-called "give-backs" should dictate the continued domination of traditional issues.

Moreover, it was felt that the quality of worklife (QWL) programs have a very low probability of becoming a common union demand within the next decade. This is despite the likely removal of some obstacles now inhibiting the spread of QWL programs in industry, such as the current law of labor relations which makes it illegal for employees to participate in company-sponsored committees. Unions will continue to see QWL and its intellectual antecedents as antiunion devices. They will be reinforced in this view by the faster adoption of QWL projects in large, nonunionized settings. However, the apparent success, or claims of success, of QWL in unionized foreign settings will not convince American unions to change their minds.

Another subject of bargaining, participation in top management, although fashionable in Europe, will have a hard time crossing the Atlantic. In the first place, workers do not become interested in participation until they have obtained job security. American workers have appreciably less job security than European workers, and until this issue is resolved they are less likely to be interested in management decision-making.

Conference participants identified several trends which may affect this situation. Some people pointed out that recent political events in France, the United Kingdom, and Sweden suggest that these societies are having second thoughts about the wisdom of achieving employment security at the expense of other macroeconomic and social goals. This may reduce the incidence of participation as a subject in Europe. On the other hand, some participants pointed out that there is a growing list of industries in the United States in which employment security has already been granted: the railroads, the printing trades, longshoring, and the Postal Service. Moreover, they noted that the passage of the Humphrey-Hawkins Full Employment Bill, the introduction of laws at the federal and state levels requiring firms to give notice of an intent to close a plant, and the federal government's willingness to help workers purchase a closed-down facility of the Youngstown Sheet and Tube Company all point to the creation of an environment in which participation has an improved chance of becoming an issue.

Perhaps the principal obstacle to participation in management among unionized firms is the longstanding resistance of unions and their leaders to sharing, and being held responsible for, management's decisions. Admittedly there have been claims recently that the scope of union interest may be expanding to include subjects such as shared control over pension funds. Also we note UAW President Fraser's attempt to block the takeover of Carrier Corporation by United Technologies, presumably because United was aggressively antiunion (*Economist*, November 4, 1978). However, such actions as these, even if they were to occur more frequently, are still best seen as new variations on the traditional attempts of unions to react to management decisions. American collective bargaining has a long way to go before it approaches the model of shared responsibility over day-to-day business decisions now emerging in Europe.

Contract Administration

The parties have until now accepted arbitration as the preferred method for resolving grievance disputes. That is not likely to change, even though the present system supposedly suffers from excessive legalism, high costs, lengthy delays, and a shortage of acceptable arbitrators. If we are to infer anything from the slow spread of expedited arbitration, it is that the parties are willing to accept the current system with its deficiencies at least for the time being. Looking ahead, following Hildebrand's analysis, arbitration will probably become even more legalistic as conflicts between the law of employment and the labor agreement continue (see, for example, Feller, 1977) and less formal approaches such as expedited arbitration are judged not to meet the union's duty of fair representation (Abrams, 1977).

The Political Activities of Unions

Recent legislative defeats over the issues of common situs picketing and labor law reform do not signal the end of the labor movement's political influence. Unions must still be considered an important political force at all levels of government in the executive and legislative branches. Should we reinstitute a mandatory incomes policy, their influence will be even greater.

Unions, nevertheless, are properly concerned with these defeats. In the legislative area, as Piore points out, unions face a new challenge in the increased political activities and resources of other interest groups. This was most evident in the well-organized and costly campaign the business community led against labor law reform. The existence of this coalition as well as of environmentalists, consumers, female and minority groups, along with changing election finance laws, the changing style of congressional operations, and the longstanding inability of unions to deliver the votes of members will continue to check the political influence of unions.

An interesting though highly speculative question is whether the unions will try to use the political arena to offset declining effectiveness in organizing and collective bargaining. In the past, when faced with threats from their enemies, unions have merely intensified their legislative activities against them rather than becoming overtly political organizations. This traditional narrow response, however, some believe is destined to failure. These people argue that only a clear departure from the past, such as the creation of a labor party, can succeed in achieving labor's economic agenda. Piore's call for the unions to forge a broad coalition of groups in the interest of social progress, a manifesto reminiscent of the old Lib-Lab Lobby, is one such analysis.

Chances are slim that a new political coalition led by the unions will emerge. Even if the unions could overcome their conservative political tradition, the economic interests of the unions and other interest groups are still not sufficiently close to compel cooperation. Progressive groups outside the labor movement find it difficult to forgive the unions for their unwillingness to sacrifice their self-interest for what these other groups define as social progress. Likewise, portions of the labor movement object to any analysis which defines the union as a conservative force in society and fails to give the labor movement some of the credit for such social advances as civil rights, equal employment programs, and women's rights.

If mutuality of interests remains the currency of political cooperation, individual unions and the AFL-CIO will join specific groups to pursue narrow objectives. Perhaps the most visible of these expedient combinations will be those between employers and unions for the purpose of brokering government policy. This pattern was evident in the joint actions of the United Steelworkers and the steel industry's effort to obtain special governmental treatment in foreign trade matters and the UAW's political efforts on behalf of Chrysler. Earlier the IAM joined with Lockheed to secure government underwriting of loans to the company. Employers who will fight unions over collective bargaining gains will find much to support in the strategic political agenda of labor, especially the issue of controlling foreign competition (*Forbes*, February 20, 1978). With further shrinkage in manufacturing employment and increased foreign competition, we can expect more such legislative cooperation between unions and companies.

Last, any discussion of unions or politics should not give the impression that all unions share a common political agenda or are equally influential. Thus the big industrial unions in manufacturing are likely to lose some political influence as their membership declines and as the power of unions in the service industries and public sector grows (Shabecoff, 1979).

Concluding Observations

It has been too long since we examined unions and collective bargaining in the manufacturing sector. The reexamination presented here seeks to determine whether the system of industrial relations in manufacturing has changed significantly since its inception over forty years ago, and whether it might change significantly in the next decade. It is our feeling that as we enter the 1980s, collective bargaining in unions is still adequately described by what can be called the classical paradigm of American industrial relations. The union is still a workplace institution, formed by workers to achieve economic welfare and job security. Unions rely upon collective bargaining as the principal mechanism for regulating employers and for achieving the goals of the rank and file. The power of unions to achieve these goals through bargaining stems from their ability to organize workers in an industry, the strength of the industry's product market, the tightness of its labor market, and the public's support of or opposition to trade unionism. The involvement of unions in politics is in effect an extension of worker and organizational interest and not an effort to change society.

There are those who take a contrary position. Without change, some contend, the union will become the industrial age dinosaur, unable to survive in the postindustrial age (Schrank, 1979). Lodge and Henderson (1977), from another view, believe that institutional change has already started and point to the development of a new ideology based on cooperation instead of competition. Whatever merit these ideas may have, we believe that the fundamentals cited above will survive the next decade.

Perhaps the best way to view this decade is as a period of equilibration in relationships among the actors, induced by shifts in manufacturing's sociopolitical environment, the product market, and the labor market. Some employers will gain power, while some unions will lose power. Unions and their leaders will seek control and authority over members who desire more autonomy. Within old-line CIO unions, the prestige and influence of the manufacturing divisions will face competition from other segments of the organization. Within the AFL-CIO, leadership of the CIO unions will face even more rivalry from unions in the public industries and the service industries. The most visible sign of the changing balance of power will appear in the political arena where the persuasiveness of other interest groups, most notably business, will rise.

The 1980s in many ways will be the same as the 1950s and 1960s for manufacturing unionism. Economic conditions are unstable, there is foreign competition for manufactured products, and there is low public support for unions. The 1980s, however, should differ from the 1950s and 1960s in the amount of conflict we are liable to see brought on by the anticipated realignments of power and organizational effectiveness. The potential for conflict has been readily apparent in each of the areas discussed by this conference: the general economic environment, the anticipated competition for new union members, the increase of employer resistance to unions and greater militancy in negotiations, the restructuring of bargaining relationships, the changing character of internal union affairs and structure, and the competition among unions, business, and others for political influence. Moreover, tensions in industrial relations will be exacerbated over the next decade by the labor market frustration of mid-career employees who will be in oversupply and by the continued intervention of government in the employment relationship to secure gains for targeted groups.

While the future may be a difficult time for unions in manufacturing, there is ample cause for confidence in the institutions and processes of collective bargaining which have proven to be highly creative and adaptive to prior challenge.

References

Abrams, Roger I. "The Integrity of the Arbitral Process." *Michigan Law Review* 76 (December 1977):231-264.

Feller, David E. "Arbitration: The Days of Its Glory Are Numbered." *Industrial Relations Law Journal* 11 (Spring 1977):97-130.

"Hands Off." *Economist*, November 4, 1978, p. 84.

Hendricks, Wallace. "Conglomerate Mergers and Collective Bargaining." *Industrial Relations* 15 (February 1976):75-87.

"Labor on the Defensive." *Forbes*, February 20, 1978.

Lodge, George C., and Henderson, Karen. "Changing Relationships among Labor, Business and Government in the United States." Paper for Trilateral Commission, October 1, 1977.

Lublin, Joann S. "More Women Enroll in Unions, Win Office, and Push for Changes." *Wall Street Journal*, January 15, 1979, p. 1.

Schrank, Robert. "The Future of the Labor Movement." Speech delivered to The Conference Board, March 1979, New York.

Scoville, James G. "Influences on Unionization in the U.S. in 1966." *Industrial Relations* 10 (October 1971):354-361.

Shabecoff, Philip. "Big Merged Union May Tip Labor from an Industrial to Service Base." *New York Times*, July 18, 1979, p. A18.

Smith, Lee. "The UAW Has Its Own Management Problem." *Fortune*, May 21, 1979, p. 70.

"Two Stevens, New York Life Directors Resign in Another Textile Union Victory." *Wall Street Journal*, September 13, 1978, p. 8.

Weber, Arnold R. "Casual Approach to Labor Supply May Haunt Business." *Wall Street Journal*, January 30, 1978, p. 12.

Index

Abel, I.W., labor leader, 74
Absenteeism, problem of, 125
Accountability, employer, 65
Activism and activists, rank and file, 104, 131, 143
Administration practices; agencies for, 179; and collective bargaining, 105-112; and contracts, 101, 160-161, 205, 208; and employees, 21; and personnel, 161-162; structure of, 37-38, 203-205
Adversary processes and relationships, 66-67, 76, 83-84, 132-134, 170, 192-194
Age: factor of, 69, 101-102, 124; prime, 98-100
Agriculture, decline of, 7, 10, 13
Alaska, timberland of, 155
Allegheny Ludlum Industries, 39
Altruism, ghost of, 191-194
Amalgamated Clothing and Textile Workers Union (ACTWU), 50, 90, 92, 188, 201
Amalgamated Meat Cutters (AMC), 45, 50, 89, 92
American Center for Quality of Work Life, 127, 134
American Federation of Labor (AFL), ideology of, 71, 77, 185
American Federation of Labor-Congress of Industrial Organization (AFL-CIO): Executive Council, 199; Industrial Union Department, 120; influence of, 50, 82, 99, 101, 132, 140, 156, 177, 187, 190-192, 194, 209; leadership of, 193, 210; research by, 164
American Federationist, 130
American Telephone and Telegraph Corporation (AT&T), 128
AMTRAK railway system, 39
Anaconda Brass Company, 119
Anti-intellectualism, 174, 191-192

Apparel industry and union of, 50, 75-76, 83, 90-91
Arab-owned subsidiaries, 155-156
Arbitration, processes of, 65, 74, 91, 161; and grievances, 68, 113; voluntary, 104-113
Associations: and bargaining, 88, 90, 98-99; employer, 119, 159; quasi-professional, 56; trade, 29
Atlanta Constitution, 165
Attitudes: changing, 100, 117; cultural, 143; and labor relations, 169; top leadership, 130-131; union toward quality of work life, 130-134
Austria, management policies in, 142
Authority: governmental, 6, 100; managerial, 98; rejection of, 122
Automation and automatic adjustments, 68, 73
Automobile industry, 19, 46-47, 73, 76, 90

Baby boom, postwar, 97, 122
Baltimore and Ohio Railroad, 138
Bargains and bargaining: association, 88, 90, 98-99; central, 194; coalition, 90, 99-100; coordinated, 69; crisis, 74; distributive, 133, 139; effectiveness, 63, 66-71; integrative, 133, 139; multiple-plant, 78, 88-90; organization, 63-66; political, 69-70; rights, 61; single-plant, 88-90, 98; structures, 45, 60, 65, 98-100. *See also* Collective bargaining agreements and negotiations
Beatrice Foods Company, 136
Behavioral norms and measures, 5, 125
Behavioral scientists, 122
Belgium, 154
Benefit programs, supplemental and fringe, 74, 141, 162
Black population: opportunities for, 188-189; workers, 57, 72, 76, 176-177

213

About the Contributors

Jack Barbash is John B. Bascom Professor of Economics and Industrial Relations in the Department of Economics and Industrial Relations Research Institute at the University of Wisconsin-Madison.

Frank H. Cassell is professor of industrial relations at the J.L. Kellogg Graduate School of Management of Northwestern University.

Milton Derber is professor of labor and industrial relations at the Institute of Labor and Industrial Relations at the University of Illinois at Urbana-Champaign.

Clifford Hathway is vice president of labor relations of the Caterpillar Tractor Company.

George H. Hildebrand is Maxwell M. Upson Professor of Economics and Industrial Relations in the Department of Economics at Cornell University.

Michael Jay Jedel is professor of management and associate director in the Industrial Relations Program at Georgia State University.

Arthur Loevy is assistant manager for the Chicago and Central States Joint Board of the Amalgamated Clothing and Textile Workers Union, AFL-CIO.

Michael J. Piore is professor of economics in the Department of Economics at Massachusetts Institute of Technology.

Lee E. Preston is Melvin H. Baker Professor of American Enterprise in the School of Management at the State University of New York at Buffalo.

Richard Prosten is research director for the Industrial Union Department, AFL-CIO.

Albert Rees is professor of economics in the Department of Economics at Princeton University.

Stanley Ruttenberg is president of Ruttenberg, Friedman, Kilgallon, Gutchess and Associates.

George Strauss is professor of business administration and associate director of the Institute of Industrial Relations at the University of California, Berkeley.

Joseph A. Tierney is director of labor relations for Michelin-USA.

Lloyd Ulman is professor of economics and director of the Institute of Industrial Relations at the University of California, Berkeley.

John C. Zancanaro is national representative for the Federal Mediation and Conciliation Service.

About the Editors

Hervey A. Juris received the A.B. degree from Princeton University and the M.B.A. and Ph.D. degrees from the University of Chicago. He is associate dean for academic affairs and professor of industrial relations and urban affairs at the J.L. Kellogg Graduate School of Management of Northwestern University. From 1965 to 1970, Dr. Juris taught at the School for Workers, University of Wisconsin-Madison. He is coauthor of *Police Unionism: Power and Impact in Public Sector Bargaining* (Lexington Books, 1973), and his work on collective bargaining in the public and private sectors is widely published.

Myron Roomkin received the B.S. degree from Cornell University and the M.S. and Ph.D. degrees from the University of Wisconsin. He is associate professor of Industrial Relations and urban affairs at the J.L. Kellogg Graduate School of Management of Northwestern University and also has taught at Case Western Reserve University and the University of Chicago. His research on collective bargaining and human resources policy has been published in several professional journals.